ON MORAL
PERSONHOOD

ON MORAL PERSONHOOD

Philosophy, Literature, Criticism, and Self-Understanding

RICHARD ELDRIDGE

The University of Chicago Press
Chicago and London

Richard Eldridge is associate professor of philosophy at Swarthmore College.

The University of Chicago Press, Chicago 60637
The University of Chicago Press, Ltd., London
© 1989 by the University of Chicago
All rights reserved. Published 1989
Printed in the United States of America

98 97 96 95 94 93 92 91 90 89 5 4 3 2 1

Library of Congress Cataloging-in-Publication Data

Eldridge, Richard Thomas, 1953–
    On moral personhood : philosophy, literature, criticism, and self-
    understanding / Richard Eldridge.
        p. cm.
    Includes index.
    ISBN 0-226-20316-6 (alk. paper)
    1. Literature—Philosophy.   2. Philosophy in literature.   3. Self-
perception in literature.   4. Kant, Immanuel, 1724–1804—
Aesthetics.   5. Philosophical anthropology.   6. Literature, Modern—
History and criticism.   I. Title.
PN45.E467   1989
801'.3—dc20   89-30497
                                                                          CIP

For Joan

For this commandment which I command thee this day, it *is* not hidden from thee, neither *is* it far off.

It *is* not in heaven, that thou shouldest say, Who shall go up for us to heaven, and bring it unto us, that we may hear it, and do it?

Neither *is* it beyond the sea, that thou shouldest say, Who shall go over the sea for us, and bring it unto us, that we may hear it, and do it?

But the word *is* very nigh unto thee, in thy mouth, and in thy heart, that thou mayest do it.

     Deuteronomy 30:11–14

What we deny is that the picture of the inner process gives us the correct idea of the use of the word "remember." We say that this picture with its ramifications stands in the way of our seeing the use of the word as it is.

     Ludwig Wittgenstein, *Philosophical Investigations*, §305

CONTENTS

    Coleridge's "Frost at Midnight"   126
    1. Naturalism and Romanticism   126
    2. Humean Skepticism and Romantic Autobiography   128
    3. Recollective Reflection and Onwardness with Others   131
    4. Actuality, Imagination, and the Sustenance of
       Relationship   139

6. Ideality, Materiality, and Value: *Pride and Prejudice*
    and Marriage   141
    1. The Difficulty and Interest of *Pride and Prejudice*   141
    2. Two Conceptualizations of Marriage   151
    3. Courtship, Criticism, and the Transfiguration of
       Experience   159

7. Epilogue: The Uses of Narrative—Partiality and Difference,
    Self-Understanding and Value   181

    Notes   189

    Index   205

ACKNOWLEDGMENTS

The readings that follow articulate a conception of the expression and sustenance of one's personhood in one's understandings and activities. A leading theme of this conception is that autonomous achievements of understanding and value are inextricably intermingled with relations to others. A further theme is that cooperation in such achievements, embodied in open-endedly purposive activities involving criticism and conversation, is the essential possibility of human life that most fully promises us joy and dignity as persons. I am thus moved to acknowledge those who have shaped and shared in this work not only out of pleasure but also out of a sense that these others have enabled my own ways of being. For this I am to them deeply grateful.

This work has been long in preparation. My longest-standing and most continually renewed intellectual debt is to the writings on Wittgenstein, aesthetics, criticism, literature, and movies of Stanley Cavell. What made this debt possible, however, is something even greater, namely, what I owe to my teachers, who encouraged me to go on with a way of doing philosophy that they at times must have found opaque and quite possibly irresponsible. Their own work as readers and critics of both canonical philosophers and my own tentative writings served for me as an image of what criticism might aspire to, and they showed enormous patience in sorting through with me various half-formed thoughts about philosophy, literature, modernism, grammatical necessity, and human freedom. For both patience and inspiration, I must thank Ted Cohen, Alan Donagan, Manley Thompson, Stanley Bates, Timothy Gould, and Dennis O'Brien.

As fortunate as I have been in my teachers, I have been equally fortunate in my colleagues. At Swarthmore College, at Purdue University, and at the Illinois Institute of Technology, I found departments of philosophy—there cannot be so many—that made it possible for me to teach and work on Wittgenstein and Romanticism, and friends who read and carefully criticized what I was beginning to produce. At IIT I must thank Fay Sawyier, Bob Ladenson, and Jack Snapper, each of whom took an interest in what I had to say about the visions and fears expressed, but not directly argued for, in philosophical writing and in the possibilities of a deepening of vision through reading narratives. The earliest writing in this work dates from my time at Purdue, where William Rowe arranged for me to teach in literature, and where he and Larry May, Bill McBride, Cal Schrag, Lilly Russow, Jim Stephens, Rod Bertolet, and Martin Curd took these first formulations seriously.

The remainder of the writing has been done at Swarthmore College. Two of the essays—those on Conrad and Austen—were virtually written in the corridors of Papazian. I am able to mark the record of conversations with Hugh Lacey, Hans Oberdiek, and Richard Schuldenfrei almost line by line throughout them. In responding both to my work and to that of others in similar terrains that we heard together, Hugh Lacey has continually broadened my vision and forced on me a sense of the weight social life places on our moral imaginations and of the responsibility we bear for engaging with it. His reminders and admonitions were often in my ear as I wrote. Much of my understanding of Kant's moral philosophy is traceable to Hans Oberdiek's deepening of the work of my earlier teachers of Kant, as are various thoughts about Wittgenstein and necessity. I further owe to his conversation and his comments on my early drafts uncountable particular points about voluntariness and freedom, moral pride, and other aspects of motivation and character. Richard Schuldenfrei crucially helped me to give up worrying too much about philosophical methodology in favor of getting on with the work of reading. Conversations with him were vital in my coming to see my own readings as themselves enactments of a moral vision, as a moral enterprise that could have no prior ground in value-neutral essentialism. Dorothea Frede generously read the entire penultimate draft with sympathy and encouragement; she suggested many important improvements in expression and pointed me to further background distinctions and influences.

Various Swarthmore undergraduates suffered and responded to not only my public worries about agency and responsibility but also my private thoughts and first drafts, thus becoming more colleagues than students. Joanne Wood and I worked through Kant, Hegel, and Conrad together over a summer; I further owe to her a deepened appreciation of the liabilities of idealist criticism in general and of idealist criticism of Austen in particular. Exchanges with Kristen Kann also helped to shape the reading of Austen. Conversations and correspondence about Charles Taylor, Kant, Hegel, postfoundationalist philosophy, and practical reasoning have substantially shaped my thinking. Many exchanges took place over a period of years between me and Martha Matthews, Paul Cohen, Martin Estey, David Sussman, and Elise Bjørkan, as well as others whom I associate less with particular points, but equally with an atmosphere of seriousness.

Early stages of various pieces of writing were presented to a number of audiences. In addition to formal presentations to the ASA, IAPL, and MLA, a continuous, generous, and spirited hearing for my thoughts on Wittgenstein and essentialism, and on morality, has been provided by the working group of the Philadelphia Philosophy Consortium. Together with my colleagues at Swarthmore, I have found with Joe Margolis, Michael Krausz, Bill Sullivan, Jack Caputo, and Richard Shusterman a genuine philosophical community. All of them have generously criticized my work on morality and on interpretation for some years as we have regularly exchanged manuscripts and talked things out. Richard Shusterman kindly read the entire manuscript in its penultimate form, and his comments had a particular influence on the readings of Conrad and Austen. Work on Wordsworth was presented at Albright College, where I must thank Jeff Barker, and work on Conrad at Bucknell University, where I must thank Richard Fleming and Jeffrey Turner for comments, and Mary Devereaux for comments and for philosophical friendship now of some years.

As a philosopher coming to work on literature, I have had to depend on the patient guidance shown to me in Wordsworth studies by Kenneth Johnston and James Chandler. They have both suggested better formulations of my points and encouraged me in my ways of reading, responding with interest to them as neither stale nor trivial. This has helped me to keep on.

Correspondence on the relation between literature and moral philosophy, and on aesthetics and criticism, has helped me over a period of years to arrive at my final formulations. Earlier ones were tested out on Charles Altieri, Anthony J. Cascardi, Arthur C. Danto, Martha Nussbaum, J. B. Schneewind, and Roger Shiner. Each of them has also commented generously on pieces of my work that are either included here or indirectly drawn upon. Exchanges with P. M. S. Hacker, and at a late stage with John Hyman, were crucial in sharpening my understanding of Wittgenstein (even where they may not share it), which figures in everything I write. Stanley Bates read the penultimate manuscript and suggested numerous valuable additions and improvements, therein continuing and deepening his teaching. Comments from anonymous readers both provided an occasion for and encouraged last revisions I had been saving up. Suzanna Sherry has read most of my work and drawn me out in conversation on its significance for public life, thus encouraging me to think that it had some.

It proves specially awkward and misleading in considering interdisciplinary work of this kind, and of this length of preparation, to assign particular influences to particular figures. I regret slighting the contributions of many to various topics and to my vision and sense of plausibility. I can remedy this in part, though only in part, by mentioning what I owe to the styles and attitudes of the now-dispersed group known on occasion as the Gnu critics—Lorna Gladstone, Paul Gudel, Françoise Meltzer, Stephen Melville, and Andrew Parker. To Stephen Melville in particular, I am further indebted for continuous nurturing of my understandings of Hegel and of contemporary criticism.

Two of the essays below are somewhat revised versions of essays that appeared in the journal *Philosophy and Literature*. It is very little exaggeration to say that they could not have appeared anywhere else. Apart from its reception of my work, it remains my judgment that both philosophy and literature as disciplines are much improved by its life in both of them. I am grateful in particular to its editor, Denis Dutton, and associate editor, Jesse Kalin, for encouraging my work and holding my style and arguments to the journal's standards of interest and clarity.

A Eugene Lang Faculty Fellowship from Swarthmore College funded a sabbatical during which much of this writing was done. The Ford Foundation and Bryn Mawr College funded research and teaching in Romanticism with Carol Bernstein and Kathleen Wright that later figured in these essays. Fran Cuneo typed much of the manuscript.

There is no adequate way of acknowledging what I owe to my parents, to my children, and above all to Joan Vandegrift, my wife. It is too little to say that she has read every line and improved many of them, though this is true. It is too abstract to say that but for her I would have nothing like the understanding of either literature or human beings that I do, and nothing like whatever stores of patience and sympathy I may have, though these things are also true. What I have had to say about Jane Austen and marriage comes closest to standing as what I would regard as an acknowledgment, though going on with her has been, so far as I can judge, both better, and better acknowledgment, than these fixed words can express.

OPENING: THE SPACE OF READING

There is only the fight to recover what has been lost
And found and lost again and again: and now, under conditions
That seem unpropitious.
>   T. S. Eliot, "East Coker"

One might say that the subject we are dealing with is one of the heirs of the subject which used to be called "philosophy."
>   Ludwig Wittgenstein, *The Blue Book*

How should one live? And how might one come to know how one should live? What differences in answers to these questions are made by different local situations, projects, and relations? Are there any answers that may have general force for us, against our local situatedness? Though leisured reflection on these questions has often been an impossible luxury, raising them is virtually natural to persons. Children and grownups of any time and place can scarcely fail to see that there are differences in taste, temperament, talent, interest, activity, and relationship among us. Various ranges of differences, sometimes wide, sometimes narrow, will be evident in various times and places, as will various opportunities for becoming more like one or another person in different ways. Then these questions will arise, even if they are often then foreclosed, as we attempt to "true our asymmetries," internal and external, to lead more whole and fulfilling lives.[1]

While raising these questions is virtually natural to persons, going on in taking them seriously and in articulating answers to them has been made specially difficult and urgent over the past two hundred years. Both naturalism, which sees human conduct as stemming from either purely individual or impersonal imperatives, forces, and choices rather than from a partial understanding of a divinely arranged plan, and capitalism, which in the names of efficiency and rationalization undoes traditional roles and relations and encourages the exclusive pursuit of personal satisfaction, have helped to make social life more flexible and less foreign to many. But at the same time they have flattened and distorted our lives, leading us to see our choices and lives as insignificant effects of either the brutely individual or the impersonally physical rather than as achieved and assessable products of rational deliberation. Some underlying unhappiness with this situation where it is most advanced is evident in such things as the prevalence of psychotherapy and in rapid moves through successive styles of taste, opinion, and fashion. But are there genuine alternatives to lives based on purely individual or anonymous local imperatives? If there are, then how can we come to know and value them? And how might any universal and autonomously generated imperative be given expression in the world?

The great project of modern philosophy in the seventeenth and eighteenth centuries can be understood as an effort to give simultaneous expression to our sense of our dignity or autonomy in the face of a mechanized nature and to our sense of our embeddedness in nature and society. (This project itself bears recognizable affinities to, for example, Plato's simultaneous arguments in favor of the immortality of the soul and efforts to understand the sensible world in which we live as an image of the intelligible. Our senses of our autonomy and of our embeddedness within an independent world are not solely historical artifacts.) Thus Descartes argues that individual reason can establish a priori both that the will is free and that the world exists, is knowable, and can be mastered. Yet this expression of our senses of self and world—a kind of success for modern philosophy—ends in a kind of failure.[2] Reason doesn't prove what Descartes says it can; substantive assumptions that are open to doubt appear in his arguments, and mind-body interaction remains a mystery. (Perhaps it should be a mystery, yet we can still ask how our mindedness and embeddedness can be expressed and expressed well, and what exemplars of such expression there might be—questions over which Descartes does not linger.)

The great effort of Descartes's successors is then to give fuller and more stable expression to these somewhat opposed senses of our autonomy and our embeddedness in the world. Spinoza achieves a measure of clarity and consistency and defends the idea of our being essentially related to the world via God, but at the price of conceding too much to a form of determinism. Leibniz upholds our autonomy at the price of disengaging all genuine individuals, monads, from interaction with one another. Kant's effort to uphold both our moral being and our capacities to know founders on the unintelligible relation between phenomena and noumena. Hegel moves toward making this relation intelligible, but only through tending implausibly to deny the finitude of our reason and through appealing to history as a process of the resolution of all conflicts between individual and society, desire and reason, and particular and universal. In all these ways, the great project of modern philosophy comes to an end.

But then if our senses of ourselves as simultaneously autonomous and embedded in the world cannot be given full and coherent expression through the reasoned articulation of a *theory* of our being in the world, and if these senses nonetheless persist in us, then how can these senses be expressed? Can there be, if not a theory of our being in the world, at least a coherent practice of its expression, and wisdom within that practice? A central moment of the awareness of this problem is to be found in Kant's *Critique of Judgment*. Having described the knowable causal structure of the world of experience in the *Critique of Pure Reason*, and having stated the formula of our autonomy and noumenal freedom in the *Foundations of the Metaphysics of Morals* and the *Critique of Practical Reason*, Kant's leading problem in the *Critique of Judgment* is how we can appreciate and achieve our autonomy in the world, acknowledging both the requirements of universal moral principle and the pull on us of the world and society. Can we do this at all? If so, how? And how might the way to do this become evident to us? Or are moral imperatives, in consisting in the self-legislation of our noumenal nature, simply cut off from the world?

Kant's delicately nuanced answer to these questions is that the route to such awarenesses and achievements of autonomy in the world as we can manage is to be found in aesthetic experience, in particular, of the beautiful and the sublime in nature and in art. These experiences are curiously at odds with each other. In experiencing the beautiful in nature, we feel the world to be in harmony with our rational nature, to provide a home for it. To experience the beautiful in art is similarly to be struck by a feeling of the ultimate intelligibility of others as it is manifested in their freely produced works, and hence of our social life with them. In experiencing the sublime in nature, we are in contrast made to feel our apartness and autonomy, our dignity as rational beings of independent worth against nature. To experience genius in art is similarly to be struck by our difference from one another and to be moved to awareness of the kinds of achievements in expression of self to which we aspire. Both kinds of experiences, in Kant's accounting, are central to our full sense of ourselves. (Wordsworth registers a similar point in recounting what Hartman has called his experiences of *akedah* and *apocalypse*.[3]) The awarenesses achieved through these kinds of experiences all at once have particular occasioning circumstances, are manifested in feeling, and suspend one another or call one another into question: they are balanced against one another only through their repeated alternation in time. In all these ways, the awarenesses achieved in these experiences differ from achievements of general theoretical knowing. To the extent that the route to the full and coherent expression of our being in the world and of our senses of it runs through these experiences, the expression of our being is not to be achieved in knowing, but in *acknowledgment*.[4] Such acknowledgment of our being—with its occasioning circumstances and alternating aspects—can have no logic, but only partial and anxious exemplars.[5] As a result, our moral self-understanding must take the form not of a *theory*, but rather of an ongoing *practice* of interpretive and critical engagement with these imperfect exemplars.

How then are we to go on as persons to manifest and sustain our being in the world? From what landmarks in our courses can we take our bearings? The readings that follow approach these questions by sorting through and balancing competing accounts of the roles in our lives of universal principles and demands of our nature, themselves associated with our autonomy, on the one hand, and the effects and demands of particular projects and relationships rooted in our connectedness to nature and society, on the other. The texts under study are preoccupied with conflict and its resolution between principle and practice, universality and particularity, *Moralität* and *Sittlichkeit*, and Kantian and Hegelian moral philosophy. The Hegelian idea that others matter fundamentally to the development and exercise of our capacities for self-understanding and for flourishing is played off against the Kantian idea that these capacities have at the same time a partially independent and morally significant ground in us simply as persons. Balances and resolutions are achieved in these readings through tracing the developments in protagonists of increasing understandings of the weight, nature, and possibilities of lived acknowledgment of the demands of the particular and the universal. These developments in understanding are set out against the background provided by the understandings and lives of other figures and by the earlier understandings through which the protagonists have moved. The work of these texts, and of reading them, is to make these developments of understanding and lived acknowledgment on the part of the protagonists explicit and to show their relations to, and terms of criticism of, various traditional and contemporary moral and psychological theories. In each reading, the suggestion is that the development of the protagonist is both recognizably human and exemplary, involving a discovery of a dimension of our shared best possibilities of life as persons in the world, a discovery that places and criticizes alternative conceptualizations of what we can achieve. Yet at the same time each such discovery remains marked by particularity, so that no discovery is perfect; partially divergent successes and failures in self-understanding and in activity appear in each case.

Within these readings, a posteriori interpretive stances, inspired by Hegel's work on the phenomenology of self-understanding, now more or less naturalized, and by Wittgenstein's work on self-understanding as ongoing narrative-interpretive activity, are taken up to yield Kantian results about the universal demands our nature places on itself. These demands are expressed in a principle of morality and acknowledged by the protagonists in its implicit acceptance. Their acknowledgments of principle are simultaneously given exemplary but partial embodiment in their lives, as their relations and activities take shape around them. At the same time, these acknowledgments and achievements remain both partial and crossed by the particular circumstances and contexts of their emergence. We see in the careers of these protagonists both the possibility and the importance of coming to "treat humanity, whether in your own person or in that of another, always as an end and never as a means only,"[6] and also how divergent, imperfect, difficult to sustain, and socially shaped any actions moved by a sense of the importance of this must be. What thus emerges from these readings is a kind of broken, socialized Kantianism of this world, with an emphasis more on Kant's concern with *dikaiosyne* and rightness than on rights, more on our imperfect duties to ourselves that at the same time involve attention to others than on our perfect duties of noninterference. Our lives as persons, as they are shown to us through the lives of these protagonists and their communicants, emerge as expressions of our being fated to succeed and fail, partially and along various dimensions, in coming to know our nature and to act on principle in an ongoing, fulfilling, and cooperative way.

Taken as moral philosophy, this recovery of a Hegelianized Kantianism, wherein reason and sensibility reciprocally affect one another in and through social life, rather than being assigned separate realms, invites comparison with the work of Rawls. In certain respects, *A Theory of Justice* looks very much like an articulation, shaped by a historical narrative, of the universal demands our nature places on itself. It is possible to read Rawls as providing an account all at once of the nature of our *awareness* of the nature of justice, as modeled by historically informed reflections in the original position; of our *development*, psychological and social, that makes this awareness possible; of the *content* of our awareness, embedded in the principles of justice; and of our *motivation* to be just, insofar as the course of development toward this awareness is itself both natural and fulfilling. In chapters 8 and 9 of *A Theory of Justice*, Rawls is concerned to show that a just state would be stable, in the sense that persons raised within an ideally just state would naturally come to care about justice, or at least to take seriously efforts to regulate their conduct and assess their institutions by reference to the principles of justice. To show that the sense of justice is in this way natural to us is to show that "moral attitudes are part of our humanity."[7] To lack a sense of justice, itself defined by the principles of justice, "would be to lack part of our humanity."[8]

As Rawls describes it, the natural course of development toward having a sense of justice has roughly three stages. First, within a justly ordered family, children come to recognize and reciprocate their parents' love for them. Second, persons within a just social arrangement come to trust and care about others who maintain the justice of institutions. Third, persons come to care about the principles of justice themselves, as they reflect on how they have benefited from institutions and relations ordered in accordance with these principles.[9] Here it looks as though we are to come to acknowledge the principles of justice, themselves specified through reflective reasoning, through a posteriori, interpretive reflection occurring within the textures of our familial, social, and emotional lives. It might then be possible to regard the historical emergence of the circumstances of justice, and of our capacities both to reflect on these circumstances and to develop a sense of justice, or to acknowledge its principles, as themselves part of a kind of Hegelian emergence of reason and justice in the world, an emergence that undoes the dualism of phenomena and noumena by showing us that what we naturally do is rational. Simultaneously emotional, social, and reasoned acknowledgement of principles of social life is here cast as a valuable emergent possibility of our nature.[10]

Despite its elegance, however, this interpretation of Rawls faces both textual and philosophical difficulties. Already in *A Theory of Justice* Rawls insists, first of all, that his remarks about psychological development "are not intended as justifying reasons" in favor either of the relevance to us of reflections carried out in the original position or of the principles that emerge from them.[11] More recently, he has emphasized this point even more strongly: "The conception of justice that I have called justice as fairness," Rawls writes, "does not . . . depend on [any] . . . claims to universal truth, or claims about the essential nature and identity of persons."[12] The principles of justice are instead, as it were, to stand on their own, as the principles that would reasonably be chosen by disinterested free and equal persons. The account of our psychological development under certain ideal social conditions is intended to show only that a social order based on these principles would be stable. That is, all that is to be shown, according to Rawls, in talking of psychological development is that "this conception [of justice as fairness] is more stable than other traditional conceptions with which it is compared, as well as stable enough."[13] The defensibility of the principles of justice is established independently.

Philosophically, the reason for this is that Rawls suspects that any effort to underwrite a conception of justice metaphysically as grounded in the nature of persons *must* be antidemocratic and authoritarian.

> Philosophy as the search for truth about an independent metaphysical and moral order *cannot*, I believe, provide a workable and shared basis for a political conception of justice in a democratic society. . . . *No* political view that depends on these deep and unresolved matters [viz., "questions of philosophical psychology or a metaphysical doctrine of the nature of the self"] *can* serve as a public conception of justice in a constitutional democratic state. . . . We apply the principle of toleration to philosophy itself: the public conception of justice is to be political, not metaphysical.[14]

The thought here is that any more explicitly teleological account of the natural emergence of reason within certain familial and social structures would be too constraining. It would suggest that certain developed identities and institutions ought to be maintained, and this suggestion is seen as an intolerant intrusion on the legitimate claims of individuality to less constrained self-development.

Two questions can now be raised about this view. (1) Is the stronger, more Hegelian view necessary, either epistemologically or as an element of an adequate moral self-understanding? Or can the principles of justice be upheld on their own, as those that would reasonably be chosen by free, equal, and disinterested persons, *without* relying on any background account of how ordinary people, in initially nonideal circumstances, might come to acknowledge what Rawls claims to be the verdicts of reason? Epistemologically, it is a matter at least for some worry that Rawls provides no account of how ordinary people may develop toward an appreciation of reasonableness, construed as mandating the choice of certain principles. Perhaps the theory remains so ideal that we are not able to enter into it fully, especially if we have been harmed, rather than helped, by the developed institutional arrangements that structure the initial intuitions about persons and the social scientific knowledge on which Rawls has his original contractors draw.[15] Morally, a self-understanding that denies that our achieved relations and institutions are bound up with our reasonableness, as it is expressed in a commitment to abstract political justice, seems to sever the private and historically concrete too much from the public and the ideal. Achieved relations and actual institutions seem to be too strongly cast as stemming from the contingencies of desire and circumstance alone, rather than in part from the same reasonableness that attaches us to abstract political justice. The result is that our domestic and historical lives seem morally unstable insofar as we are unable to see our particular attachments and institutions as reasonable, and hence worthy of continuance, in anything like the way in which ideal justice is worthy of pursuit. (It is noteworthy that Rawls explicitly allows that moral theory may diverge from political philosophy and that his account of how political ideals may be constructed in the original position, and hence upheld, may not be appropriate for moral ideals.[16] He provides, however, no specific account either of moral reflection or of how its results might stand in relation to results in political philosophy.) Both epistemologically and morally then, there seem to be some reasons to prefer a more thoroughly Hegelianized version of Kantianism than Rawls's, a version in which reason and nature, and public and private, are brought at least into partial accord with one another. The readings of narratives that are here put forward are aimed at showing the emergence in the world of these partial accords.

(2) Is it in fact the case, as Rawls seemingly urges, that our specific, concrete attachments and institutions stem significantly from contingencies of desire? If so, then any Hegelian effort to cast particular attachments and institutions as rational fulfillments of our nature in the world *must* be nothing more than authoritarian efforts to constrain the development and expression of divergent but fully legitimate desires. Are all teleological interpretations of existing attachments, institutions, and activities necessarily antidemocratic and repressive, as Rawls charges?

It is hard to know how to respond to these questions in advance of a developed interpretation of specific achieved attachments, institutions, and activities. But it is at least possible abstractly to cast some doubt on the view that all teleological interpretations are *necessarily* intolerant and antidemocratic. For all that they are genuine and exemplary, the achievements in the fit expression of our nature—in attachments, in institutions, in activities, in feeling, and otherwise—that are surveyed in these readings are all nonetheless *partial*. None of the imagined lives under scrutiny is perfect throughout its defining ranges of attachments, institutional settings, and activities. In each of them, the achievement of autonomy is precariously balanced against the achievement of cooperative meaningfulness, and the different balances struck in different lives stand in criticism of one another. As a result, considerable tolerance of these different ways of striking these imperfect balances is called for. Insofar as the terms of this necessary tolerance are marked out by principles of equal basic liberties establishing rights to noninterference, democratic and liberal political schemes and schemes of public education will be in order. But now these political and educational schemes will themselves be understood as structuring public life so as to allow various and divergent strikings of these imperfect balances, shaped by both reason and desire. In this way, a democratic and liberal political scheme, together with its way of drawing the public/private distinction, will be seen as reasonable in virtue of what it allows and promotes in the private sphere. (This is not to imply that a suitable liberal political scheme might not be somewhat more socialist, say, than Rawls's, but only to establish that basic individual liberties such as those of religion, speech, and private conduct can have a full place within a teleologically oriented moral theory in which the partialness of our best achievements is emphasized.)

The important differences between Rawls's views and a Hegelianized Kantianism thus do not lie in political philosophy, where the views are in rough agreement. They lie instead in contrasting conceptions of the nature of value and of how we may come to acknowledge its nature and to articulate our acknowledgments. Where Rawls's view is generally constructivist, in seeing political ideals and principles of justice as constructed in response to a particular, albeit persistent and important, public political problem only, a more Hegelianized Kantianism represents our commitment to a moral principle as resting on a discovery of the universal demands of our nature, so that the account is realist, not constructivist. Where Rawls emphasizes the independence of political philosophy and issues of public justice from moral philosophy and from issues in domestic life,[17] a more Hegelianized Kantianism emphasizes, following Kant, both the fundamental importance of duties to oneself in moral and political philosophy alike and the dependence of the resolution of issues about public justice on the resolution of normative issues internal to our domestic lives. Finally, and most important, where Rawls puts forward an ideal *theory* of justice, what is here put forward does not aim at achieving the closure or completion of morally significant self-understanding. Insofar as only imperfect and partial achievements of lived acknowledgment of the demands of our nature are surveyed and interpreted as fallen exemplars, what emerges from the interpretations does not have the form of a theory. Rather, the description and assessment of these cases, as well as of countless others that lie against them, must be understood as an ongoing interpretive and moral practice, as itself an effort, partial and perennially open to criticism, at lived acknowledgment of our nature, as an effort to achieve and express practical wisdom. (This rejection of theory runs counter to Hegel along lines of thought opened by Wittgenstein.) Within our lives in the world, we must hope for neither less, nor more, understanding than this: we stand in need of the grace of forgiveness.

Taken as literary criticism, these readings in support of a Hegelianized Kantianism invite comparison with such movements as deconstruction; New Historicism, in all its ranges from the Foucaultian to the Hegelian; and politicized poststructuralism, mixing Adorno with Derrida and emphasizing the imperialism of commodity-exchange culture in shaping all thought and expression. Like the interpretive work carried out within each of these critical movements, these readings take for granted the claim that thought, feeling, personal identity, and expression all have significant linguistic and cultural dimensions, without which they are impossible. We are what we are only through our languages and cultures, and their pasts; there is no Cartesian or Husserlian self-present, independently cognizing ego standing as the unshifting locus of experience and source of action and expression, as the container behind the contained. As Hegel urged,

> What we *are* we are at the same time in history; . . . in what we *are* our common imperishable lot is linked inseparably with the fact that we are in history. . . . [What we have that makes us what we are] is essentially an inheritance and, more precisely, the result of labour, the labour of all the preceding generations of the human race. The arts of the externals of our life, the mass of means and skills, the arrangements and customs of social and political associations, all these are the result of the reflection, invention, needs, misery, and misfortune, the will and achievement of the history which has preceded our life of today.[18]

But nothing follows from this about the ultimate determinants of language, culture, and history. It remains so far as our explicit historicity goes an open question whether these things are principally conditioned by our neurophysiology, by our innate neurally encoded grammars for possible languages, by laboring activity and the growth of forces of production, by the life of the unconscious and the gender antagonisms inscribed in it, by practical reason and individual will, by religion and God, or by absolutely nothing, so that cultural and linguistic formations just brutely emerge by breaking with their predecessors. To the extent that literary criticism takes place through unreflectively assuming one or another stance on the historical development of language, culture, and expression, it is itself ideological and premature. Too much criticism simply ignores what has gone on in such areas as analytical assessments of Marxist economics and historical social theory, behavior theory, philosophy of language and transformational linguistics, philosophy of mind and theory of action, and so on. Perhaps we cannot establish with certainty what *the* logic of historical development and human action is; perhaps there is no one logic. But these very thoughts ought to cast some doubt on confident assertions that human agents and their expressions are nothing but effects of linguistic codes or material forces or unconscious life or gender oppositions or whatever. Any such assertions, and hence the strategies of literary criticism that they motivate, presuppose specific narratives of the historical development of languages and cultures. None of these narratives has any founding privilege against the others; each must justify itself by its results in yielding an understanding that furthers our self-consciousness and the integrity and wholeness of our lives.

Once we see that various ways of reading, along with the various, implicit, systematic understandings of language and culture and agency on which they rest, themselves emerge out of conflicting narratives of historical development, then we seem moved toward the thought that it is in and through narrative itself that we lead our lives as persons, that we come to our strategies of reading, our claims to systematic understanding, and our expressive activities as readers, writers, social theorists, and agents in general. It would at least be unwise to rule out a priori, in advance of the work of criticism, the thought that

> our lives are ceaselessly intertwined with narratives, with the stories that we tell and hear told, those we dream or imagine or would like to tell, all of which are reworked in that story of our own lives that we narrate to ourselves in an episodic, sometimes semiconscious, but virtually uninterrupted monologue. We live immersed in narrative, recounting and reassessing the meaning of our past actions, anticipating the outcome of our future projects, situating ourselves at the intersection of several stories not yet completed.[19]

And all this seems to be true of us as critics, as readers, as social theorists, and as agents in general.

Strong suspicion of any sharp contrast between the real and the merely fictional or literary follows immediately from such a narrativist conception of persons and agency. There is a perfectly straightforward sense in which Jim and Marlow, the narrator-protagonists of the poems of Wordsworth and Coleridge, and Elizabeth and Darcy do not exist, do not occupy space and time, act, wish, fear, hope, marry, or die. But this does not mean that the narratives of what these protagonists do are disconnected from us as idle and misleading merely aesthetic objects. Persons are not, it seems, "just" real material entities either. They lead lives out of ongoing narratives, make choices out of them. These narratives and the lives and choices that they shape are in turn structured by assumptions about narrative unity, coherence, and closure that are tested in narrative writing in general, and in particular in fiction, where the influence of contingencies can yield to the imper-

ative to achieve coherence. It is for this reason that Aristotle observes
that

> the poet's function is to describe, not the thing that has happened, but a
> kind of thing that might happen, i.e. what is possible as being probable
> or necessary. . . . [The historian] describes the thing that has been, and
> [the poet] a kind of thing that might be. Hence poetry is something more
> philosophic and of graver import than history, since its statements are of
> the nature rather of universals, whereas those of history are singulars.[20]

While this remark seriously undervalues history, which is not mere
chronicle but itself involves the construction of narratives, the general
point remains that narratives are important in making manifest connections among beginnings, middles, and ends in order that the
shapes of actions may be discerned and judged. The work of literature,
and of the criticism that continues it, is the very work that we implicitly
and under various pressures of contingency carry out in our own lives
as persons. Literary narratives come from our expressive acts and their
narrative backgrounds; the narrative backgrounds of our acts are structured by assumptions that literary narratives help to make manifest. It
seems that literary narratives and personhood are, one might say,
internal to one another.

If it is plausible to see an internal relation between personhood
and literary narrative, then it is further plausible to see something of a
common personhood variously manifested in different narratives. It
then becomes sensible to say, with Northrop Frye, that persons live

> not directly or nakedly in nature like the animals, but within a mytholog-
> ical universe, a body of assumptions and beliefs developed from
> existential concerns. Most of this is held unconsciously, which means
> that our imaginations may recognize elements of it, when presented in
> art or literature, without consciously understanding what it is that we
> recognize. Practically all that we can see of this body of concern is socially
> conditioned and culturally inherited. Below the cultural inheritance
> there must be a common psychological inheritance, otherwise forms of
> culture and imagination outside our own tradition would not be intelligi-
> ble to us. But I doubt if we can reach this common inheritance directly,
> by-passing the distinctive qualities in our specific culture. One of the
> practical functions of criticism, by which I mean the conscious organiz-
> ing of a cultural tradition, is, I think, to make us more aware of our
> mythological conditioning.[21]

If, so far, this is plausible, it then becomes possible to ask, What
are the fundamental terms of our background, culturally shaped my-
thologies that themselves more deeply reflect existential concerns

stemming from our common personhood? Reading literature and doing criticism with this question in mind will require, as poststructuralist, neo-Marxist, feminist, psychoanalytic, and New Historicist criticisms have variously emphasized, continuous alertness to local linguistic, material, and psychological pressures in shaping the expression of our continuing fundamental concerns as persons. What we can see of our concerns, in the texts that give them expression, *is* socially, materially, linguistically, and psychoanalytically conditioned. There will be real dangers of aestheticism in criticism, resulting from the premature abstraction of continuing concerns from various narratives, without sufficient attention to the contingencies and pressures that make various expressions impure and partially divergent. One will have to be alert to the ways in which concerns can be compromised, and their expressions made incoherent and self-undermining, by these contingencies and pressures. Contingent facts of desire, class, shifting linguistic usage, and culture do give shape to what is expressed. It will hence be wise, as Martha Nussbaum puts it, to read various narratives "side by side,"[22] so that each may call into question the fullness of the visions of our concerns that are expressed in the others. And yet, despite all this, we may still be able to discern the continuing, albeit varied, presence of fundamental concerns—here, particularly, concerns with autonomy and embeddedness—in the expressions that we confront.

Autonomy and embeddedness may thus through our criticism emerge as fundamental values to be balanced as we seek to express and embody respect for persons, ourselves and others. They may stand as the fundamental terms of the mythology, the narrative of our deepest concerns, that discernibly structures the actual culturally embedded expressions and narratives that we receive and construct. Traces of these concerns may then become legible even within those critical theories that urge either that fundamental concerns do not exist or that they are vastly different from those set out here. Much poststructuralism will then appear to be encouraging the autonomy of the reader or receiver by insisting on the incoherencies and self-underminings of the texts that are read, which are then no longer to be taken as authorities. Or, insofar as it is more materially and politically engaged, deconstruction, together with recent neo-Marxisms, may then appear as pointing to the fact and to the varieties of our material embeddedness within a capitalist economy and its institutions or within a linguistic community and its institutions. These institutions and social relations may then be taken within this criticism as things to be embraced, reformed, or resisted, in the name of a renewed vision of autonomy within embeddedness. Likewise, even the high modernist

writings of the twentieth century that initially appear to resist a concern with general values of autonomy and embeddedness in favor of a
kind of detachment and self-corroding irony, wherein the seeker and
seer of value is taken as a figure either of tyranny or of fun, may turn
out in the end to express a concern with autonomy and embeddedness
in a desperately fallen time: witness, for example, Wallace Stevens, as
Helen Vendler and Harold Bloom have taught us to take him, as concerned to discover an authentic American sublime,[23] and as achieving
a "curious late radiance" stemming from "an alliance [in him] between
naturalism and a visionary faculty."[24] ("One must," Stevens wrote,
"make concessions to others; but there is never a necessity of smutch-
ing inner purity."[25] "It is not, then, a matter of eluding human pathos,
human dependence. Thought is part of these, the imagination is part
of these and they are part of thought and imagination."[26]) Any criticism that aims at making fundamental concerns legible and objects of
acknowledgment must be tentative and revisable and must win its
convincingness through its treatment of cases, not a priori. But we may
nonetheless be able to take the work of criticism, together with that of
its objects, to be that of achieving an articulation of the continuing,
culturally manifested concerns of persons.

Thus if these readings are to do the work of showing us to ourselves, then they must do it of themselves, for one of the principal
implications of the Hegelian and Wittgensteinian rejection of epistemology as first philosophy is that the question of a criterion of
interpretation cannot and need not be answered. No proof can be
given of why these texts of Conrad, Wordsworth, Coleridge, and Austen must be read or must be read this way. At best, we can say that
these texts, together with others, neighbor, come from, and inform the
texts of our lives and concerns in ways that make these concerns salient
for present criticism. These texts, these readings, and the understanding of our moral personhood in the world that they develop will be true
or successful not because a known method or criterion tells us so, but
only insofar as we take them up, live them, make sense and assessments of our lives in their terms. There can be no assurance that we will
do this; the ways in which these texts neighbor and inform one another
may give out. And even were we to take these texts up and live against
them, some divisions within ourselves and in our social lives would
nonetheless remain. Failure in self-understanding is a permanent possibility, and failure of perfect self-understanding and perfect self-
realization is a permanent fact.

Not only is a kind of failure our ineliminable lot; the present times
also make likely certain forms of conspicuous failure in the effort to
realize one's personhood in the world. The cultural conditions under

the private ownership of massive amounts of capital are far from propitious for realizing our best shared possibilities. The likelihood that most will be frustrated in attempting to live meaningfully and well in turn can warp our readings and self-understandings. And even were we to feel guided by our responses to these texts and readings to understand and assess our lives along Kantian lines, we could not be spared the work of using these Kantian terms of criticism to read our lives, of testing to what extent they enable us to make sense of who we are, and perhaps of revising or abandoning them. The assessment of cases that proceeds from a commitment to principle is dependent on readings—is creative, not algorithmic—and our commitments remain revisable under the pressure of our further readings. Wittgenstein marked liabilities of this kind in the preface to *Philosophical Investigations:* "It is not impossible that it should fall to the lot of this work, in its poverty and in the darkness of this time, to bring light into one brain or another—but, of course, it is not likely. I should not like my writing to spare other people the trouble of thinking. But, if possible, to stimulate someone to thoughts of his own."[27] Philosophy, bringing terms of description and assessment to bear on one's life and others', is, one might say, not a body of results, but an activity that admits neither of closure nor of full success. Cases may diverge. And yet it is not impossible that some light should be cast by these readings, that something like their work should be taken up and should help us toward partial achievements of understanding and value in our own lives.

The claim that our nature makes demands on us to achieve autonomy and connectedness—demands that are articulated in Kantian principle, known to us through our responses to their acknowledgment and refusal in particular lives, and acknowledged and refused by us along various ranges in our own social lives—runs against not only the public culture of the age, but also, unsurprisingly, its intellectual habits. A school of critics of Kantianism, who have also been concerned with literature, seems often to argue that Kant was an a priorist, that no a priori arguments about morality are sound in the face of our freedom to make of ourselves what we will, and that hence Kantianism is a flawed doctrine. But this argument is logically invalid: it is possible that the substance of Kant's views, with suitable shifts in emphasis, survives the failure of his arguments in favor of them, and that our freedom, though persistent, is a freedom to acknowledge or refuse what our nature demands of us.

Readers of narratives who are hostile to Kantianism, and more broadly those who would refuse any principled assessment of either others' lives or their own, have resorted to two main strategies to avoid recognizing the demands of our nature that are partially acknowledged by the protagonists of these texts. Either they have taken refuge as critics in the supposed scientific authority of psychoanalysis or Marxism, or they have taken refuge in the supposedly impenetrable particularity of literature and criticism ("That's just how I read or see it"), reducing both to gratuitous emotivisms or trivial acts of personal expression. Both strategies tend to deny that morality is or can be of this world. If their practitioner is tough-minded and impressed by science, this will mean "so much the worse for morality"; if sentimentally religious, "so much the worse for this world." Both strategies further offer ways of maintaining one's authority and detachment as a reader. Knowing the laws of the unconscious or of class struggle, or at the very least knowing one's own mind about what one sees in the text, it becomes possible to refuse identification with protagonists and their developments and terms of self-criticism and in this way to free oneself, one's life, and one's reading from the possibility of criticism. Here the complexities of psychoanalytic or deconstructive or Marxist criticism can sometimes serve as a screen between the reader and the moral claims of the text, even where they can also sometimes remind us of the fragility and partiality of any achievement of the expression of our shared personhood. In the terms of the readings here enacted, in contrast, we would be better served as readers were we to refuse methods, theories, and criteria of reading that act primarily as props to our private authority and were we to read cooperatively and in responsiveness to the criticism of our lives that may be implied in opposing narratives of development.

What is needed is to bring the real insights of the newer necessitarian and quasi-scientific criticisms together with those of the more traditional idealistic and aesthetic criticisms in order to elaborate a way of reading that is alert to both the partiality and the genuineness of the achievements of self-understanding and value on the parts of protagonists. No judgment, including the judgments of the necessitarian and quasi-scientific critics, can be altogether free of implicit aesthetic and political ideals; innocence of the ideal cannot be won through a turn to the unconscious or the history of class struggle, for these turns themselves arise in part out of underlying aspirations. Yet no judgment comes wholly from the ideal either; our articulations of ideals and the agendas and readings that emerge out of them remain marked by the particularities of individual desire and by their being generated in response to particular instances of partial injustice and partial success in the expression of personhood in the world. What is needed is not the quasi-scientific criticism that produces the frisson of a new line of fashion in deflating the pretensions of literature and art,[28] and not the criticism of the repetition of empty, decontextualized ideals, but instead the criticism of nonsovereign reminder, a criticism that leads us to see our own dimensions of possible partial success and failure in expressing and sustaining our personhood in the world with others against the background of the partial successes and failures of the protagonists of the narratives we read.

The criticism of nonsovereign reminder—unlike the self-image (but like the fact) of both necessitarian, quasi-scientific criticism and traditional idealizing criticism—shares with its narrative objects both a rootedness in the particular and the implicit presupposition of ideals. In the generation of narratives of human action, of all sorts, and criticism, we are ourselves at stake. Narratives and criticism are alike elements of our efforts to manifest and sustain our personhood in the world in response to particulars. In these efforts, as in our lives, only certain ranges of achievement are possible. There can be no perfect and final narrative of human action, or criticism, or moral philosophy. But there can likewise be no escape from the effort to manifest and sustain our personhood in the world, and no escape from the influence of ideals on this effort. The criticism of nonsovereign reminder would then see in narratives, in criticism, and in our lives successions of what Charles Altieri has called *expressive acts*, "projections that claim an aspect of identity before a community," actual takings of "responsibility for agents' capacities to stage themselves as the kind of persons who can perform deeds in certain ways that establish aspects of this identity for an audience."[29] Such projections, takings, and stagings are ongoingly particular and original in being free from full subjection to an absolutely sovereign specific ideal. Yet, at the same time, in succeeding as projections that are intelligible to us and that serve as reminders of our shared personhood and its tasks, they are acts within what Anthony J. Cascardi has called "a field for the realization" of the moral, not only of the ethical;[30] they manifest in part our shared nature and its demands, not only discrete individual willings. Though Bernard Williams is right to distinguish the ethical from the moral,[31] there is more to be said for the claim that we have a common moral nature than Williams thinks: the moral in part shows itself in our expressive acts and our responses to them.

What then is it to lead the life of a person, and to lead it well, if it is not only to be responsive to the particular pressures of the unconscious, of class, or of personal imperatives? How can an understanding of this be approached? As Richard Wollheim has urged, the question of what it is to lead the life of a person is properly prior in seeking self-understanding to the questions of what it is to be a person and of what a lived life is. The priority involved here might be called *dianoietic* or decisive for the possibility of understanding: "In order to understand the thing that is the person, or in order to understand the product that is the person's life, we need to understand the process that is the person's leading his life."[32] If instead we focus directly on what we imagine to be the thing that is the person or on the relations among events or states imagined of themselves to constitute a person's life, putting aside the question of what it is to live as a person, then we will end up attempting to *explain* ourselves as complex or constructed objects or events falling under nomological laws. Thus we would end up scanting our distinctive capacities as subjects for self-responsibility; we would devalue and misunderstand the contributions we make as agents to our own lives. As Charles Taylor paraphrases Wollheim's view, which he traces to Kant's criticisms of Hume's conception of personal identity, "any adequate description of human life must make reference to our projects and careers as active beings."[33] Or, as Wollheim has it, it is crucial that there is a "way in which [a person's life] comes about,"[34] a way having to do with our activity. Were we to deny this, and live out this denial so far as possible, we would refuse our best possibilities, miscasting ourselves as things, not persons.

There can be no direct and fully convincing demonstrative argument for these claims. Wollheim himself says that a crucial consideration in establishing our active role in our lives is "the dependence of mental states on underlying mental dispositions and the further fact that these dispositions must be housed somewhere—and where else could they be housed but in a person?"[35] To this, one might well feel inclined to say that mental dispositions, for all Wollheim's claims show, might "simply be lodged in the brain."[36] Indeed the idea that it is the setting up and reinforcement of *dispositions*—especially those to remember, imagine, and anticipate—that constitute leading the life of a person might well encourage a reductive treatment of our putative activity as subjects, for dispositions are the sorts of things that might plausibly be taken to be implanted in us by our experience and biology.

Beyond demonstrative argument, however, Wollheim, under the influence of psychoanalytic theory, attends closely to particular cases (notably that of Freud's Rat Man) of the development of dispositions and of the leading of lives by persons, seeking to *show* how we lead our lives, rather than arguing that we must lead them in a certain way. One should not altogether resist the sort of story Wollheim tells of the sometimes decisive and sometimes devastating effects infantile experiences can have on our development. But, even without questioning too closely either Wollheim's account of the Rat Man or the suggestion that some lives can be shaped by the sorts of experiences the Rat Man had (the suggestion that our mental lives have, among others, a structure that permits this), one may well wonder whether *all* our actions and understandings are largely the effects of such experiences and structures. Moreover, even the weak value-laden assessments of the Rat Man's fantasies and actions as pathological or dysfunctional—assessments that Wollheim carefully avoids, but that psychoanalysis as therapy seems to require—seemingly presuppose a capacity on our part, independent of our infantile experiences and our mental structures of response to them, for assessing the shape and goodness of a life. Similar remarks might be made about accounts of the influence of class experience on the shapes of our lives.

Yet how compelling are such criticisms of the significance of Wollheim's readings of cases? How much support for morality do these criticisms yield? Just what are our capacities? It is not at all clear that theoretical remarks about what we must be able to do will take us very far. For example, Charles Taylor has similarly urged, against various reductionisms, that we do make an independent contribution as evaluators to our lives. As he puts it,

> To be a full human agent, to be a person or a self in the ordinary meaning, is to exist in a space defined by distinctions of worth. A self is a being for whom certain questions of categoric value have arisen, and received at least partial answers. Perhaps they have been given authoritatively by the culture more than they have been elaborated in the deliberation of the person concerned, but they are his in the sense that they are incorporated into his self-understanding, in some degree and fashion. . . . Our identity is therefore defined by certain evaluations which are inseparable from ourselves as agents. . . . Shorn of these we would lose the very possibility of being an agent who evaluates; . . . we would break down as persons, be incapable of being persons in the full sense.[37]

Taylor then goes on, albeit tentatively, to suggest that the structure of our capacity to evaluate not only rests upon what is given in our cultures, experiences, or personal motives, but also includes the potential to "feel called upon *qua* rational being, or moral being, or creature made by God in his image, in other words capable of responding to this like God, that is, out of agape."[38] How far is this so? How are our evaluative capacities incorporated into us? Through introjection and socialization, as Wollheim suggests? Or are they somehow, at least in part, independently emergent, as Taylor suggests? Alone—apart, that is, from attention to cases (narratives that make sense and engage us) of the emergence and exercise of our evaluative capacities—such claims, as Taylor more or less recognizes,[39] hang in the air. So far as close attention to substantial narratives is lacking, we can no more find ourselves in these abstract claims than in the claims Humeans or Freudians make about the structure of our capacities to evaluate. Without attention to cases, we are left torn between Humean-Freudian imagery picturing understanding and evaluating as products of impingement and Platonic imagery picturing them as decontextualized vision. Either way, we fail to countenance the possibilities, marked by Hegel and Wittgenstein, that self-understanding is centrally an ongoing activity and social phenomenon, bound up with both criticism and conversation.

If we are to go on in self-understanding, avoiding an unending alternation between theoretical characterizations of us that tantalize us—those of Humeans and Freudians by grounding us in the world and promising us science, those of Platonists and Kantian noumenalists by exalting our dignity and autonomy—but that we cannot wholly live, then all we can do is attempt to find ourselves in cases, in narratives of the development of persons. Such generalizations about our capacities as there can be will emerge only as we show ourselves to ourselves through the work of reading. All we can do— we are perhaps fated to do as we lead our lives, in any case—is engage in, take our bearings as agents and evaluators from, *insistence*,[40] *criticism*,[41] *redescription*,[42] or *reading*,[43] directed at cases in the service of the elaboration of a *perspicuous representation*[44] of who we are, of what our nature as persons is and demands of us. This will be an open-ended arrangement of cases, narratives, admitting of multiple points of entry, standing in complex relations of mutual criticism and reinforcement, and yet fitting together, each leading us to the others along various strands of characterization, continuing and deepening our responses, as these strands in intertwining compose and recompose an account of the manifestation, sustenance, and partial betrayal of our moral personhood and our fundamental concerns in the world.

Elaborating a perspicuous representation of our personhood will itself be a moral enterprise, not a detached cognitive exercise. As we go on in developing our readings of cases and our strands of characterization of our personhood, taking our bearings as agents and evaluators from these developments, we will be making something of ourselves, taking up or abandoning one or another possibility for our personhood, in ways that will themselves be open to assessment. Our readings enact possibilities of practice in ways that are themselves open to moral assessment. Our insistences, criticisms, redescriptions, and readings will themselves be expressive acts—it would be a mistake to think of these, in the manner of Rorty,[45] as necessarily either discoveries or proposals—and will take their places alongside the expressive acts that are their objects, rather than setting once and for all the terms of assessment of all acts. There is no fixed foundation for either our reading or our going on[46]—though this is not to say that we may not find ourselves in possession of relatively stable readings of cases and relatively firm commitments to principle. Yet such progress in reading and practice as we can make is also not merely a matter of achieving coherence. Certain readings and changes in practice may be revolutionary in requiring transfigurations of our activities and concerns and may put us more deeply in touch with our personhood. In looking back, we can sometimes see clear mistakes in prior understandings, not only intuitions to be balanced against others.

When our reading through particulars proceeds without fixed foundations and yet nonetheless may stably draw on and support certain general characterizations of our nature and its demands, then any hard distinction between literature and philosophy begins to dissolve. Narratives of the particular are always embedded within general presuppositions about persons and about what makes sense (literature is implicated in philosophy), and general presuppositions gain their sense and intelligibility only from the particular narratives that draw on them (philosophy is implicated in literature). The central texts—those of Homer and Plato, Augustine and Dante, Descartes and Cervantes, Tolstoy and Wittgenstein, and so on—from which the normalized disciplines of literature and philosophy in some unfaithfulness take their bearings are perhaps best understood as readings of a particularized common human being in the world, so that these works resist ready classification into the simply particular and the simply theoretical. As T. S. Eliot casts the relation between poetry and philosophy, "What poetry proves about any philosophy is merely its possibility for being lived. . . . For poetry . . . is not the assertion that something is true, but the making that truth more fully real to us; it is the creation of a sensuous embodiment. It is the making the Word Flesh."[47] What remains to be added is that without this poetic Flesh there can be nothing that we will honor as the Word, nothing that we will count as a genuine understanding of our nature and its demands. And without the Word, or a partial articulation of it in a general characterization of the person, there can be no coherent or recognizable poetry or narrative, no Flesh. Hence philosophy must both resist and embrace the perennial temptation to achieve full closure of understanding, to deny the potentially revolutionary importance of new cases, as it must both move toward general characterizations and retain its responsiveness to the particular. And hence literature must both embrace and resist its perennial temptation to concentrate solely on the particular, as it must respond to what is new and contingent while still drawing on general characterizations in order to focus our attention. And to say all this is to say that philosophy and literature must simultaneously embrace and resist one another. Writing that responds to these imperatives, no matter whether it is called literature or criticism or philosophy, will fall, as it were, somewhere between the Book and *l'écriture*. It will be neither the sacred solution to life nor mere unguided intertextuality. In Wittgenstein's words, "Thus this book is really only an album."[48]

THOUGH THEY CAN neither do the work of the readings, nor justify them, nor even have any sure claim of following what is there among them, some preliminary tracings of the characterization of our shared moral personhood in the world that will emerge may help to articulate these readings' commentary on and continuance of one another. The texts of Coleridge ("Frost at Midnight," 1798), Wordsworth (*Prelude*, 1799, 1805, 1850; "Resolution and Independence," 1802), and Austen (*Pride and Prejudice*, 1813) that are under study were all largely written in England within a span of fifteen years. Conrad completed *Lord Jim* in July 1900. Each writer was thus well placed both to have a re-membrance, despite advancing secularization, of a lived religious conception of human life and dignity and simultaneously in that re-membrance to encounter and criticize emergent materialism and capitalism. (The Poland of Conrad's youth was both more religious and less industrialized, culturally more like the England of the early nineteenth century, than the England of the 1860s and 1870s.) This is noteworthy, again, not in justifying their grouping, but in pointing us to what may, after reading, emerge as a common responsiveness both to a cultural moment or condition that may still persist in part and to our persistent natural senses of ourselves as both autonomous and in the world. That is, the response of these writers to a cultural moment or condition may itself be a figure and a prominent manifestation of our recurrent situation in feeling torn between our aspirations to wholeness, integrity, and spirituality and the demands and facts of our material needs and circumstances, between our autonomy and our embeddedness. There is perhaps a certain particular courage and per-ceptiveness in these writers in facing this sense of being torn, in seeking an honorable resolution of it, and in acknowledging the partial character of the resolutions they project.

In each text, the route toward partial resolution and self-under-standing is presented as involving multiple and ongoing activities of reading and interpreting. Jim of his past; Marlow of Jim, the French lieutenant, Brierly, and himself; Wordsworth of his past and of his present moods; Coleridge of his vexed meditations, of the film on the grate, of his childhood, and of his and his son's futures; Elizabeth and Darcy together of each other's motives and capacities—all appear as readers or interpreters, attempting to understand and express themselves and their natures in the world. In each case others—whether as subjects of interpretation, occasions for interpretation, or co-interpreters—play significant roles in enabling the work of reading. There is a variety of these roles, from the bare presence and example of the leech gatherer of "Resolution and Independence," to the absent friend and addressee (Coleridge) of the *Prelude*, to the imagined shapers, audiences, and inheritors of the *Prelude* and "Frost at Midnight," to the co-interpreters and co-protagonists of *Lord Jim* and, most fully, *Pride and Prejudice*. In each case, our competence in seeking self-understanding as readers or interpreters is shown to depend on our already being in relationship with others. (This is thematically most explicit in Wordsworth, most fully actualized in Austen.) These images of socially contextualized, cooperative reading or interpreting, with its occasions and outcomes, demand to be set against such alternative images of routes to self-understanding as Plato's allegory of the cave, with its individualistic and nonlinguistic emphases, and Hume's and Freud's parables of graceful submission to irresistible forces.

Continually balancing in these texts a sense of the role of others in coming to self-understanding is a sense of the *content* of self-understanding as including an awareness of what activities and relations befit a person, or enable personhood's maintenance and furtherance, or answer to our fundamental concerns. This awareness is figured as the acknowledgment of Kantian principle and its contextual requirements in Jim and Marlow, as Wordsworth's uncovering of the possibility and importance of poetic activity, personal and political, as Coleridge's casting of his future well-being as involving his serving as a teacher, and as Elizabeth and Darcy's discovery of the possibility and value of joint purposiveness and responsive conversation. These modes of awareness inform one another. Wordsworth's commitment to a way of activity and relationship as fit for a person and Coleridge's similar commitment to teaching show us the structures of activity that we must develop in respecting and attending to persons, and show us what Elizabeth and Darcy may together aspire to. The progress in relationship of Elizabeth and Darcy shows us the social conditions of the acknowledgment and achievement of respect for persons and of cooperative engagement in activities of value. It shows us part of what may be imagined to have taken place between Jim and Jewel, as Jim discovers the fact and value of her need for him. The scope and limits of the progress of Elizabeth and Darcy show us how hard it must be under unjust social conditions to sustain our respect for, attention to, and nurturance of ourselves and others as persons. Our concerns for autonomy and embeddedness cannot be fully balanced against each other under conditions of social injustice, of which unconstrained individualist capitalism and bureaucratic authoritarianism are alike types. A sense of limits to genuine but particular moral achievements is the political dimension of each text. These writers do not so much deny the political as see it as omnipresent in the fine details of domestic and daily life, where partial, but only partial, solutions to moral problems may be achieved. These achieved solutions may then point toward the transformation of the political and the public, even where inertia in these realms proves too strong to be overcome in private achievement. Marlow's marking of the demands of the principle of respect for persons as internal to our nature, in contrast with the appeals of honors and rewards, articulates the difference Elizabeth and Darcy come to feel between the use of others for satisfaction that is generally prevalent around them and the subjecthood for one another that they come to achieve and value. And so on, as the protagonists' awarenesses of our nature as persons and its demands grow along various dimensions.

Further internal to the development of each awareness is a sense of the impossibility of self-sufficient moral authority. Every interpretation of our nature and its demands is at the same time an egoistic violation of them. Any interpretation can be ratified only in general social life, as others freely take it up and live it out. No such ratification can be complete, insofar as the expressive acts of others will stand alongside and criticize the partial achievements of any protagonist. Thus Marlow must tell Jim's and his story "many times in distant parts of the world," Wordsworth and Coleridge compulsively project, as though out of deep knowledge of the onwardness of social life and the partial otherness of others, the reception of their visions of our possibilities, and Elizabeth and Darcy rehearse their interpretations for each other and criticize each other's lapses, perhaps therein escaping a world they cannot master. We nonetheless remain always tempted by inflexibility—tempted, that is, to flee from reading and to regard our stance as something sublime and immune from criticism—and we continually, in reading and in action, reinforce norms always imperfectly and in the absence of finally founded knowledge. (This is perhaps much of what is comprised in the religious doctrine of original sin.) Yet authority persists only in the continual extension of community in expressive acts that are intelligible to others.

And thus each work acknowledges the impossibility of the full and final closure of authority. There will always be new others to test any interpretation of our personhood, and their responses cannot be mastered a priori. There are unavoidable risks in going on, in philosophy and in life. Marlow ends his narrative with a question put to us;

Wordsworth projects a future and wishes for, but cannot force, a response from us; Coleridge leaves us with the image of the poet as icicle, reflecting itself and its place in the order of things to us but also melting into nothingness; the conversations of Elizabeth and Darcy are dominated by their shared dark thought of the limits of education, of words, in bringing us to shared self-understanding, in the face of the onwardness of human life. Can we go on, in understanding and in practice, from the cases here considered: from Jim, Marlow, the French lieutenant, and Brierly; from the Wordsworth of rationalist revolution and the Wordsworth of social-poetic activity; from Coleridge the outsider and Coleridge the teacher; from Charlotte Lucas, Lydia, Mr. and Mrs. Bennet, Darcy, and Elizabeth? How—with what capacities, concerns, tasks, and self-understandings as persons in the world—do we go on?

THE PHENOMENOLOGY OF MORAL CONSCIOUSNESS: PRINCIPLE AND CONTEXT, KANT AND HEGEL

1. Consciousness, Relativism, Rationalism, and Literature

It is tempting to see our lives as wholly driven by the particular. When we think back over our lives, we are likely to attempt to explain their courses by saying that we did such and such because we wished to please someone or because we had internalized a role set by others' expectations of us. Such explanations are often in order, and the development of various psychological and revolutionary therapies in the twentieth century has made us more alert to their variety.

As we have become more sophisticated in explanation, a natural consequence has been the replacement of morality by therapy, of responsibility by inevitability, and of praise and blame against a moral standard by talk of causes and cures. Action on moral principle and the demand for it have come to many to seem impossibilities, and moral assessment has come to be etiolated. A certain strand in contemporary moral philosophy, evident in the writings of such figures as MacIntyre, Foot, and Williams, and rooted in various ways in Nietzsche, Freud, and Hume, has sharply circumscribed moral authority, denied the universalizability of moral judgments, and rejected any accounts of practical reasoning that are cast in terms of abstract principles that emphasize fairness and equality and that fail to accord overriding conduct-relevant value to specific persons or communities or desires. Such a circumscription of moral authority and disjoining of it from a grasp of abstract principles is clearest in Williams's attack on moralities of impartiality and defense of multiple moralities of the perfection of particularized characters. In thinking about the rationality of impartial conduct, Williams observes, one necessarily comes up against the thought

that such things as deep attachments to other persons will express themselves in the world in ways which cannot at the same time embody the
impartial view, and that they also run the risk of offending against it.
   They run that risk if they exist at all; yet unless such things exist,
there will not be enough substance or conviction in a man's life to compel
his allegiance to life itself.[1]

Thus, according to Williams, reasoning about how to act arises only in
the context of particular given desires, projects, and attachments that
are of an overriding importance to those who have them.

My present projects are the condition of my existence, in the sense that
unless I am propelled forward by the conatus of desire, project and
interest, it is unclear why I should go on at all: the world, certainly as a
kingdom of moral agents, has no particular claim on my presence or,
indeed, interest in it.[2]

This circumscription of moral reasoning to reflection that acknowledges the importance of given particulars stems from a
relentlessly naturalistic conception of deliberation and of human
thinking generally. Deliberation and conceptualization are ineluctably
shaped by the particular circumstances of their appearance. As MacIntyre puts it, "Concepts are first acquired and understood in terms of
poetic images, and the movement of thought from the concreteness
and particularity of the imaged to the abstractness of the conceptual
never completely leaves that concreteness and particularity behind."[3]
A kind of moral relativism is an immediate consequence of the ineluc-
table and overriding influence of the particular, for, when two persons
from substantially different communities and historical contexts confront one another, "each will represent the beliefs of the other within
its own discourse in abstraction from the relevant tradition and so in a
way that ensures misunderstanding."[4] As a result, consensus about
rightness or permissibility or *dikaiosyne* or *Recht* or *devoir* will not be
forthcoming; the parties to such confrontations are not even talking
about the same thing.
   Against such a background phenomenology of conceptualization
and deliberation, an insistence on action motivated by abstract universal principles will seem to urge a substitution of arid legalism for
graceful submission to the natural bonds of love and to promote both a
narcissistic failure of responsiveness to others and, in the end, a kind
of self-mutilation, severing the self from those commitments that make
its life in expressive action possible. When human deliberation is so
understood, the result of an insistence on principle is that even "a
deeply rooted and natural love is degraded to the status of a gratifica-

tion of the self"[5] that is of no moral significance. Instead of being grounded in the articulation and application of abstract principles, moral deliberation from this perspective is more properly aretaic and relative to circumstance, devoted to figuring out by reference to examples the best that can be done in particular situations.

A sharply contrasting rationalist strand in contemporary moral philosophy, inspired largely by Kant and evident in the writings of such figures as Gewirth and Donagan, finds relativistic, aretaic moral theory, and its associated phenomenology of deliberation, both deeply problematic on its own account and insensitive to our genuine capacities of rational reflection. The sort of aretaic theory espoused by Williams, MacIntyre, and Foot is, from this latter point of view, crucially "morally indeterminate,"[6] in Gewirth's phrase. Aretaic theory offers us no rules or criteria of rightness or permissibility by reference to which we might decide what is obligatory and what is permitted in any given situation. (MacIntyre might admit this and claim that only religion can save us from indeterminacy; Williams would accept indeterminacies that stem from conflicting particular commitments as crucial to the texture of the ethical life.) But morality must be determinate, in that there must be objective analyses of fairness, rightness, and so forth if these concepts are to have application at all. Genuine virtue, on this latter rationalist reading, consists in an ongoing disposition to reflect on and live according to rationally knowable universal moral rules. Where aretaic theorists see moral narcissism and a flight from commitment in appeals to principles, rules, or criteria, moral rationalists see in aretaic thinking a failure of seriousness and a kind of moral anomie insofar as aretaic theory regards human beings less as self-legislating than as directed by their particular given cares and commitments.

Aretaic thinking and its yoking of deliberation to the particular are mistaken, according to moral rationalism, precisely because we are capable, as agents and rational beings, of grasping universal laws of right conduct. As Gewirth puts it, "The existence of human rights [as specified in principles constraining permissible action] logically must be granted by *every* agent."[7] Failure to abide by this "must" is a failure of rationality, for the principle that rights and hence rule-delineated constraints on permissible action exist "signifies . . . what agents are logically committed to hold or accept insofar as they are rational in the sense of being able to follow out the implications of the concepts of agent and action, and hence of their own activity as such."[8] No matter what our particular circumstances, we are all capable of rational reflection on what it means to be an agent, and such reflection is sufficient to lead us to recognize the existence of rights and to keep to the principle of respecting them. The respect for rights that is brought about by adherence to the moral rules has the function of promoting the exercise of the capacities that are characteristic of agents in general.

> The ultimate purpose of the rights is to secure for each person a certain fundamental moral status: that of having rational autonomy and dignity in the sense of being a self-controlling, self-developing agent who can relate to other persons on a basis of mutual respect and cooperation, in contrast to being a dependent, passive recipient of the agency of others.[9]

The seriousness of the rationalist conception of the moral life is compelling. Yet, armed with the notion that there is a competing Humean-Nietzschean phenomenology of deliberation and conception of agency, one must wonder whether a life lead in its terms would be either possible or valuable. A measure of perhaps overconfident a priorism infects the rationalist conception of agency and the moral life. Why aren't deliberation and agency Humean? (Gewirth simply *says* in passing that "Aristotle's analysis of voluntary action is just as relevant and true for modern and contemporary agency as it was for his own time."[10]) If agency is Humean, then the "must" in the Gewirthian "all agents *must* . . ." will not be categorical and necessary but will instead be hypothetical and contingent on one's projects. (MacIntyre, treating the "must" as hypothetical, objects that "I must have freedom," which he then reads roughly as "I want freedom," does not entail "I have a right to freedom";[11] Gewirth replies that the "must" is categorical and necessary, that I must as a rational agent have freedom.[12] Which, then, is it? Which conception of agency is correct?)

Or why isn't agency Hegelian—something which can be fully exercised not by individuals no matter what their circumstances, but whose exercise requires the active cooperation of others in mutually sustaining projects directed toward a single, coherent, overarching end? From such a point of view, Gewirthian cooperation among individuals who suppose themselves capable of full voluntary agency on their own, and who respect one another's rights, will look like a form of *competition*. To a Hegelian, representing freedom as a requirement of sheer voluntariness, as Gewirth does, leads to a seriously incomplete understanding of freedom, which is a rich social concept; what individuals require for mere voluntariness—mostly, absence of coercion, perhaps not even that—falls far short of a genuinely freedom-enhancing and person-furthering social system. From this point of view, Kantian-inspired moral rationalism substitutes legalistic *Moralität* for genuine agency-nurturing *Sittlichkeit*, rationalizes a liberal system of economic distribution and exchange that materially and spiritually impoverishes many, and leaves us with a self-conception that inhibits the development of social forms in which full agency *can* be exercised. *If* the exercise of full agency is possible only within a perfected *Sittlichkeit* or institutionally embodied communal self-understanding, then individualist moral rationalisms will be either impoverishing and uncritically conservative of the status quo or empty of content insofar as they fail to promote some *Sittlichkeit* or other, where some background *Sittlichkeit* always shapes and remains necessary for even minimal agency and reflection. Hence, unless it uncritically rationalizes what is, individualist moral rationalism cannot tell us how to enter into agency-nurturing projects, commitments, and relations. Individualist moral rationalism thus enforces a kind of liberalism, against the background of which, as one critic has put it, "all our particular attachments and commitments appear as mere inclinations with respect to which we are *passive;* they do not express anything significant about our moral personalities."[13] Individualist moral rationalism prescribes nothing about what attachments and relations we are to enter into in order to nourish the capacities for agency, rationality, self-expression, and social interaction that the Hegelian model of agency sees as closely linked. It represents our desires and interests as given; their pursuit may be checked by reason but not educated by it.

One must then wonder whether an analysis of the concepts—our concepts—of *agency* and *reasons* can reveal even our own obligations and aspirations, let alone everyone's. If the obligations and aspirations that actually move us are rooted in either the community or the particular, then appeals to universal principle *will* be narcissistic refusals of connectedness. And yet there are the threats of indeterminacy and anomie to trouble aretaic thinking and particularist conceptions of agency.

IN CONFRONTING THESE sharply distinct relativist and rationalist strands in contemporary moral philosophy, one may find oneself to be deeply pulled both ways: both narcissism and anomie are genuine problems in the moral life. Despite this, very little has been done to reconcile the insights embedded in these two strands of moral philosophy. Accounts of the moral lives of persons that proceed from the relativist and rationalist standpoints tend to pass each other by in mutual incomprehension, and this largely because they fail to rest on a shared understanding of the phenomenology and possibilities of human deliberation and action. Concrete accounts of the pull of specific attachments on certain exemplary figures are pitted against sketches of our ability to reflect on what is abstractly right and universally required.

Yet it is not clear that relativist-aretaic and rationalist-universalist accounts of our moral life *must* pass each other by, and one might hope that a suitably full phenomenology of deliberation and action could make a place for the claims of both particular attachments and universal principles, that such a phenomenology could even articulate their interaction for us. What is the best illustrative account—the account into which we are imaginatively able to enter most fully, recognizing ourselves as potential protagonists—of how we come to deliberate and to act rationally and responsibly? How, in such an account, are the claims of the particular and the universal aligned against each other?

Any plausible phenomenology must acknowledge that, as Williams and MacIntyre have emphasized, human deliberation and action actually emerge only in various specific conditioning circumstances, whether or not what emerges is then subject to certain universal constraints set by our rationality and agency. Particular projects and commitments to others *are* ontogenetically prior to our reflective normative thinking. And one may, as it were, remain stuck in the particular, with all one's actions driven by an overriding demand, produced by particular circumstances, for revenge or affection or respect. (Consider Thomas Sutpen in *Absalom, Absalom!*) Serious injuries to our projects and commitments are moral tragedies in that they can detract from the worth of our lives as persons, crippling our capacities for reflection in conversation with others and for envisioning and entering into projects expressive of both our particular selves and our humanity. One can be diminished by the loss of friends, justice, or liberty in such a way that leading the life of a person, exercising the given capacities that are distinctive of one's personhood, is no longer seriously possible in practice.[14] Madness is one of the threats of such losses. One's capacities as a moral person may be prevented by loss or injury from developing into actual abilities to be engaged in the world as a moral person, just as one might have a capacity to speak Hindi but lack or be prevented from developing the ability to speak Hindi (one may be capable of speaking Hindi, but not able to speak it).[15]

In light of such facts, views such as those of Kant and Gewirth that simply identify our capacity for rational reflection and our obligations to act according to reason as categorial features of rational agents per se, without elaborating how we have exercised this ability concretely, are not helpful. Unless we can see ourselves as concretely exercising abilities reflective of our deep capacities as moral persons, our grip on our possession of these capacities will become attenuated, and a Humean-Nietzschean conception of agency will seem more plausible. With what reason do we regard ourselves as having deep capacities for principled deliberation and action if we cannot see these capacities expressed in manifested abilities and in particular choices?

Human persons may normally and naturally have certain capacities, and this may entitle them to certain forms of respect, but these capacities, while perhaps normal among humans and categorial among rational beings, are at least subject to injury and loss. We can be injured as persons when our bodies and attachments and social lives are wounded deeply enough. And this means that how those capacities normally develop into abilities in us and what claim their fostering makes on us are serious issues that cannot be settled solely by general characterizations of what it is to be a rational agent. Indeed, if the influence on us of particular harms and goods is great enough, can really prevent our being *able* in practice to lead the lives of moral persons, then, one may begin to fear, perhaps we have no deep given capacities as moral persons at all; perhaps our particularity goes deeper than our personhood. How human beings (normally and naturally) become capable rational and moral agents in the world and why and how their so becoming *must* be fostered are issues that require a phenomenology of human agency in the world, not remarks about rationality per se. As one sympathetic critic of Kant has put it,

> Kant located our rational nature and its attendant dignity out of this world, outside experience and even time. In so doing, he distilled out of the conception of persons and moral psychology the urgency and immediacy of morality which is so evident in and integral to being in the world.[16]

And in doing this Kant may have made impossible our recognition of ourselves as moral persons within the world. If our particularity is a fact of our lives in our differing attachments and projects—and it is—then to locate our universal capacity for rational self-governance out of this world, isolated from the influence of particularity, is to locate it out of our lives, so that our moral personhood becomes an idealistic illusion.

But while any serious phenomenology of deliberation and action must acknowledge the rootedness in the world of our deliberating and our living, it does not follow that deliberating and living cannot be informed by universal principles. Is it possible for a sense of principle that transcends one's particular attachments and projects to emerge within the very framework of our living that they set? If so, how? Not, as Kant supposed, by our coming to recognize our membership in an intelligible world—unless Kant's account of our recognition of ourselves as noumenal is metaphorical for some more complex act of self-recognition. What is the phenomenology of coming to see that one is bound by principle? How is this achievement both shaped by the particular and partially transcendent of it, so that it may inform our further attachments to particulars? What social requirements might there be for such an achievement? Could it enable us to overcome both moral narcissism and moral anomie? How?

ATTENTION TO NARRATIVES is of crucial importance in thinking through the answers to these questions, for narratives (fictional, poetic, biographical, autobiographical, and historical) contain the fullest reflective accounts there are of deliberation and action in specific circumstances. When such accounts are concerned with motives, ideals, changes in self-understanding, and the like, then—whether they are fictional, poetic, biographical, autobiographical, or historical—they are not directly and unambiguously verifiably true or false of particular persons, times, and places. Somewhat surprisingly, this makes them of considerable value as vehicles for self-reflection on our personhood and its moral dimensions, for, in narratives of action, descriptions of deliberation, motivation, and action vary (within some limits set by facts) at the author's discretion, so that ranges of narrative test and establish the limits of the possible in human deliberation and action. As a result, the narratives of art—that is, the ones we and others over time respond to most deeply and enter into most fully—will (it is plausible to surmise) reflect to us the most serious demands on and possibilities for our moral lives as persons. A narrative of this kind, in Danto's phrase, gives "me to myself for each self peering into it . . . , [transforms] the self-consciousness of the reader who by virtue of identifying with the image recognizes what he is."[17] Or, as Charles Altieri puts it, the works of the literary canon, while they are not fixed a priori and must always be judged and rejudged "from within the canon as it develops over time," nonetheless provide "examples of what ideals can be, of how people have used them as stimuli and contexts for their own self-creation, and of when acts in the present can address more than the present," can even "articulate what Jürgen Habermas calls our emancipatory interests."[18] Moreover, if and only if we take seriously the reflection of ourselves to ourselves by works of narrative art as a source of action-shaping self-understanding will it be possible to avoid the errors of both pure a prioristic idealism (according to which action-guiding changes of consciousness can come from pure reflection, not connected with particulars) and materialism (according to which changes in consciousness are always driven by material forces, psychological or biological or social, not by independent achievements of self-understanding). Even if we cannot achieve a complete and perfected self-understanding through reflection on our responses to narrative art, we may nonetheless hope through these responses, reflections, and the activities and relations to which they lead us to maintain and further our personhood in the world.

Once we take narrative art seriously as a vehicle of self-reflection, then the most moving and critically absorbing accounts of deliberation and action, and of their circumstances, successes, and failures, can enable us to test to what extent we see ourselves as commanded by principle as part of our highest aspirations for ourselves as persons and for our projects, in specific social and institutional circumstances. *If* acting on principle has a proper place in our lives as persons, then it must be evident to us in the deliberations, actions, and self-recognitions of those protagonists in narrative art whom we recognize as reflections of ourselves and who have managed to reconcile particulars, principles, social relations, and aspirations in a way that is expressive of their ongoing recognition of themselves, and our recognition of them, as human persons in the world. What such protagonists do with the particular, how they bring universal principles to bear on it, to the extent that they do, can be exemplary for us in reflecting on our own moral lives as persons.

In order, however, initially to develop a fuller sense of the shape of the problem of how we *may* come to act on principle, it is useful to survey both Kant's theory of morality and practical reason and Hegel's richly developed criticisms of it. A survey of Kant's account of our capacity as rational beings to acknowledge and act on principle, and of Hegel's reasons for denigrating this capacity, can point us toward an understanding of just what sorts of circumstances, achievements, needs, social relations, and other abilities the exercise of this capacity in human persons may presuppose and rest on. We may further come to appreciate the existence of limits to even our best efforts to exercise and sustain our capacity for practical reason. Through surveying certain criticisms, not all sharply distinct and not all consistent, of Kant's account of the exercise of agency in the world, and through developing responses to them that depart to varying degrees from Kant's official exposition of agency, it becomes possible to see just how acting on principle *may*, even while marked by particularity, be both possible and valuable in the world, not out of it.

2. Kantian Morality: Problems and Responses

1. The most common classic charge against Kant's moral philosophy (a charge, for example, quickly made and upheld by MacIntyre,[19] and surveyed and rejected by Donagan[20]) is that Kant's analysis of permissibility is, in virtue of its failure to refer to any specific desires or desired ends as material for willing, an empty formalism: anything is

permitted. Kant, so the criticism runs, first of all gives us no independent reasons to adopt a principle of respect for persons.[21] He fails really to explain why one must always "treat humanity, whether in your own person or in that of another, always as an end and never as a means only."[22] Second, even were we to have reasons as rational agents for adopting a principle of respect for persons, there are no criteria of respect. For all Kant says, it remains open to a Nietzschean to hold that he respects and even loves his enemy as he stabs him in the back. Respect and treatment as an end are notions that are too plastic to make anything objectively impermissible. Finally, though rational agents must indeed be consistent, the consistent universalizability of my maxim, or description of what I aim at in doing such and such, that is enjoined by the first version of the categorical imperative is too weak a constraint to rule out any action as impermissible. Anything I might desire to do can be justified under some maxim or other that is consistently universalizable. As MacIntyre puts it, "All that I need to do is to characterize the proposed action in such a way that the maxim will permit me to do what I want while prohibiting others from doing what would nullify the maxim if universalized."[23] All I need do is say that I am doing such and such in order to benefit *me*, with all my particular qualities. Or, as Hegel, who first lodged this criticism, put it, "Just because the criterion is a tautology, and indifferent to the content, one content is as acceptable to it as its opposite."[24] Because in it "no transition is possible to the specification of particular duties," Kant's moral philosophy is a mere "empty formalism."[25]

One way to reply to this charge and to find content in the first version of the categorical imperative is to insist that I may not cast about for any universalizable maxim at all under which my proposed action considered consequentially might be permitted; instead I must test for consistent universalizability the actual maxim or description of my aim in doing such and such that has occurred to me and led me to contemplate acting. But the difficulty with this reply is that I may be radically uncertain about my own aims and maxims. I may, for example, find myself lifting weights.[26] Why? To maintain my health or become strong? To mortify my flesh as a punishment for transgressions? Narcissistically, in order to become a loved *object* (again)? To make a show of my seriousness in preferring exercise to entertainment? Unless there are stable criteria for calling specific actions, described physically and consequentially, actions in the pursuit of specific ends, radical uncertainty about ends and hence about maxims is always likely to undermine the application of the permissibility test embodied in the first version of the categorical imperative. There will be stable criteria linking actions (considered physically and consequentially) with ends only when people regularly employ them, that is, publicly interpret their own and others' actions according to them, educate their children in them and their application, and in general articulate and make use of them. Here, then, is one presupposition of the applicability of Kant's morality of principle: there must be criteria linking actions and ends, criteria adverted to in the life of a community of persons.

The same presupposition, further explicitly connected with a conception of value for persons, emerges in considering the applicability of a principle of respect for persons. If there are stable and publicly acknowledged forms of respect for persons (criteria connecting actions, described physically and consequentially, with the achievement of respect for persons), then the notion of respect will *not* be overly plastic and will enable us to classify some actions as objectively impermissible. If, furthermore, we clearly regard the instancing of these forms of respect for persons, or acting according to the criteria of respect, as·an expression of something personhood requires, then we as persons will have a reason for acting according to a principle of respect for persons.

Crucially, and contrary to Kant, the establishment and testing of both the application of criteria of respect and the value of acting according to them *cannot* be the work of individual consciousness or conscience alone. Alone, individuals will founder in attempting to see both how to express respect and what makes its expression valuable, just as they will founder in attempting to formulate the maxims they are to test for universalizability. Criteria are established publicly, as they are articulated and lived out by the members of a form of life. The articulation of moral principles, their public application to specific cases, and their value for persons all proceed together only against the background of a *Sittlichkeit*, of shared ways of life and discourse.[27]

Equally crucial, however, and contrary to Hegel, appeals to a principle of respect for persons can be made by individuals in criticism of a particular community and are not beside the point. On certain occasions, a present and local community can develop practices contrary to the requirements of a principle of respect for persons. Individuals may come to see this and engage in well-founded protest. Similarly, individuals have a central role in creatively envisioning how to extend the requirements of principle to new cases—though whether such creative extensions are apt will itself be a matter for others also to judge on the basis of their own grasps of principle in application to past cases. Judging practices, individual and communal, as a competent moral agent is a crucial feature of the moral lives of persons. It is possible only against a background of stable and embodied, but also open-ended and revisable, criteria for the expression of respect for persons, conformity to which is seen by us as central to what is valuable for persons in general. When, and only when, there are both stable criteria of respect and a background history of their applications, is it then possible to acknowledge one's obligations as a person to act on principle and to judge actions according to it. One must be able to draw on past cases of acting well on principle, that then lead us to see against them how to act well on principle in new cases. As Michael Oakeshott's nice analogy has it, the competence of a moral agent resembles the competence of a speaker of a language who has come both to observe and to be capable of extending and transforming various regularities of usage. The kind of extension and transformation of criteria of respect for persons that a competent moral agent can accomplish "is analogous to the change to which a living language is subject: nothing is more habitual or customary than our ways of speech, and nothing is more continuously invaded by change."[28] And, at the same time, as linguistic competence may or may not be, moral competence—if it is to be a real and necessary expression of our nature as persons, over and above a looser ethical competence—is given shape and structure by the very principles and criteria it is capable of extending and revising.

Thus Kant's moral theory can be rescued from the charge of emptiness if and only if (1) there are stable yet revisable criteria for the expression in action of respect for persons, and (2) we regard those who live against or through these criteria as incarnating a fundamental value for persons, one to which we, considering them, are drawn by our personhood, not our contingent wants. We must recognize ourselves in the actions of others who act well on principle. Hence the fundamental questions that remain in considering whether we are bound to respect persons are whether there are criteria for respecting persons and whether we regard value for our personhood as exemplified in acknowledgment of and conformity to them.

2. When a principle of respect for persons is taken seriously, it is clear that moral agents can be required by it either to avoid or to break from certain attachments to others, certain projects, and certain prevailing practices. Any plausible criteria for respecting persons will prohibit, *ceteris paribus*, persecuting the innocent, treating others as disposable commodities to be used up in the service of one's own projects, or helping others to do either of these things. The world is a more or less tragic place to the extent that I am prohibited by principle from pursuing my projects and attaching myself to others without constraint, and, if we are bound to respect persons, then I may have to sacrifice some of my attachments and projects.

Recently, the thought has been urged by Bernard Williams and others that this cannot be right. I cannot be bound as a person to give up the attachments and projects that make it possible to lead the life of a person at all. Since a Kantian morality of principle will sometimes require such sacrifices, inasmuch as the commands of principle will not always be consistent with the promptings of apparently essential inclinations, then it must be wrong. As Williams argues,

> For [Kantian] morality, if the conflict really does arise [between moral principle and a "ground project" of an agent], must be required to win, and that cannot necessarily be a reasonable demand on the agent. There can come a point at which it is quite unreasonable for a man to give up, in the name of the impartial good ordering of the world of moral agents, something which is a condition of his having any interest in being around in the world at all.[29]

According to Williams, then, quite particular and primitive projects and attachments to others give a basic structure and character to the life of a person. These projects and attachments are, at least initially, unmediated by principle, and, in the event that principles of impartial respect come into conflict with the most basic of them, these principles must be sacrificed in order for the agent to go on living as a person at all. Hegel likewise makes this criticism in preferring not "individual [law-giving] consciousness . . . conscious of itself as universal will," but rather "specific personality" that has moved away from universal law-making and to "one kind of activity and being."[30] Apart from this, Hegel suggests, there is nothing that can genuinely be called action or the life of a person.

There is more than a little point to this criticism. Prideful misinterpretation of the requirements of principle *can* lead to sterile self-congratulation and alienation that are expressed in either stoical withdrawal from the world, when the prideful interpreter lacks power, or narcissistic tyranny over others, when the prideful interpreter has power. Thus, when power is lacking, an agent putatively yet pridefully hewing to impartial principle may find himself "distancing himself so brutally from his sense of what is essential to him that his capacity for participating actively in his own life would be deeply impaired."[31] Or, as Hegel put it, the knight of virtue, acting on his own consciousness, determined to incarnate goodness, yet lacking power, is able in the world to take a "part in the fighting [that] is, strictly speaking, a sham-fight which he *cannot* take seriously, . . . a sham-fight which he also dare not allow to become serious."[32] Lacking power, yet committed pridefully to acting on principle, rather than participating immediately in what is, "the individual who professes to act for such noble ends and who deals in such fine phrases is in his own eyes an excellent creature, [afflicted with] a puffing-up which inflates him with a sense of importance in his own eyes and in the eyes of others, whereas he is, in fact, inflated with his own conceit."[33] With power, prideful acting on principle is even worse. The actual legislation of individual consciousness in power, having abstracted itself from its prior attachments and projects, displays a "tyrannical insolence which makes caprice into a law."[34] For a consciousness so separated from attachments and projects and with the power to act in the world, "there is left only . . . negative action, . . . merely the fury of destruction."[35]

No moral principle is self-interpreting. Prideful misinterpretation is always possible. Further, in interpreting the requirements of principle—that is, in figuring out how in the present to extend and conform to the criteria for respecting persons—it is surely necessary to attend to the forms of expressing respect prevalent in one's own culture and in whatever culture one is confronting, not to abandon attention to what is in favor of retreat into soliloquy and self-congratulation. Projects and attachments to others *do* arise prior to an acknowledgment of moral principle in the life of a person, and they *can* conflict with principle. In various extreme material situations, it may even be rational as a person not to insist on some particular and locally favored line of action on principle, since it may be unclear, especially to an outsider, how any action could further the emergence of a community of respect. In such situations, hasty insistence on principled action will be tyrannical. Crucially, however, even here not any culture in extreme circumstances is worthy of sacrifices of principle and of normal criteria for the expression of respect; such sacrifices must always be aimed at developing a moral community of respect out of the culture so threatened by circumstances. No culture without the potential for this development—if there is *any* such culture (Germany in 1943? the Soviet Union in 1935?): too hasty identification of one *is* prideful and tyrannical misinterpretation—is worthy of any such sacrifice. Our aspirations to a moral community founded on principle plausibly figure in our reflections on action even in extreme situations, where it is radically unclear how in any immediate way to inaugurate a kingdom of ends.[36] Further, even in nonextreme situations attention to prevailing ways of life and practice as potential expressions of respect for persons is necessary in interpreting the requirements of a principle of respect for persons. Without attending to what others do, an individual runs a deep risk of tyrannically imposing groundless ideals of the expression of respect on others from whom the interpreter might rather learn new modes of respect. What is needed, in Martha Nussbaum's elegant phrasing, is not "blunt and blind . . . duty without perception," but rather a "loving dialogue" of principle and attention.[37]

Kant clearly acknowledged in his casuistical writing the proper roles, in interpreting the requirements of principle, of both engagement in ongoing modes of activity within a culture and attention to others' views about and ways of expressing respect for persons. Work, participation in ongoing activity in the world, is nearly indispensable for self-discipline, that is, for raising one's capacity to act as principle requires rather than acting out of prideful misinterpretation of principle.[38] Further, "each of us needs a friend . . . to whom we can communicate our whole self" and "who will help us to correct our judgment when it is mistaken. This is the whole end of man, through which he can enjoy his existence."[39] The burden of moral personhood can genuinely be borne only socially. To acknowledge this is to enjoin persons to interpret the requirements of principle in conversation with one another, attentive to both already employed and newly emergent criteria of respect.

The remaining issue then is whether value for persons is more fully expressed by attention and commitment to existing projects and attachments alone, or rather by such attention and commitment shaped and mediated by principle. Does our personhood lead us to aspire to share a world in which each member both attends perceptively to particulars and on principle respects persons? Or do our personhood and its local sites of emergence rather draw us to aspire at best to the cultivation of existing attachments and projects, as though we were in the end always huddled around local campfires? With whom is it possible to be most intimate and most fully to express one's personhood? Those to whom one is attached by contingency alone, or those to whom one is so attached and with whom one further shares a commitment to acting on a universal principle of respect for persons? If one prefers attachment unmediated by principle, then one has, it may be suspected, bought "into an extremely romantic notion of love . . . and unconditional friendship"[40]—unless, of course, the most careful and sensitive observance of moral principle is itself sometimes necessarily destructive of the most valuable forms of attention and attachment to particulars.

Thus it is clear that a necessary condition of persons' being bound by a principle of respect for persons is that the shape of a principled life must not be either unrealizable in the world or destructive of forms of attention and attachment that *are* crucial to personhood. And this requires in turn that there be relatively stable yet revisable criteria for respect, against the background of which a community of interpretants lives and can take its bearings, and the acknowledgment of which we find to be valuable for persons. Absent such criteria, through which we recognize our commitment as persons to principle, acting on principle *will* alienate us from attachments and projects and result in either stoical withdrawal or frenzied tyranny. When there are such criteria of respect that serve as a background to self-recognition, then the subordination of principle to particular attachments and projects will itself be, what Kant thought it to be, a form of

> moral fanaticism and exaggerated self-conceit [indulged in by those who] produce in this way a shallow, high-flown, fantastic way of thinking, flattering themselves with a spontaneous goodness of heart, needing thereby neither spur nor bridle nor even command, and thereby forgetting their obligation, which they ought to think of rather than their merit.[41]

There must be criteria of respect whose acknowledgment in action we recognize to be valuable for persons if we are to be bound as persons to act on principle. If there are, then it is the morality of immediate attachment to others and to projects that is either unrealizable or tyrannical.

3. When acting on principle, out of respect for persons and acknowledgment of the moral law, is taken to be necessary for having a good will, and hence for being a worthy person, then, it has come to be argued, the role in the lives of good persons of so-called nonmoral motives for action such as love and sympathy is seriously undervalued. Love and sympathy, so the criticism runs, are properly among the motives of the actions of genuinely good, even worthy people, who fully exemplify the best possibilities of personhood; to hold otherwise is to sacrifice natural human affections on the altar of duty, grounded in the acknowledgment of a principle of respect for persons that is often alienating. (Clearly this charge is intimately connected with the previous one.) Explicitly criticizing Kant along these lines, Iris Murdoch has pointed to "the fact that love is a central concept in morals."[42] Williams has observed that "the deeply disparate character of moral and of non-moral motivation, together with the special dignity or supremacy attached to the latter [by Kantian views], makes it very difficult [within a Kantian framework] to assign to those other relations and motivations the significance or structural importance in life which some of them are capable of possessing."[43] Julia Annas has called the "sharp separation of the motive to be moral . . . from all *inclinations* . . . the core of the defect in Kantian morality"[44] and has attempted to illustrate through analysis of a literary work the im-

poverishment that occurs in the life of an individual when love is sacrificed to duty. This criticism too is rooted in the work of Hegel, who, in opposing concrete ethical life to moralities of principle, praised marriage "as the immediate type of ethical relationship" characterized above all by "self-conscious love."[45]

It is clear why Kant insisted that the worth of a person consists only in the person's being actually motivated by respect for persons and acknowledgment of the moral law; any other putatively valuable characteristic of a person—Kant mentions, among other things, intelligence, wit, courage, perseverance, wealth, contentment, and coolness—in fact produces goodness in the world only under specific conditions. If these conditions are not satisfied—if, for example, coolness is possessed by a villain—these characteristics produce neither good in the world nor worth for persons. Thus "nothing . . . can possibly be conceived which could be called good without qualification except a *good will*,"[46] a will actually motivated by respect for persons grounded in an acknowledgment of the moral law.

As a result, persons, who are beings objectively directed by reason to the incarnation of worth, "must disregard every object to such an extent that it has absolutely no influence on the will, so that practical reason (will) may not merely minister to an interest not its own but rather may show its commanding authority . . .";[47] the willing of a worthy person, one who acts *from* duty, "wholly excludes the influence of inclination."[48] *How* this could be is a deep issue, but refusing to allow oneself to be motivated by inclinations and material objects of willing is clearly constitutive of the essential worth and dignity of persons, given Kant's equation of autonomy from the empirical, noumenal causality, pure practical rationality, and the expression of personhood in action: "Man must give [the] autocracy [of the soul] its full scope; otherwise he becomes a mere plaything of other forces and impressions which withstand his will and a prey to the caprice of accident and circumstance."[49] When rationality and autonomy and rightness are so equated, "morality consists in this, that an action should arise from the impulsive ground of its own inner goodness."[50] Here the dismissal of inclination as a legitimate motive in actions that are expressive of rationality and personhood readily suggests the sort of stern, proud, and aloof ascetic perfectionism that Nietzsche saw in Kant. When, according to Kant, autonomy for persons is rightly understood, it becomes clear that "inclination . . . is blind and slavish; . . . even the feeling of sympathy and warm-hearted fellow-feeling, when preceding the consideration of what is duty and serving as a determining ground, is burdensome even to right-thinking persons."[51]

Nonetheless, despite these striking formulations and despite the requirements stemming from the equation of autonomy from the empirical, pure practical rationality, and worth for persons, what exactly does the requirement that the will be free from determination by inclination really come to? Kant elsewhere observes that the "distinction of a principle of happiness [viz., empirical inclination] from that of morality is not for this reason an opposition between them, and pure practical reason does not require that we should renounce the claims to happiness; it requires only that we should take no account of them whenever duty is in question."[52] Similarly, he explicitly opposes the "misanthropic ethics . . . of moroseness [that] sets moral conduct in opposition to all pleasures."[53] These passages suggest that there may be occasions when duty is not in question; there is, it might be held, no risk of my damaging either others' personhood or my own in setting to read either *Adam Bede* or *Daniel Deronda*. Hence it is permissible in choosing between these alternatives to allow inclination to determine my will. Developing this line of thought, Barbara Herman has suggested that deliberation about the requirements of autonomy and of respect for persons properly arises only when there is a risk of "moral danger" in one's proposed course of action. Such situations of moral risk are identified for review against the principle of respect for persons by stable yet open-ended "rules of moral salience," or, roughly, common moral precepts. If an action proposed by my inclination possesses no morally salient features—it does not involve physical harm, deceit, the furtherance of addiction, or other things condemned by common moral precepts (an open-ended list)—then I may act as my inclination prompts me. My practical rationality and moral personhood are primarily expressed not in every action I undertake, but in my ongoing determination to employ the rules of moral salience to identify cases in which duty is in question, to revise those rules as necessary, attending closely to particulars as new varieties of harm to persons emerge, and to act always as respect for persons requires when duty is in question.[54] Similarly, Alan Donagan has urged that a Kantian theory of morality has a much narrower compass than the topic of goodness for persons: "A life the sole object of which was to obey the moral law would be aimless and empty";[55] some content for a life well led must be furnished empirically.

Yet, despite its obvious attractions, this way of leaving room even in a maximally good life for the promptings of inclination fails to do justice to the genuine perfectionist strain in Kant's moral philosophy and leaves reason, contrary to Kant's aim, with a relatively narrow role in structuring our aspirations as persons. Specifically moral worth, grounded in action from duty, is more nearly definitive, according to

Kant, of genuine worth for persons than this line allows. (Attention to rules of moral salience is necessary but not sufficient for a morally worthy life.) Thus Kant represents it as a commandment of morality that we must develop our faculties rather than occupy ourselves with idle amusements, even when no specific defilement of personhood, but only its general deliquescence, would result:[56] "With regard to contingent (meritorious) duty to one's self, it is not sufficient that the action not conflict with humanity in our person as an end in itself; it must also harmonize with it."[57] Thus, by way of the notion of meritorious duties to oneself, the injunction to seek to be morally worthy becomes a command to which we must conform, not only when specific harms to oneself or others threaten to stem from our actions, but also whenever we act. This command properly structures our aspirations by defining general goodness for persons as the incarnation in some developed way of life of the general expression of respect for persons. (There can be latitude in the development of a way of life that does this, as there cannot be any latitude in the observance of necessary non-meritorious duties. Special latitude is left to us in virtue of the fact that we have imperfect or meritorious duties both toward ourselves and toward others. There may then be widely divergent yet still exemplary ways of striking a balance between these two types of imperfect duties. This, rather than free rein for every caprice consistent with respect for others' rights, is the essence of Kant's particular liberalism.) Pointedly, "our duties towards ourselves constitute the supreme condition and the principle of all morality; for moral worth is the worth of the person as such."[58] Given this equation of the worth of persons with moral worth, an equation that stems from the prior equation of human rationality and dignity with autonomy from the empirical, the more relaxed line (according to which we are free to act on inclination except when there are specific dangers of harm to personhood) is surely not Kant's. The commandment to actualize our rational selfhood through action somehow motivated by respect for persons is wide-ranging and comprehensive. For moral worth and the expression of personhood in action, it is necessary that an action be sufficiently motivated by respect for persons grounded in acknowledgment of the moral law.

But now the criticism that Kant seems to have too narrow a conception of worth in action for persons seems to press even more closely: surely the actions of good and even worthy persons are sometimes motivated by love and sympathy. Can this point be accommodated within a comprehensive morality of principle, and, if so, how?

To retain Kant's equation of moral worth and worth for persons in general, but also to allow inclinations, including love and sympathy, to play some role in the motivation of action that is worthwhile for persons, one must see reason as not only checking action on inclination when it is contrary to respect for persons, but also as educating and informing inclinations and passions. Inclination alone can never determine the will in a worthy action; to that extent inclination must be checked. But reason can also operate upon initially unruly and polymorphous passions, partially transform them, and thereby attach our inclinations and feelings to actions and ongoing modes of activity or ways of life that have been taken to express respect for persons. (Kant sometimes distinguishes *passions*, which are original, in conflict with reason, and likely to overwhelm the will, from *feelings*, which can be informed by reason and in harmony with good willing.) There can be, for example, a deep inclination to bring about distributive justice, itself shaped by our rational understanding of the requirements of respect for persons on social distribution in various circumstances, and upon such reason-shaped inclinations it is permissible, and even praiseworthy, to act. Here reason educates and transforms passion in a way that goes well beyond the occasional hindrance of action on inclination, for the character of the object to which the passion is attached, for example, justice, is itself determined by the requirements of the rationally knowable moral law. To the extent that an inclination toward the inauguration of things like justice, the structures of which are determined by reference to the moral law, can shape our entire lives, extending into our relations of friendship and marriage and ranging through our commitments to modes of work and discipline, then inclinations can motivate action that is morally worthy.[59] That the object of our feelings, in cases in which it is both permissible and worthwhile to be motivated (in part) by them, must be defined by reference to the rationally knowable moral law and pursuable in all facets of our living is perhaps highlighted by the third formulation of the categorical imperative, according to which we are to act always under "that legislation through which alone a kingdom of ends is possible."[60]

Kant pointed clearly in his casuistical writings to the way in which it is valuable for persons for reason to educate passions: "If the feelings and passion are so bound up with reason that their soul is in harmony with reason, they can quite well be in keeping with our duties toward ourselves."[61] This binding of the feelings and passions to reason takes place principally by way of the production in us of the feeling of respect, consequent upon our grasp of the moral law: "Respect . . . is a feeling produced by an intellectual cause."[62] It is "possible through a prior (objective) determination of the will and the causality of reason."[63] Similarly, we are commanded by reason, which itself here defines the object of our feeling, to "endeavor after" the practical disposition of "love [of] one's neighbor," to attempt "to like to practice all duties toward him."[64] Commanded as we are by pure practical reason to seek to have it, this sort of love or liking, in which inclination is positively directed by reason, is a virtue, part of moral worthiness and worthiness for persons.

The principal mode of the education of feeling by reason is *habit*. The practice of willing the rationally determined object of proper willing, a kingdom of ends, itself transforms our feeling. When it is so shaped, "love from inclination is also a moral virtue: commencing by doing good from obligation through habit we can end by doing it from inclination."[65] Moral feeling is likewise nourished by habit. Self-mastery, "the subjective condition of the performance of duties to oneself," and hence of all duties, and hence itself commanded of us by reason, is acquired through practice and habituation: "By constant practice, [he who wishes to discipline himself morally] will strengthen the moral grounds of impulse, through self-cultivation he will acquire a habit of desire and aversion in regard to what is morally good and bad."[66] Feelings and inclinations, inculcated by the habitual attempt to inaugurate a kingdom of ends, itself defined by reason and pursuable throughout one's living, thus have a legitimate role to play in motivating morally worthy action that is expressive of personhood.

Yet, if habituation is required to produce the self-mastery necessary for acting from duty, or if feeling of some kind *must* be given a legitimate though subordinate role as a partial motive for worthwhile action, then there is something wrong with the picture Kant elsewhere sketches of practical rationality and autonomy as consisting in noumenal causality or independence from the empirical. The image of imperial reason coldly subduing essentially unruly feeling in action from duty *is* an overly simple and crude picture of how worth for persons is expressed in action; the actual transactions between feeling and reason, even allowing absolute priority to reason in its specification of the proper object of good willing, are murkier and more temporal than this simple picture suggests. Once habit is given an ineliminable role in moral development, and once feelings are legitimated as motives, then the proper image of the expression in action of the dignity and value of persons cannot be that of action grounded in the control or hindrance of our lower animal nature by our higher rational nature. We are—as the importance of habits and feelings shows—too much in the world to find that image a full expression of value for persons, and practical rationality must consequently be located in the world, not out of it.

This fact has serious consequences for the ways in which it is possible to defend the claim that Kantian moral worth is worth for persons. If our full picture of moral worth or moral competence now includes feeling and inclination within the complex structure of worth-making motives, then we cannot be obliged, simply because we are rationally capable of pure noumenal causality and ought to do that of which we are rationally capable, to strive to be morally worthy in Kant's rich sense. Just what makes Kantian moral worthiness—the motivation of action by reason in harmony with and educative of feelings—constitutive of goodness for persons? Given that feelings, especially respect and love, have some place in motivating morally worthy action, then why ought they not to have a greater place? Why should we not prefer, say, a morality of *agape* to a morality of respect, attention, and self-development? To answer "because we are rational" or "because we are potentially noumenal causes" will not do, for we are evidently not able, at least not without distortions of our personhood, to free ourselves entirely from the influence of inclination; even within a Kantian framework, what we are to hope to have motivate us is inclination transfigured by reason. Why ought we to hope for that, rather than for comprehensive inclinations of love, compassion, and service?

To respond to this difficulty, one must be able to draw on criteria of Kantian morally worthy action. That is, there must be criteria for identifying various actions as expressing motivation by the reason-transfigured inclination that appears in Kant's full account of moral worth. And we must then find conformity to these criteria, to the extent that it can be ascertained, to express the deepest demands of our personhood—as though we found ourselves asking "Is so-and-so (fully, genuinely, really) a person?" *by* asking "Does so-and-so acknowledge in action, or have the capacity to acknowledge, the fundamental value for persons of acting on that legislation through which alone a kingdom of ends is possible, of acting motivated by inclination transfigured by reason and so attached to a kingdom of ends?"

Inclinations, feelings, and emotions—especially love and respect—can thus have a place as motives within a Kantian rationalist morality of principle as long as reason is capable of specifying their proper objects, which themselves can be pursued comprehensively rather than merely occasionally, and so of giving them shape and direction. Whether such a rationalist morality of principle is correct turns then on the issue of how we understand ourselves: as beings who flourish when reason comprehensively transfigures inclination or as beings for whom inclination and feeling are, at some deep level, always simply given.

4. As part of his project of showing that we can know a priori that

the categorical imperative is binding on us as rational agents, Kant attempts, in the first section of the *Foundations*, to derive the formula of a categorical imperative from the mere concept of a categorical imperative. Kant's a priorism requires him to attempt some such derivation, for, if we are to be able to know a priori that we are bound by it, then our knowledge of just what the fundamental principle of morality is must not be grounded in any particular experience. Kant begins by claiming that the moral worth of an action, which depends on its being done from duty (not on its outcome), is a matter of the will's being determined purely formally, by no material object of inclination. If the will's being so determined formally is what action from duty consists in, then, Kant goes on to argue, the sole formula of action from duty must be that the will should be determined only by universal legislation, which has no specific material content furnished by inclination: "Since I have robbed the [dutiful] will of all impulses . . . , nothing remains to serve as a principle of the will except universal conformity of its action to law as such. That is, I should never act in such a way that I could not also will that my maxim should be a universal law."[67]

Unfortunately, however, this derivation is both built on empirical assumptions and not clearly sound. One might agree that the moral worth of an action—intuitively, its expression of the value and dignity of personhood—turns on its motivation, and even its motivation by duty, not its outcome. Various cases of the ascription of moral worth support this thought: Beck observes, for example, that we regard two soldiers, each of whom volunteers for a dangerous mission out of a sense of duty (to the extent that this can be ascertained), but only one of whom succeeds, as equally *morally* worthy.[68] Similarly, we are led by our intuitions about Kant's cases of the dutiful and the prudent merchant to regard moral worth as a matter of how the will is motivated.[69] Yet clearly our so regarding these cases is a fact of empirical psychology. To the extent that Kant's equation of moral worth with a quality of motivation is dependent upon our acquaintance with such examples, he has clearly failed to establish that we know the formula of the categorical imperative a priori. (Kant also has an independent argument, running through the *Critique of Practical Reason* and sections 2 and 3 of the *Foundations*, for the claim that we know a priori that we are bound by the second version of the categorical imperative, the principle of respect for persons. If that argument succeeds, then we would be obliged in virtue of this a priori knowledge to see cases of moral worth as Kant sees them, and empirical psychology would be beside the point. But that argument, it will become clear, is not unproblematic either.)

Second, even if it is conceded that the moral worth of an action is a matter of its motivation, not its actual outcome, it does not follow that the motivation of a morally worthy or dutiful action can itself make no reference to outcomes. Yet Kant assumes that it does follow: "[The] moral value [of an action], therefore, does not depend on the realization of the object of the action but merely on the principle of volition by which the action is done, *without any regard to the objects of the faculty of desire*."[70] The addition of this last phrase is insufficiently motivated inasmuch as there might be material incentives or objects of desire—general happiness, for example—that are properly categorial for human beings. As Robert K. Shope notes, "If there are ends which it is objectively, morally necessary to have, we might be able to claim that these provide a priori incentives, and Kant has said nothing to rule out the possibility that the worth of an action derives from a maxim whose object, end, and purpose is such a morally necessary end."[71] Kant's reason for rejecting the suggestion that the principle of volition motivating morally worthy action might refer to a categorial material end is that happiness is the only plausible candidate for a universal material object of inclination, yet the subordinate inclinations of persons are so diverse that no definite content can be given to the concept of happiness.[72] But clearly these judgments are a posteriori, interpretive, and dubitable. We might all, for example, as rational persons be inclined to preserve our lives with some security within a society, so that maxims that make for moral worth could be construed as determinations to follow rules for a stable social life, roughly in the manner of Hobbes. The end of leading a stable social life might either furnish a definite content to the concept of happiness or be categorially desired by rational persons apart from any desires for deeper particular happinesses. Kant's remarks about happiness do not rule out these possibilities. Thus Kant's derivation is not clearly sound.

Instead then of an a priori derivation of the formula of a fundamental principle of morality, what is needed is an a posteriori, interpretive *legitimation* of a particular formula. The best candidate for a formula to be so legitimated is the second version of the categorical imperative, the principle of respect for persons. As Alan Donagan has shown, versions of a principle of respect for persons have been affirmed throughout most of Judaic and Christian theological history.[73] That principle has been one around which, at least officially, considerable numbers of persons have organized their lives. Thus it is possible that the principle of respect for persons could be legitimated as binding on persons *if* lives based on conformity to it can be judged through interpretation to be expressive of the requirements of valuable personhood in the world—cases of conformity to the principle of respect for persons thus leading us to understand how principle can valuably inform a life in particular ways, while the principle organizes and articulates the shared value of a number of distinct cases. If there are stable yet open-ended criteria of the expression of respect, and if we can interpretively judge conformity to them to be valuable for persons as such, then there will be a route to the legitimation of a specific formula as a fundamental principle of morality, not purely a priori, but contrastively and interpretively, through a perspicuous representation composed of these cases. The issue thus becomes how we understand our personhood and its value to be expressed—well or poorly—in cases of conformity to stable yet open-ended criteria for the expression of respect for persons.

5. The concept of impermissibility has a central role in Kant's moral theory. Kant's version of the principle of respect for persons— "Act so that you treat humanity, whether in your own person or in that of another, always as an end and never as a means only"[74]—is most naturally understood as laying down a criterion of impermissibility. No person may be treated as a means only; anything other than treatment of persons as means only is permitted.

This focus on impermissibility has been thought both to prevent Kantian morality from having anything serious to say about our proper aspirations and, as a result, to make it impossible to justify any fundamental moral principle objectively and universally. Although Kant holds that justice and truthfulness are specifically moral virtues, in that unjust and untruthful acts are inconsistent with treating persons as ends, justice and truthfulness are in fact, so the criticism runs, merely *secondary* virtues; they are not deeply connected with human flourishing, and no one can structure a life around an aspiration to be just and truthful. As MacIntyre puts it, "[The] existence [of such rule-circumscribed things as truth and justice] in a moral scheme of things as virtues is secondary to . . . the notion of another primary set of virtues which are directly related to the goals which men pursue as the ends of their life."[75] Further, since moral rules definitive of specifically moral virtues can be justified only as delineating actions instrumental to the realization of the proper human aspirations, Kant's argument that we are bound by a principle of respect for persons *must* fail inasmuch as it makes no reference to proper and comprehensive human aspirations.

Kant's failure to understand the importance of aspirations and goodness in moral theory is traced to his acceptance of the modern invention of the decontextualized individual, that is, the view that persons are *not* existent only through "inherited modes of thought and practice" and through "social relationships,"[76] but are self-subsistent. When the essence of personhood is thus isolated from inheritances and relationships, then empty sincerity will tend ultimately to become the sole virtue. This has happened from the seventeenth century on, and this development is poignantly expressive of the decadence of modern life. Kant and modernity, it is urged, have left us bereft of objectively valuable aspirations, not knowing how to go on, and bereft in such a way that anything is permitted, as long as inclination is sincere.

This line of criticism too was begun by Hegel. From the master-slave dialectic in chapter 4 of the *Phenomenology* on, persons are treated as essentially existing in relations to one another of increasing richness. Modern individualism, with its emphasis on sincerity, beginning in the Renaissance and finding expression in philosophy in the seventeenth century, is then understood as an imperfect attempt to inaugurate a new and better community out of the ashes of a medieval religious world that had failed to leave room for autonomy. This attempt takes place within a particular context of communal relations—though it is in part a rejection of them—within which persons lead their lives, and this attempt is ultimately to be replaced by a yet fuller lived understanding of how goodness in the lives of persons occurs only in and through community.

Whatever the vices of modernity, this line of criticism rests on a misreading of Kant that amounts to travesty. It is true that Kant does not offer us a morality of happiness; the concept of happiness is too indefinite for that. But there is a strong and comprehensive morality of aspiration embedded in Kant's treatment of duties to oneself. One has a duty as a person to express and realize one's personhood in action in the world; in this sense, Kant's moral theory is fundamentally shaped by a conception of the aspirations and ends proper to persons. Duties to oneself are, as already noted, the foundation of all other duties: "The self-regarding duties are conditions under which alone the other duties can be performed."[77] Since there are duties to oneself, the proper end of human life cannot be happiness, even in the sense of the general satisfaction of one's common needs and interests. Rather, genuine, *characteristically human* happiness presupposes worthiness to be happy.[78] One will not be happy *as a person*, with the dignity and autonomy persons possess, but will instead only be *satisfied*, if one fails to respect persons in the name of some personhood-extrinsic end. This shows in our willingness to forgo satisfactions, and even life, if our dignity as persons would be compromised through an abandonment of principle: "To observe morality is far more important [than life]. It is better to sacrifice one's life than one's morality."[79] This aspiration, not to happiness as satisfaction, but to the expression and realization of personhood through conformity to the moral law, ranges throughout our lives, by way of the notion of duties to oneself, and structures all our acts as persons. Rightly read, in light of the importance of duties to oneself, both the treat-persons-as-ends and kingdom-of-ends versions of the categorical imperative are less criteria of impermissibility than injunctions to structure one's life around the expression of personhood. This will also, as already noted, require one to develop friendships of disposition with others, who will share the burden of moral personality that no one can bear alone; a grasp of principles and their requirements can be attained only cooperatively and conversationally.

While this reading of Kant's moral theory sees aspirations, ends, and social relations of a certain sort as central to it, the correctness of this reading as moral theory presupposes that we *do* find contextually informed action on principle, grounded in a reason-shaped harmony of reason and inclination, to be the best expression of our personhood. If we do find value for our personhood so expressed, then our findings must be capable of being elicited and brought to consciousness through our reactions to specific concretely embodied forms of expressing respect. There must, that is to say, be criteria of respect for persons, conformity to which we judge to be an expression of fundamental value for personhood. The issue is whether we understand value for persons to be exemplified in acting on principle.

6. According to Kant, the possible existence of the highest good is a necessary condition of our being bound by a principle of respect for persons. The highest good is defined as the necessary coincidence of virtue and happiness; in it, "virtue and happiness are thought of as necessarily combined."[80] Given the tragedies that trouble finite human life, the necessary coincidence of virtue and happiness will be possible only if both the soul is immortal and God exists as the coordinator of merit and reward. Thus, insofar as we regard ourselves as bound by a principle of respect for persons, we are further obliged to believe in the immortality of the soul and the existence of God. In sum, then, Kant's argument is:

> (i) If the moral law is valid, then the highest good as the necessary coincidence of virtue and happiness is possible: "Since, now, the furthering of the highest good . . . is an a priori necessary object of our will and is inseparably related to the moral law, the impossibility of the highest good must prove the falsity of the moral law also."[81]
> (ii) The moral law is valid: "The moral law is given, as an apodictically certain fact, as it were, of pure reason. . . . [The objective reality of the moral law] is firmly established of itself."[82]
> (iii) Therefore the highest good is possible.
> (iv) The highest good is possible only if the soul is immortal and God exists: "[The] highest good is practically possible only on the sup-

position of the immortality of the soul."[83] "[The] highest good is possible only on the supposition of a supreme cause of nature which has a causality corresponding to the moral intention."[84]

(v) Therefore the soul is immortal and God exists—or at least we must believe these things insofar as we will the highest good, a necessary object of the will of a being bound by the moral law. Each of these claims is thus "an inseparable corollary of an a priori unconditionally valid practical law."[85] Each of them "now becomes an assertion"[86] elicited from us as agents bound by principle.

The motivating thought behind premise (i) is that we are, as embodied and temporalized beings with inclinations, also beings who necessarily seek happiness, and not only beings subject to the moral law. Happiness is part of "the entire and perfect good as the object of the faculty of desire of rational finite beings."[87] Given that we are, as rational finite beings with desires, categorially "in need of happiness,"[88] it would make no sense—our nature would be permanently at war with itself and would not be a rational nature—were worthiness to be happy not as a matter of necessity further crowned with happiness, at least in our possible further existence. Thus happiness and virtue are together elements of the highest good as a result of the combination in our nature of objective directedness by the moral law with a fundamental need for happiness. The possibility of the highest good is then assured by the further assumption that all natures and their elements are at least problematically rational, in the sense that they are not necessarily in irreconcilable tension. That is, the full version of premise (i), in which all its underlying commitments are explicit, must be: If the moral is valid, and if we are categorially directed toward happiness, and if natures are at least problematically rational, then the highest good is possible.

But now, once premise (i) is so expanded, it is by no means clear that the three conjuncts of its antecedent are true. That we are categorially directed toward happiness in some rough sense is not likely to prove controversial. That the moral law is binding on us, as premise (ii) claims, is supposedly proved a priori, principally in sections 2 and 3 of the *Foundations* and in the first half of the *Critique of Practical Reason*. Whether that proof is sound will be an important issue. But there is also an immediate issue about whether natures in general are rational. The assumption that they are, that things make sense according to a scheme of their harmonious development, is so deeply presupposed in Kant's moral philosophy that he scarcely questions it, qualifying the assumption only by noting that it is problematic. Strictly speaking, however, it is a fundamental tenet of Kant's immanent critical philosophy that the rationality, as harmonious end-directedness, of things cannot be known. Such knowledge would be of a transcendent ground or condition of all conditioned things, while the most we can do in the way of acquiring knowledge, according to the *Critique of Pure Reason*, is to trace chains of conditioned events and to establish both the logical infrastructure of our ability as self-conscious beings to do so and our entitlement as self-conscious beings to regard our claims about conditioned events as objective and universalizable. Inquiry into unconditional conditioning grounds necessarily comes to nothing. Nonetheless, that natures are rational remains a problematic assumption within the moral philosophy and an assumption that, the *Critique of Judgment* argues, is lent compelling subjective yet intersubjectively valid support by the experience of beauty, an experience that reveals in feeling a harmony between our material sensibility and its manifold stimuli, on the one hand, and our freer conceptual capacities, on the other.

From a modern, generally Cartesian point of view, however, the idea that natures are rational and harmoniously end-directed is an illusion of unscientific consciousness. To the extent that things have natures or essences at all, natures just are, and talk of ends and harmony is explanatorily beside the point—so the modern thought runs. Morality may then seem to be an empty irrelevance in light of the way that the world of real natures seems to go on its own, as, in various ways, Nietzsche, Freud, Lacan, and Foucault have all held at times. Once this modern thought has arisen, it is hard to see how talk of merely problematic rationality and end-directedness inherent in natures can defeat it. What is needed, it seems, to combat this modern thought is a demonstration that natures are in fact rational and that goodness is in fact being realized in the world. Talk of problematically rational natures and possible highest goods beyond this world comes to nothing. Either natures are rational and harmoniously end-directed, and binding morality accords with our directedness to happiness, or they are not, so that our natures are divided and the commands of morality (if they even still have force) cannot be reconciled with the demands of happiness. To say simply "*If* morality is valid, *if* we're directed toward happiness, and *if* natures are rational, *then* the highest good is possible" is *not* to help us to know how we are genuinely, perhaps contradictorily, directed in the order of things. Saying this leaves us bereft of action-guiding self-understanding of our full nature, so that all we can then do is fall back into prideful individual willfulness. Individual moral conscience, directed by both moral command and the demands of happiness in ways that can never be seen in this world, in the end turns prideful and scorns the world entirely.

Hegel originally laid this charge against Kant's account of rationality as possibly realized in the world but also necessarily always beyond it.

> On the one hand [morality] is supposed to have validity simply and solely as the unreal "thought-thing" of pure abstraction, and then again equally to have no validity in that mode; its truth is supposed to consist in its being opposed to reality, and to be entirely free and empty of it [insofar as full rationality that is effective in bringing the highest good into being is not evident in *this* world, which is inhospitable to morality], and then again to consist in its being reality [insofar as God effectively assigns rewards according to the laws of morality].
>
> The syncretism of these contradictions which is set forth at length in the [Kantian] moral view of the world, collapses internally, since the distinction on which it rests, the distinction between what *must* be thought and postulated, and yet is at the same time *not* essential, becomes a distinction which no longer exists even in words [as we become concerned with what our nature really is]. . . . Consciousness comes to see that the placing-apart of these moments is a "*dis*placing" of them, a dissemblance, and that it would be *hypocrisy* if, nevertheless, it were to keep them separate. But as pure [Kantian] moral consciousness, it flees from this disparity between the way it thinks and its own essential nature, flees from this untruth which asserts that to be true which it holds to be untrue, flees from this with abhorrence back into itself. It is a pure conscience which rejects with scorn such a moral idea of the world. . . .[89]

There *is* an enormous tension in Kant's view that rationality that effectively coordinates virtue and happiness is possibly in the world, but also necessarily out of it (since we are never in acting rationally and morally to take seriously our worldly directedness toward happiness). But this view also has its own strengths against the actual demonstration of the rationality and goodness of this world that Hegel attempts to put in its place. Hegel's diagnostic historical uncovering of rational and good-incarnating teleologism in the world, from his early efforts in chapter 6 of the *Phenomenology* to his later *Lectures on World History*, is forcedly selective and overly smooth. Given, moreover, the widespread lack of emergence since Hegel's writing of justice and freedom in the world by his own lights, it is hard to believe that history is comprehensively teleologically organized: there is and has been too much backsliding, oppression, and unreason for that. Thus a quasi-Kantian, quasi-Hegelian view, according to which socially circumstanced individuals have the capacity to grasp the dimensions of their rational nature through moral *Bildung* but who frequently fail to do so, either through bad faith or through the decay of public languages of self-understanding, and who frequently act evilly when they so fail, is much more plausible. It may even be urged that the world as an arena for ongoing cooperative moral struggle to grasp our nature and its requirements, and further to display this grasp in action, is a more significant and better place than a world in which virtue is automatically both increasingly apparent and rewarded. Moreover, the experience of beauty in nature that evokes in us a sense of the purposiveness of things and the experience of significance in art that evokes in us a sense of our shared nature (experiences analyzed in the *Critique of Judgment*) may have some force in shaping our understandings of our personhood. There *is* an experience of beauty in nature that is important for philosophy (as John Wisdom confirms[90]) and transfigurative of self-understanding, an experience that is powerfully suggestive of rational purposiveness in things, an experience of the sort described by Wordsworth in "Tintern Abbey."

> And I have felt
> A presence that disturbs me with the joy
> Of elevated thoughts; a sense sublime
> Of something far more deeply interfused,
> Whose dwelling is the light of setting suns,
> And the round ocean and the living air,
> And the blue sky, and in the mind of man:
> A motion and a spirit, that impels
> All thinking things, all objects of all thought,
> And rolls through all things.[91]

And there is a further experience of something like beauty in art, an experience that awakens us to our common human interests, drifts of response, and directedness toward an end. (This is something ultimately to be shown in critical reading of particular works, not only said abstractly, though perhaps it must also be said.)

A morality that allots a fundamental role to a principle of respect for persons can thus be critically and interpretively legitimated in the world, not beyond it, if, in recognizing ourselves in works of literature (fictional, autobiographical, biographical, or historical) as directed toward an end as part of a rational system of natures (though one which is corruptible by human evil and cannot be simply known either a priori or experimentally), we further recognize that our directedness is fundamentally shaped and articulated by a principle of respect for persons. That is to say, there must be stable yet open-ended criteria of respect for persons, conformity to which is shown to be possible for us in works of narrative art. And these criteria of respect must, according to our self-recognitions, then further be criteria of value for persons. We must, if a Kantian morality of respect is to be upheld, find fundamental value for our personhood expressed in lives reflectively recounted to us that are, to the extent that we can tell, deeply and thoroughly informed by respect for persons.

7. In section 3 of the *Foundations* and in the first half of the *Critique of Practical Reason*, Kant offers an argument using only a priori knowable premises for the claim that we are obliged by our rational nature to obey the categorical imperative. (Elsewhere Kant remarks that "the objective reality of the moral law can be proved through no deduction, through no exertion of the theoretical, speculative, or empirical reason"; rather, "it is firmly established of itself."[92] Yet many people—among them, say, Mill and Nietzsche and Williams—deny that morality is so established, and there *is* in Kant's texts an argument designed to prove that the moral law is objectively real. Thus it seems to be in order to ask whether this argument is sound, and, if not, further to wonder what kind of self-warranting fact—if it is a fact—the fact of morality is.)

Kant's argument begins roughly from the thought that we are able, so far as we can tell, effectively to think about what to do, rather than always being determined to act by immediate inclination. Sometimes we can use our rational capacities to determine that we should forgo immediate satisfaction in favor of greater satisfaction in the long run, say by not eating crackers before dinner in order to savor the *canard à l'orange* more fully later. Our responses to stimuli have a rationally informed plasticity distinct from what is evident in the behavior of other animals: "Now man really finds in himself a faculty by which he distinguishes himself from all other things, even from himself so far as he is [merely] affected by objects. This faculty is reason."[93]

To the extent that reasonings sometimes inform our actions, we necessarily regard ourselves as negatively free, not wholly determined to act by material stimuli and their bodily effects: "Every rational being who has a will also has the idea of freedom and . . . acts only under this idea."[94] Thus we are really practically free inasmuch as the idea of freedom and our rational calculations are effective in moving us to act: "Every being which cannot act otherwise than under the idea of freedom is thereby really free in a practical respect."[95]

But genuine freedom is not exercised in actions based on rational calculations about satisfaction; it is, rather, *autonomy*, the ability of a rational creature with a will to govern itself by self-generated laws not grounded in sensual promptings: "What else, then, can freedom of the will be but autonomy, i.e. the property of the will to be a law to

itself?"[96] Thus the freedom we have not to act on immediate inclinations is not merely a freedom to use our reason instrumentally to
maximize long-term satisfaction; it is freedom to act according to what
seems objectively best, giving ideals and an objective law to oneself,
rather than taking inclination as always the ultimate basis for action.
The initial ideas that we regard ourselves as practically rational and
negatively free have alerted us to a further positive capacity for self-
legislation, a further ability not only to exercise our practical rationality
instrumentally but also to establish ends that are not grounded in
inclination: "The [initial] definition of freedom is negative and therefore affords no insight into its essence. But a positive concept of
freedom flows from it which is so much the richer and more fruitful."[97]

But full autonomy now consists in acknowledging and acting
according to the first version of the categorical imperative, which is the
formula of autonomy or self-legislation not grounded in material inclinations: "The proposition that the will is a law to itself in all its
actions, however, only expresses the principle that we should act according to no other maxim than that which can also have itself as a
universal law for its object."[98] Beings who are capable of such self-
legislation are, furthermore, ends in themselves and consequently de-
serve respect as such, so that the principle of respect for persons is also
binding on us in virtue of our ability to act autonomously. Thus our
initial sense that we are minimally practically rational and negatively
free leads us to acknowledge that we are bound by a fundamental
moral law we lay down to ourselves through pure practical reasoning.
Initially negative but then finally positive and person-respecting freedom is "the *ratio essendi* of the moral law."[99]

Two transitions in this argument obviously call for comment.
From the fact that we *regard* ourselves as minimally practically rational
and negatively free not to act on immediate inclination, it by no means
follows that we *are* practically rational and negatively free. We may on
the basis of introspection typically misreport the deep structure of
motivations for action. There is no doubt that we do forgo some immediate satisfactions. But it is not at all clear that our doing so is an
exercise of agency that is grounded in an independent sense that it is
either best or right to do so. It may be rather that a passion that is not
immediately satisfiable—say for tasting *canard à l'orange* with a clear
palate and a ready stomach—is simply *stronger* than an immediate
passion—say for crackers—not that it seems to a reflective agent objectively directed to values to be *rationally better* to desist from cracker
eating now. Our deepest senses of objective value may, if Freud is
right, be based on introjections and projections of others that have
been causally induced by stimuli in early childhood. In one way or

another, the apparent plasticity and objective value-directedness of our behavior may be an illusion that masks deeper controlling empirical regularities. Against such naturalisms that locate our actions within a material causal order in the world, Kant's only move is somewhat hollowly to locate our exercises of practical reason in a distinct "intelligible world," in "an order of things which only the understanding can think."[100] But if practical rationality has no expression in the world, then naturalist accounts of human behavior become all the more compelling.

Kant's reply to this charge is that we have an immediate consciousness of the moral law that enters into even our most minimal exercises of practical rationality. Thus our apparent genuine practical rationality does not ultimately consist in stronger passions overruling weaker ones; the moral law is "the *ratio cognoscendi* of freedom."[101] But this will not do, for what is at issue is whether it is an illusion that we have consciousness of an objective moral law, where such consciousness is effective in action and is part of the structure of our ability not to act on immediate inclination. Whether we are genuinely even negatively free is surely not immediately a priori knowable without appeal to cases. Neither is whether the structure of our negative freedom includes a positive freedom and objective directedness toward respect for persons and a kingdom of ends.

But while appeals to cases are relevant to an analysis of practical rationality, they are *interpretively* relevant, not relevant as theory-free data. It is out of the question to look to cases to specify a causal mechanism for our commandment by practical reason to respect persons. Rather, the best we can do is search for cases of actions that are plausibly expressive of a respect for persons grounded in practical rationality and then try to see whether these actions manifest fundamental value for persons. What the deep structure of possible motives for action is must be tested interpretively through producing the best accounts we can, accounts that elicit self-recognition, of human motivation, practical reasoning, and action.

There is a sense in which the knowledge of our freedom and of the power of reason to be practical that might emerge from the interpretive consideration of cases could even be called a priori, if *any* attempt to make sense of *any* case of *human action* or *behavior*—the proper event description will be crucial—without ascribing both negative and positive freedom (perhaps poorly exercised) to human persons breaks down in incoherence. But it might be better to call the necessity of the judgment, itself emergent from the interpretation of cases, that persons are positively free and practically rational *interpretive* or *grammatical* necessity, since it is now clear that it is only by way of our recognition of the expression of personhood in cases of action of which we have reflective accounts that we can come to know the characters of our practical rationality and our moral lives.

This suggestion about the relevance of cases is not entirely foreign to Kant (though it *is* contrary to his talk of an intelligible noumenal world), in that he observed that "if pure reason is actually practical, it will show its reality and that of its concepts in action, and all disputations which aim to prove its impossibility will be in vain."[102] And Kant offers us cases—most notably those of the dutiful merchant,[103] the despairing nonsuicide,[104] the nonsympathetic philanthropist,[105] and the honest witness who pays for his honesty with his life, his fortune, or his friends[106]—that are intended to elicit from us a recognition of our personhood, our practical rational capacities, and what is valuable for us. It is through the consideration of cases, and not through the stipulation that we are practically rational as members of a noumenal world, that our objective directedness as persons by a principle of respect can be established.

This thought points us to and is reinforced by a second difficulty in Kant's a priori argument. From the facts that we are genuinely free and practically rational, it does not follow that we are bound by the categorical imperative, in either its first or second version, as the formula of self-legislation, for, as already noted, Kant's a priori argument for the claim that the law that our maxims must be consistently universalizable is the sole possible piece of categorial self-legislation is defective. It is possible, contrary to Kant's connection of particularity with materiality and universality with pure form, that our common directedness as persons to material happiness in the world might furnish us with a law that is categorial for persons and is in that sense a piece of self-legislation on the part of persons as such, not a mere object of particular willing. But if our knowledge of our moral personhood and its demands thus waits upon the consideration of narratives, rather than being achieved a priori, then moral self-knowledge will not be the achievement of an isolated rational consciousness, and the moral law will not be legislated by a self in isolation or as a member of a noumenal world. Kant's individualism is compromised by the failure of his pure a priorism. We can attain moral consciousness only as we see our personhood and its demands reflected to us in the lives of others that are recounted to us in narrative art, while our collective responses themselves determine narrative art's relevant and proper exemplars. Our achievement of moral consciousness is then not a purely individual one, and Kant's claim that our genuine freedom is exercised in conformity to a piece of individual a priori self-legislation cannot be sustained.

We can know our freedom and our personhood only interpretively, as they are reflected to us in accounts of action that elicit our self-recognition. There must, if a Kantian morality of respect for persons is to be upheld, be criteria of respect, conformity to which we recognize to be fundamentally and comprehensively valuable for persons. This interpretivist stance is deeply at odds with much of Kant's a priorism, in particular with his insistence that considerations of particular cases do not bear on what is a priori knowable. Notoriously, Kant observes in the *Foundations* that "our concern is not whether this or that was done but that reason of itself and independently of all appearances commands what ought to be done. Our concern is with actions of which perhaps the world has never had an example. . . . Nor could one give poorer counsel to morality than to attempt to derive it from examples."[107] The principal reason why such counsel would be poor is that no necessary and universally binding law could ever be grounded in a particular empirical claim: "It is a clear contradiction to try to extract necessity from an empirical proposition . . . , and it is equally contradictory to attempt to procure, along with necessity, true universality to a judgment."[108] "It is clear that no experience can give occasion for inferring the possibility of . . . apodictic laws of duty."[109] The moral law "needs no further support from theoretical opinions on the inner character of things, on the secret final end of the world order, or on a ruler presiding over it in order to bind us completely to actions unconditionally conformable to the law."[110]

Yet it is not immediately clear why this is so and where the mistake in attending to examples lies. It *would* be a mistake to try to establish a moral law inductively by reasoning "A^1 acts well and does X^1, A^2 acts well and does X^2, A^3 acts well and does X^3, and so on; therefore to act well is to do X." Although we are entitled to make universalizable judgments about causal relations, for example, on the basis of experience, such judgments are always in principle corrigible by further experience and are not fully necessary and knowably universal, as the moral law is held to be. But if instead the premises are rather of the form "A reflective account of A's behavior, motives, and consciousness shows that A's behavior expresses respect grounded in A's awareness of the dimensions of personhood and its objective end, *and* I recognize my personhood in this account of what A thinks and does," then enumerating cases in order to support generalizations inductively becomes beside the point, and the argument that stems from such a treatment of cases will be an interpretive and not an inductive one. The truth in such an interpretive argument comes in giving content simultaneously to "I recognize my personhood in what A thinks and does" and "A is aware of the dimensions of personhood and its objective end." What could these claims mean? How could we test them, especially when interpretivism denies us pure a priori knowledge of a criterion of value for personhood?

Satisfactory answers to these questions *cannot* be given abstractly, but only through the actual work of critical interpretive reading. What it is to see our personhood and its end in an account of an agent's actions, motives, and self-understanding is something that can be specifically *exhibited* only through the generation of accounts of action and critical reflection on them. And, curiously, despite his a priorism, the idea that our personhood and its end and specific dignity can be exemplified in accounts of actions, which then enable us to establish a necessary moral law interpretively, has some roots in Kant's writing. In the section of the *Critique of Practical Reason* called the "Methodology of Pure Practical Reason," which treats "the way in which we can secure to the laws of pure practical reason access to the human mind and an influence on its maxims,"[111] Kant urges "educators of youth . . . after laying the foundation in a purely moral catechism, [to search] through biographers of ancient and modern times with the purpose of having examples at hand of the duties they lay down."[112] Kant himself then goes on to set before us the fictional case of the witness who suffers the losses of fortune, friends, freedom, and possibly even life for the sake of his honesty.[113] Though such examples are, officially, supposed only to refine our judgment concerning cases and to enliven our feeling for a moral law that commands us purely a priori, it turns out that the strategies of moral education for the young may in the end be not so different from the only mode of anyone's access to the moral law. That is, even in critical moral philosophy a fundamental use of examples seems to be required in order to uncover the formula of the moral law and to establish that it binds us. This uncovering and establishing occur interpretively, if they occur at all, or as it were by precipitation out of cases.

> [The] example [of Newtonian science, which uncovered universal forces affecting the manifold motions of diverse particular bodies through the interpretive consideration of cases] recommends to us the same path in treating of the moral capacities of our nature and gives hope of a similarly good issue. We have at hand examples of the morally judging reason. We may analyze them into their elementary concepts, adopting, in default of mathematics, a process similar to that of chemistry, i.e. we may, in repeated experiments on common sense, separate the empirical from the rational, exhibit each of them in a pure state, and show what each by itself can accomplish. . . . In a word, science (critically sought and methodically directed) is the narrow gate that leads to the doctrine of wisdom, [which includes knowledge of] what one ought to do.[114]

Here then, in the wake of the failure of Kant's attempt to establish purely a priori both the formula of the moral law and the claim that it commands us, and in light of the threats of emptiness, alienation, cold sterility, uselessness, and hypocrisy that trouble an ungrounded morality of respect for persons, is an interpretive methodology for coming to know—if they exist—our directedness as persons and the principles that articulate it. Are there stable yet revisable criteria for the expression of respect for persons in action? How are they laid down and lived out, not by individuals alone, but in social life? Is it possible to organize a life comprehensively around conformity to them? If it is, then is such a life expressive of our personhood and its value, its objective end? (And, of equal relevance, is a life not so organized not?) These questions can be treated through the interpretive examination of cases in which (putatively) "morally judging reason," in specific social circumstances, leads an individual to resolve to respect persons and to grasp the criteria for doing so. Whether this resolution and action on it are deeply expressive of our personhood and its proper end or full possibilities of value (and contrary resolutions and actions not so expressive) is something for us to judge in thinking through accounts of cases of this kind. If they are thus expressive, then these accounts will, as it were, awaken us to ourselves, or reduce our alienation from ourselves. These accounts will display for us all at once a specific principle (respect for persons), its contextual requirements, and its role in furthering the expression of our personhood and its value in context. Do we understand ourselves and our possibilities of value, are we and our worth and dignity reflected to ourselves, in accounts of reflective conformity to criteria of respect, or not?

3. Grammatical Necessity and Transcendental Psychology

There *are* stable yet open-ended criteria of respect for persons. Such things as wanton violence directed at the innocent, lying at whim or convenience, the coercion of labor, the promotion of chemical dependencies that make impossible the expression of personality in action, and so forth are clearly contrary *ceteris paribus* to what respect for persons requires. The existence of these criteria is a signal strength of vaguely Kantian political liberalism, which opposes duty and practical love, rooted in conformity to these criteria, to pathological love, immediate attachments, and projects uninformed by principle. In political life, appeals to a principle of respect for persons have had a special force in galvanizing rational resistance to certain forms of repression and tyranny. There can be little doubt that conformity to these widely acknowledged criteria of respect is a part of human dignity and value.

But how fundamental a part is it? Are there or are there not cases in which conformity to criteria of respect inhibits the expression of value in human action, for example by reducing our commitments and attentions to others and encouraging pridefulness and moral isolationism? Is a principle of respect for persons a fundamental principle of moral theory in general, one that is a criterion of our fullest value as persons, rather than a principle useful only in isolating certain special forms of direct political and social coercion? Does a determination comprehensively to respect persons, including one's own, leave one careening (as Hegel charged) between morally isolationist and inattentive liberalism (the fate MacIntyre, Williams, and Murdoch have variously seen for a Kantian morality of principle) and unrealizable impulses to absolute self-perfection (of the sort that Fichte promoted and Nietzsche stigmatized)? Or is it first of all possible, and, second, normal, natural, alienation-reducing, and expressive of personhood to lead one's life out of such a determination? How could one tell?

Three thoughts makes these questions specially difficult to answer. The motives of persons are, as Kant insisted, not indubitably knowable; ascriptions of motives are always problematic and interpretive, developed against an always evolving background story of a person's total and only partially coherent wants, desires, projects, commitments, and needs. And if ascriptions of motives are always problematic, then judgments of the worth or value of conformity to the command that we be motivated by respect for persons will be equally so. If it is not easy to tell who is respecting persons in which ways, then it will not be easy to tell—after the failure of Kant's pure a priori arguments—whether respecting persons is fundamental to human dignity and value.

Second, the open-endedness of the criteria of respect for persons is essential to their comprehensiveness and suitability to structuring judgments about personhood in new situations. If the objections of the partialists—MacIntyre, Williams, and Murdoch—are to be met, then the complete set of criteria of respect for persons cannot be fixed once and for all. That set may have a stable basis, but, given that new material conditions and social structures that shape particular human projects and commitments can always arise, and do so regularly, conformity to a fixed and unrevisable set of criteria of respect *will* be a mode of inattention to persons and a prideful failure of commitment. (This point is registered, in a way, in the fact that Kant's casuistical writings, in particular about women and sexuality, generally strike us as dogmatic and arbitrary; a grasp of principle does not free one from the requirements of creative attention and responsible casuistry—requirements themselves grounded in the command to respect persons.)

But the necessary open-endedness of the criteria of respect for persons here too makes judgments of conformity to these criteria in particular circumstances problematic and interpretive. Again, it is not easy to tell who is respecting persons in which ways.

Finally, the question "Is the expression of respect for persons comprehensively, throughout one's life, possible and *fundamentally* valuable for persons?" is a *grammatical* and *interpretive* one, not a standard scientific, narrowly experimental one—and grammatical questions can be treated only through complex interpretive efforts at self-recognition. The question asks after the *criteria* of human value, in particular whether the expression of respect for persons is the criterion of human value. The answer will be either "grammatically necessarily yes" or "grammatically necessarily no." There is even a sense in which the answer to this question, if it has an answer at all, must be a priori knowable, as long as "a priori knowable" means *not* "deducible from immediately self-evident, nonempirical principles," but rather "grammatically necessary and interpretively legitimated." The acceptance criterion for grammatically necessary fundamental principles, in moral theory or in epistemology, is neither a priori intellection nor indubitability. Rather, as Alan Donagan, Manley Thompson, and others tracing out certain strains in Kant and Wittgenstein have variously put it, what distinguishes grammatically necessary fundamental principles is that "attempts to think in terms of their contradictories break down."[115] Crucially here, *thinking* is a matter not of calculating, but of aiming at self-recognition, at making sense of oneself to oneself as a person and of others as those who share personhood with oneself. Our grasp of grammatically necessary principles (including, if Wittgenstein is right, even *logical* principles) emerges only through such thinking, and such thinking is concerned with cases of human behavior interpretively, not with material objects in nature experimentally.

Nor is the question of the nature of value for persons a purely *analytic* one. One might initially think that it does not matter how we may narrate actions most convincingly. All that is necessary in order to establish the nature of value for persons is to consider whether, *if* someone acted out of respect for persons, *then* that person would have acted well. The theory of morality might then make do with very briefly imagined cases, philosophers' cases, not full narratives of art. Yet this suggestion cannot in the end be right, for the concepts that we may have, may use in describing cases, and may then analyze are themselves in part historical products, bound up with our evolving efforts to live well. As the failures of Kant's own a priori derivations of the formula of a categorical imperative and of the claim that we are bound by it show, there are central issues about how to describe just what is going on in the actions we analyze. Is there really such a thing as acting from good will alone, without material incentives? How and when might this be done? Is it really both possible and of value to do this? Our answers to these questions will be conditioned by our interpretive historical acquaintances with putatively exemplary cases of valuable action and with languages of action and value. Through these acquaintances, we will inevitably have senses, albeit questionable ones, of which actions are fulfilling and apt for persons. Hence conceptual analysis of *the* notion of duty cannot stand on its own. The question of what makes a principle of value for persons sound cannot be separated from the issue of how we actually come to encounter, articulate, and acknowledge such a principle and its importance. In order to find our way to morally significant understanding of value for persons, we must give ourselves over to actual, historical, interpretive thinking, directed at narratives of action.

To think in this sense, aiming at the recognition of the dimensions of personhood and the commitments to principles that it requires, is to presuppose and to articulate and make convincing in relation to cases a transcendental human psychology in which fundamental and necessary, as opposed to variable and contingent, human relations to nature, projects, needs, desires, and ends are identified. The transcendental psychology that is presupposed in Kantian moral theory (as seen through the *Critique of Judgment*) and that is to be made convincing in relation to cases shares certain crucial features with the psychology of English Romantic poetry, or, more particularly, the psychology of Wordsworth and of Coleridge in certain moments, not Shelley or Keats. These common features include (1) regarding nature as simultaneously a home for and a threat to human mindedness, autonomy, and flourishing, (2) regarding the expression of human mindedness and the incarnation of its value as essentially cooperative and social, though simultaneously advanced by mysterious individual creative vision, checked in conversation, of the specific possibilities of value in changing circumstances, and (3) the acceptance of a schema of development for human personhood according to which we move from primal innocence, communality, and attachment into an identity-developing fall into self-assertion, particularity, and role playing, and finally at least potentially into stable social relations shaped by a commitment to ideal justice that is rooted in reflection on the natures of persons and of value.

Thus, in light of the connections between fundamental principles, grammatical necessity, thinking as self-recognition of one's personhood, and transcendental psychology, a principle of respect for persons will be fundamentally descriptive of value in human life, and thinking in terms of its contradictory will break down, if and only if the principle itself specifies the most abstract and comprehensively significant criteria of value for beings—persons—with a certain transcendental psychology. The transcendental psychology of persons must be such that the best interpretation that can be given of the lives of particular persons includes the thought that they are objectively directed to respect for persons, that they are succeeding or failing in acknowledging this, and that as a result value is or is not incarnated in their lives.

And now the questions press: What is our psychology? What is it to lead the life of a person, and to lead it well? Is it to lead the sort of life that is envisioned in Kantian moral theory? That is, Is it to be in nature in that way, to be with others in that way, and to develop cooperatively and in the absence of coercion, repression, and self-misunderstanding in that way? Full and stable answers to these questions can come only from thoughtful and interpretive readings of narratives.

THE ACHIEVEMENT OF AUTONOMY: MARLOW'S TALK IN *LORD JIM*

1. *Lord Jim:* **Conrad's Inheritances and Stances**

The special relevance of *Lord Jim* to questions about character and morality lies in Conrad's obsessive concern as an author with the phenomenology and value of acknowledgment of a principle of respect for persons and of action based on this acknowledgment. That Conrad in *Lord Jim* is obsessively concerned with issues, prominent in Kantian morality, about the possibility of our autonomy in the world, its formula, and its value is generally unappreciated, at least in the present cultural climate. In his survey of approaches to *Lord Jim*, Fredric Jameson lists nine "interpretive options," none of which mentions the problem of our autonomy in the world, its formula, and its value.[1] The option that Jameson labels "the ethical" sees Conrad's works as raising "the 'issues' of heroism and courage, of honor and cowardice."[2] (Jameson's hostility to morality is evident in the scare quotes that suggest that there are in fact no real issues here.) Somewhat later, Jameson characterizes the ethical reading as one which sees *Lord Jim* as "a tale of courage and cowardice, a moral story, and an object-lesson in the difficulties of constructing an existential hero," a story that juxtaposes the "values and experience" of "feudal Poland [and] capitalist England."[3] Here Jameson's way of characterizing the issues at stake in the moral reading simply denies or ignores the very idea that there could be a moral problem of the possibility, formula, and value of autonomy in the world. The problems of morality are identified by Jameson with oppositions between the mores of different groups, such as feudal lords and entrepreneurial capitalists, as though it were an obvious assumption—one not even worth discussing—that there are no such things as objective values for persons that we might struggle morally to acknowledge and to realize in the world. Thus Jameson remarks that he is "concerned to stress . . . the paradox of the very notion of value itself, which becomes visible as abstraction and as a strange afterimage on the retina, only at the moment in which it has ceased to exist as such."[4] This seems to say that at certain times the notion of value ceases to exist. This may mean that at certain times and places value itself is not manifested in the world, which is true and trivial. Or it may mean that the word "value" has not always been in use, which is again true and trivial. Or it may mean that at certain times (when there has not been the Weberian rationalization of social life) it has not been open to people to wonder and worry about the categorial demands on personhood or the possibility, formula, and value of our autonomy in the world. *That* claim is wildly false given the persistence of such wonders and worries in ranges of texts from philosophy and literature in widely disparate cultural moments. Morality, or at least moral worry about the principled value for persons of autonomy and embeddedness, and about the relative weights of their claims, seems not to be the epiphenomenon of modern bourgeois culture that Jameson takes it to be.

If anything about *Lord Jim* is clear, it is that Conrad is concerned with objective value for persons and that he scathingly criticizes the conventionalist moralities of both feudal honor, exemplified in the figure of the French lieutenant, who emerges as a diminished or self-mutilated person, and capitalist entrepreneurialism, exemplified in the figure of the German captain, who seeks only profit and ease and who is likewise diminished or self-mutilated. Neither figure acts in ways that befit a person. And it is this question—What is it, especially in extreme situations, to act in ways that befit a person? (a question that has been raised from the beginning by Jim's case)—that is the thematic center of the novel. How, if at all, can Jim, or anyone, acknowledge failure to express one's personhood in the world and then recover to an understanding of appropriate ways to express it and of their value? Only when the novel is seen as concerned centrally with this question can it be seen as a unified and intelligible work, rather than as the failed amalgam of the psychological novel and the popular romance, an amalgam generated by the requirements of the bourgeois market, that Jameson takes it to be.[5] In the issue of the worth of Jim's conduct, in the investigation of his recovery, in the criticism of various conventionalist moralities, and in Marlow's continual probing into what one would oneself do in various situations, *Lord Jim* leaves us in no doubt that its central concern is with the possibility, formula, and value of the expression of our personhood in the world.

Conrad's concern with this topic—a concern that is perhaps natural to anyone—is heightened by a number of his own particular experiences, inheritances, and background understandings of persons and morality.

1. Conrad saw at firsthand the horrors of modern imperialism, an experience that is registered most notably in *The Heart of Darkness*, and he seems to have surmised that these horrors were contrary to, and could best be checked by the acknowledgment of, a principle of respect for persons. This surmise about the importance of principles and rules was further fueled by his experience of the importance of rules in shipboard life and in controlling his own self-destructive character. (Conrad apparently attempted suicide in 1878 at the age of twenty,[6] and he was throughout his life subject to episodes of depression and fitfulness at work.) Of his shipboard experience, Conrad wrote,

> It may be my sea training acting upon a natural disposition to keep good hold on the one thing really mine, but the fact is that I have a positive horror of losing even for one moving moment that full possession of myself which is the first condition of good service. And I have carried my notion of good service from my earlier into my later existence.[7]

The immediate duties of masters and men at sea, clearly circumscribed by rules and customs, helped Conrad to resist the loss of self-posses-sion and so to appreciate the importance of duty and principle. A ship, he observed, "is a creature which we have brought into the world, as it were on purpose to keep us up to the mark."[8] Conrad seems in part to have inherited his sense that the observance of rule-circumscribed duties is the best antidote to the loss of self-possession, either on his own part or on the part of nations tending toward imperialism, from his mother's brother, Tadeusz Bobrowski, who had assumed responsi-bility for him in 1869 following the death of his father (his mother having died four years earlier). Bobrowski, who had frequently noted Conrad's tendencies to dissipation and grandiosity (tendencies Bobrowski traced to Conrad's father's family[9]), observed to Conrad in correspondence that "if both Individuals and Nations were to make 'duty' their aim, instead of the ideal of greatness, the world would certainly be a better place than it is! . . . The devotion to duty in-terpreted more widely or narrowly, according to circumstances and time—this constitutes my practical creed [which] may be of some use to you."[10] Knowing the horrors of imperialism, his own self-destruc-tive tendencies, and the loss of family and country, Conrad appears, as Ian Watt has emphasized, "both more contemporary and more old-fashioned than his modern peers"[11] Joyce, Lawrence, Eliot, and Pound, who noted similar internal and external threats and horrors in modern life. And this is because instead of urging a withdrawal from public life into a "private system of order and value,"[12] Conrad continued after experiencing these threats and horrors to ask "But what then must I do?" where the answer was to be given in the form of a principle of conduct to be applied flexibly in light of circumstances and time.

2. While always acknowledging the importance of principle, Conrad simultaneously appreciated the fact that conformity to principle, when made a law of life by an individual inattentive to the scope and flexibility of criteria of respect, could be prideful, sterility-inducing, isolationist, and self-stultifying. Against moral individualism, Conrad maintained a sharp awareness of the social character of personhood, in the sense that the expressive activities distinctive of persons (for which all persons have capacities) can be carried out only in community with others likewise engaged in them. This awareness on Conrad's part is an inheritance from Polish romantic literature, from his father's concern with the fate of the Polish nation, from his Catholicism, and, in his subsequent literary life, from English Romanticism. As Watt has noted, "[The correction of] individualism . . . through an identification with national suffering and [the] transformation from a narrow self-concern to a larger loyalty [are] characteristic theme[s]" of Mickiewicz and Stowacki, the two Polish romantic poets "whom Conrad most admired."[13] Conrad's father, Apollo Korzeniowski, had devoted much of his life to underground political activity against the Russian occupiers of the principal part of Poland after the final 1795 partition. Apollo Korzeniowski had been imprisoned and then deported with his family by the Russian authorities to "Vologda, a cold and marshy city to the northeast of Moscow," as a result of which both of Conrad's parents ultimately died of tuberculosis.[14] Thus Conrad was made intimately aware of the connections between the fate of a nation and the fate of an individual, as his family's ancestral lands were confiscated, as his father was driven into underground political activity and then imprisoned, and as both parents were forced into periods of exile and then met untimely deaths.[15] A sense of the proper cooperativeness of human life, especially of the importance of solidarity with and service to the oppressed, is also a prominent feature of the traditional Catholic social teaching that Conrad absorbed, and this too provided a source of resistance to moral individualism. When he at last came to write, Conrad's choice to write in English, "the speech of my secret choice,"[16] and not in either Polish or French (despite his equal or greater fluency in those languages and his admiration in particular for the literary techniques of Flaubert and Maupassant), may be due in part to the explicit moral and social character of English

literature, which has attempted, at least since Wordsworth and prominently in Coleridge, Carlyle, and George Eliot among others, to
envision in closely described experiences or conversations or villages
potentials for ideally just communities and for activities ideally expressive of personhood and then further to bring us to realize these
potentials, thereby functioning as a secular scripture. This interweav-
ing of the particular with universal moral truths about human activity
and social life would have been a prominent attractive feature of English literary practice for Conrad.

Conrad repeatedly felt in his literary life a need to check his
progress as a writer against the judgments of others, as though he
could scarcely exist as a writer unless he existed together with others
who wrote with him on his topics and his treatment of them. Although
he was clearly the dominant force in it, Conrad's temporary collabora-
tion with Ford Madox·Ford was evidently enabling for him and
strengthened his sense of himself as a writer. The correspondence
related to *Lord Jim* similarly testifies to the vital role played by others in
fostering whatever conviction Conrad could maintain in his own work
and even in his own existence. Thus Conrad wrote to Edward Garnett,
the publisher's reader who had recommended the publication of
Almayer's Folly, his first novel:

> You frighten me; because were I to let you take me up on these heights by
> your appreciation the fall before my own conscience's smile would be so
> heavy as to break every bone in my body. And yet what, oh! what would
> become of me if it were not for your brave words that warm like fire and
> feed like bread and make me drunk like wine![17]

And then again to Garnett, ten-and-a-half months later, a month after
Lord Jim had been published in book form:

> This is the effect of the book upon me; the intimate and personal
> effect. Humiliation. Not extinction. Not yet. All of you stand by one so
> nobly that I must still exist. There is *You*, always, and never dismayed. I
> had an amazing note from Lucas. Amazing! This morning a letter came
> from Henry James. Ah! You rub in the balm till every sore smarts—
> therefore I exist.[18]

This sense of the necessarily communal basis and character of anything that can be called expressive and distinctively human activity
also surfaces prominently in *Lord Jim*. The novel's epigraph, taken
from Novalis, is "It is certain my conviction gains infinitely, the moment another soul will believe in it."[19] In commenting on Jim's failure
after the *Patna* incident to stay in one place and on Jim's settling in

Patusan that he and Stein are about to effect, Marlow observes that "we exist only in so far as we hang together" (136). The unnamed impersonal narrator of the first four chapters claims that "in our own hearts we trust for our salvation in the men that surround us, in the sights that fill our eyes, in the sounds that fill our ears, and in the air that fills our lungs" (14). Brierly, the French lieutenant, and the young Jim are all proud individualists who are accused of a morally narcissistic exceptionalism, of loving themselves too much.

Conrad was well placed by family, national, religious, and literary background to give voice to such sentiments and to have seen the narcissism and sterility of isolationist moral individualism. If a principle of respect for persons were to be given pride of place in the moral life as the formula of the duties and valuable aspirations of persons, then it would have to function flexibly and widely to lead us to pursue projects in cooperation with others and to seek with them to promote so far as possible the emergence of a kingdom of ends out of present situations.

3. Conrad appreciated that value in a human life must be incarnated in action in this world, not either sealed up in "inner" states of motivation that are never expressed in action or located in a transcendent noumenal world we "enter" by acknowledging the moral law and willing out of respect for it. Conrad's way of thinking about moral principles and value in human life is at odds with sharp dichotomies between inner and outer and between transcendent and empirical. This is an inheritance from English Romanticism, with its tendency to conflate mind and nature or to see mind and nature as jointly purposive (though Conrad, like Kant, never fully conflates them and quite typically also regards nature as hostile and alien), and from his Polish background, in which political commitment was inescapable, as even withdrawals from political action (such as those of his uncle) assumed a political significance.

In *Lord Jim*, removals of the exercise and expression of personhood to either a transcendent or inner realm are most notoriously criticized in Stein's remark that

> a man that is born falls into a dream like a man who falls into the sea. If he tries to climb out into the air as inexperienced people endeavor to do, he drowns—*nicht war?* . . . No! I tell you! The way is to the destructive element submit yourself, and with the exertion of your hands and feet in the water make the deep, deep sea keep you up. (130)

And that is to say, among other things, that the way of human life, and the way to incarnate whatever dignity and value it may have in it, is to act in this world, not to imagine oneself in another one. Marlow adds, "That was the way, no doubt," calling the world in which we unalterably live a "great plain on which men wander amongst graves and pitfalls" (131). And, as noted, the narrator of the first four chapters sees our salvation as occurring in this quite empirical world, in solidarity with others and in what we see, hear, and breathe.

Thus, whatever value there is in conformity to the principle of respect for persons will be incarnated in actions in this world that express this conformity, the value of achieving in nature, not out of it, the autonomy, dignity, cooperativeness, onwardness, and joy of which we are capable. We must regard nature as a home for our personhood, where its expression and flourishing are possible, though also typically threatened and never guaranteed by a comprehensive purposiveness. (The death of his father, Conrad remarked, "stripped off me some of my simple trust in the government of the universe."[20])

4. As his sense of the importance of solidarity with others and of the approbation of others in shaping one's convictions suggests, Conrad rejects pure a priorism in arguments concerning fundamental principles. He accepts instead the thought that our understandings of our personhood and the acceptances of principles woven through those understandings will be ongoing interpretive achievements. Human consciousnesses are originally and ineluctably situated within the world (Marlow remarks that man "is rooted to the land from which he draws his faith together with his life" [136]), so that any understanding of universal values that we are able to achieve must be won through interpretively seeing these values exemplified in particulars, not by contemplating goodness and rightness as autonomous abstract entities. Any such interpretive insights will further always be problematic and in principle revisable. These thoughts are natural ones for a morally serious novelist who aims at eliciting and structuring self-understanding, but who does not feel himself to be master in advance of his literary project. ("I feel how mysteriously independent of myself is my power of expression."[21]) The rejection of pure a priorism in favor of problematic interpretation is also perhaps encouraged by the experience of having been told as it were purely a priori that certain things (becoming a seaman, earning a master's certificate, becoming a writer, maintaining a Polish identity despite the Russians) were impossible and finding that they were not. What is a priori knowable in the sense of what is indubitable or deducible from self-evident principles turns out to be much less than is sometimes claimed, and the claim that something is known a priori can appear as a mask for illegitimate authority.

The open-ended, revisable, and interpretive nature of judgments about character and personhood is an obsessive theme in *Lord Jim*, registered in the impressionist technique of reordering the *récit* away from actional time, as different events become relevant to different issues, in order to emphasize the fragmentary illumination of character, and in the continual use of the symbolism of mist and fog. Marlow emphasizes that he sees Jim "in a mist" (135, 137), that he catches of him only "glimpses through the shifting rents in a thick fog" (47) or a "glimpse through a rent in the mist in which he moved and had his being" (78), and that Jim is "not . . . clear to me" (107). The force of this imagery is that judgments about character and motivations can never be made with perfect certainty. Marlow voices this thought explicitly as he refers to "that doubt which is the inseparable part of our knowledge" in remarking of Jim that "I cannot say I had ever seen him distinctly—not even to this day, after I had my last view of him" (135). If we continuously partially reveal ourselves to ourselves in action in a historical time that we cannot step out of so as to judge our characters against an independent standard, then we will not be able to know our personhood and the principles appropriate to the expression of its dignity and value unproblematically and once and for all. This is, it seems, roughly what Marlow means when he says,

> Are not our lives too short for that full utterance which through all our stammerings is of course our only and abiding intention? I have given up expecting those last words, whose ring if they could only be pronounced would shake both heaven and earth. There is never time to say our last word—the last word of our love, of our desire, faith, remorse, submission, revolt. The heaven and the earth must not be shaken, I suppose—at least, not by us who know so many truths about either. (137–38)

An understanding of our personhood and its possibilities of value, to the extent that we can come to it, will be an ongoing and problematic interpretive achievement.

2. Marlow's Progress

Lord Jim was initially begun as a study of the character of Jim, interesting in light of his, or rather his nonfictional counterpart's, role in the pilgrim ship episode. Marlow does not appear in the earliest surviving partial draft of the novel, "Tuan Jim: A Sketch," and he is not introduced until the end of chapter 4 of the completed version. Nonetheless, *Lord Jim* is, as Watt reminds us, above all else a novel about Marlow's relationship with Jim.[22] As Philip M. Weinstein has observed, it is Marlow, not Jim, who is "the figure of flexibility and survival and presence."[23] The principal action of the novel is centered in Marlow's consciousness, in the development of his evolving understandings of Jim and of himself. The structure of the novel from chapter 5 on is not directly that of the events of Jim's life, which are variously reordered and illuminated by Marlow in light of his subsequent encounters with Jim and those who knew him, but is rather that of the unfolding of Marlow's—and through Marlow's our—relationship to Jim and understanding of him. Thus the central question for a reader of the novel must be, Why does Marlow care about Jim?

Marlow's interest is neither that of a judge simply concerned to assign punishments nor that of a pathologist simply concerned to diagnose and explain according to fixed laws of behavior, though elements of these interests are woven into Marlow's. Marlow remarks early on that the object of the court of inquiry into the abandonment of the *Patna* "was not the fundamental why, but the superficial how, of this affair" (35), thereby implying, as Watt has noted,[24] that his own interest is in this deeper why, that he is concerned "to inquire into the state of a man's soul—or is it only of his liver?" (35). To inquire into this fundamental why is to ask after Jim's motives in abandoning the *Patna*. Was Jim unaware of the moral law? If so, why? What blocked his awareness? Or was he aware of the moral law but overcome by fear for his life? If so, why? What made his fear stronger than his consciousness of duty? Or, as his initial halfheartedly exculpatory remarks suggest ("'I had jumped . . . ' he checked himself, averted his gaze . . . 'it seems,' he added" [68]; "I tell you they [the ship captain and the chief and second engineers] were too much for any man. It was their doing as plainly as if they had reached up with a boat hook and pulled me over" [76]), is Jim best described as having acted involuntarily, having been pushed or pulled by forces or circumstances not under his control?

The answers to these questions are not—not to Marlow at least—of merely local concern. To ask whether Jim abandoned the *Patna* conscious of his duty but voluntarily repressing it in response to fear is to ask what are the possible and actual motivational structures of human action in general. If consciousness of what is normally called duty is a matter only of conditioning, which Jim perhaps lacked, or if Jim's fear was just *stronger*, so that he acted without volition or choice—if in either fashion our actions are determined by brute forces, internal or external, not choice—then our moral personhood and aspirations to rational, willed action in accordance with our natures are seriously compromised. Thus Marlow remarks about Jim's state of mind in jumping, "the mystery of his attitude got hold of me as though he had been an individual in the forefront of his kind, as if the obscure truth involved were momentous enough to affect mankind's conception of itself" (57). Marlow's inquiry into Jim's character is fundamentally an inquiry into his own moral personhood. Can anything be said about Jim that will plausibly represent his action in jumping ship as the result of a contingent failure—grounded ultimately in irrational choice, both immediate and woven through a history of education and practice that is not a story of simple conditioning—to act as a genuine moral law commands? If not, then we are not self-responsible moral persons of the sort that a normative principle of respect for persons requires.

It is Jim's overwhelming initial appearance of moral soundness, coupled with knowledge of his dereliction of duty, that first leads Marlow to become interested in him as a reflection of moral personhood. The case of the *Patna* had been the talk of Marlow's port prior to the deserters' arrival in it. Upon happening to see Jim and his fellow deserters first entering the port, walking along the quay toward the harbor office, Marlow is struck by Jim's looks: "I tell you I ought to know the right kind of looks. I would have trusted the deck to that youngster on the strength of a single glance, and gone to sleep with both eyes—and, by Jove!—it wouldn't have been safe. There are depths of horror in that thought" (28). Jim's appearance immediately places him in "the forefront of his kind" (57) as regards a capacity for duty.

> He was a youngster of the sort you like to see about you; of the sort you like to imagine yourself to have been; of the sort whose appearance claims the fellowship of those illusions you had thought gone out, extinct, cold, and which, as if rekindled at the approach of another flame, give a flutter deep, deep down somewhere, give a flutter of light . . . of heat! (78)

The horror in the thought of Jim's lack of faithfulness to his appearance lies in the suggestion that appearance and reality have come apart in the moral realm in such a way that the capacities, commitments, aspirations, and acknowledgments of principle that are essential to moral personhood can no longer be seen interpretively underneath the surfaces of action and aspect. In acting, we may, Jim's case suggests, not be expressing our moral personhood, our understanding of it, and our ability or inability to embody that understanding in action; we may instead be moved simply to behave. If this is true—if appearances, physical and in action, do not reflect essential aspects of moral personhood—and given the failure of pure a priorism in moral philosophy, then one loses one's grip on one's own moral personhood. Various

externals of action and aspect become no longer readable as expressions of one's moral personhood, the existence of which hence
falls into doubt. The coming apart of appearance and reality in the
moral realm reaches into the heart of one's own self-understanding
and forces an accusation against oneself of false pride in thinking
oneself capable of self-responsibility and of understanding and incarnating value for persons: "He had no business to look so sound. I
thought to myself—well, if this sort can go wrong like that . . . and I
felt as though I could fling down my hat and dance on it from sheer
mortification" (25). In Jim's severing of appearance and reality, it was
to Marlow "as though he had robbed our common life of the last spark
of its glamour" (80). The worry that Jim's case then raises, a worry
central to Marlow's understanding of his own personhood, is whether
appearance and reality can be put back together again, whether a story
can be told that plausibly represents Jim, in jumping, as betraying at
some level, through contingent error and willed choice, a common
moral personhood and a concomitant requirement to respect persons.

That Marlow's task is the rewelding of appearance and reality in
such a way as to display persons as essentially responsible and bound
by principle is more or less explicit in the account he offers of his
motives for inquiring into Jim's character as he visits, partly by chance,
the now-hospitalized and delirious chief engineer.

> Why I longed to go grubbing into the deplorable details of an occurrence
> which, after all, concerned me no more than as a member of an obscure
> body of men held together by a community of inglorious toil and by
> fidelity to a certain standard of conduct, I can't explain. You may call it an
> unhealthy curiosity if you like; but I have a distinct notion I wished to
> find something. Perhaps, unconsciously, I hoped I would find that
> something, some profound and redeeming cause, some merciful expla-
> nation, some convincing shadow of an excuse. I see well enough now
> that I hoped for the impossible—for the laying of what is the most obsti-
> nate doubt of man's creation, of the uneasy doubt uprising like a mist,
> secret and gnawing like a worm, and more chilling than the certitude of
> death—the doubt of the sovereign power enthroned in a fixed standard
> of conduct. It is the hardest thing to stumble against; it is the thing that
> breeds yelling panics and good, little, quiet villainies; it's the true shad-
> ow of calamity. Did I believe in a miracle? And why did I desire it so
> ardently? Was it for my own sake that I wished to find some shadow of
> an excuse for that young fellow, whom I had never seen before, but
> whose appearance alone added a touch of personal concern to the
> thoughts suggested by the knowledge of his weakness—made it a thing
> of mystery and terror—like a hint of a destructive fate ready for us all
> whose youth—in its day—had resembled his youth? I fear that such was

the secret motive of my prying. I was, and no mistake, looking for a miracle. (31–32)

Marlow goes on to call his hope that his doubt will be quieted by the chief engineer "imbecile," in part because he approached him "selfishly" and without "solicitude" (32). But that is not to say that his hope vanishes, and he does rather a better job in coming to terms with Jim in order to lay his doubt to rest, or at least temporarily to quell it. Partly, perhaps, as a result of his failure with the chief engineer, and partly as a result of circumstance—Jim approaches Marlow (and not the other way around) after misunderstanding a casual stranger's "wretched cur" remark—Marlow is overwhelmingly patient and solicitous. He invites Jim to dinner and lets him talk.

Marlow's efforts to allay through attention to Jim "the doubt of the sovereign power enthroned in a fixed standard of conduct" and to understand his own personhood assume the form of his repeatedly asserting to himself, and to us, that Jim is "one of us." This assertion is repeated eight times throughout the novel (as well as by Conrad in the author's preface) as Marlow keeps up relations with Jim and learns more of his character. Each time its meaning is deepened, as Marlow progressively understands himself and his commitments in relation to Jim's recovery and commitments. The variety of meanings it bears marks Marlow's progress in self-understanding, as he settles in the end on a sense for this assertion that tentatively and interpretively ascribes Kantian moral personhood in the world to Jim and to himself.

1. In its first use, the assertion "he was one of us" bears a range of meanings, including reference to Jim's appearance, to his place of origin, to his possession of certain general qualities of character such as courage and faithfulness, and to his aptitude "for mastery of the craft of the sea" (27). Among these possibilities, the one that Marlow immediately takes up and develops, apparently seeing it as fundamental to other aspects of character, is the last. After quickly mentioning Jim's appearance and place of origin and the aptitudes they typically suggest, Marlow goes on at length to detail Jim's fitness to serve at sea:

. . . he was outwardly so typical of that good, stupid kind we like to feel marching right and left of us in life, of the kind that is not disturbed by the vagaries of intelligence and the perversions of—of nerves, let us say. He was the kind of fellow you would, on the strength of his looks, leave in charge of the deck—figuratively and professionally speaking. I say I would, and I ought to know. Haven't I turned out youngsters enough in my time, for the service of the Red Rag, to the craft of the sea, to the craft whose whole secret could be expressed in one short sentence, and yet must be driven afresh every day into young heads till it becomes the component part of every waking thought—till it is present in every dream of their young sleep? (27)

Marlow's thoughts about his own experience of his craft and his role in training his successors ("Don't I remember the little So-and-so's!" [28]) continue along these lines until he reaches the culminating charge: "I couldn't believe it. I tell you I wanted to see him squirm for the honour of the craft" (28). Here the initial range of muddled possibilities of meaning for the assertion that Jim is one of us has been narrowed to the idea that Jim literally received training in the craft of seamanship that he subsequently betrayed. Apparently, in Marlow's first accounting, to be one of us means principally to have been apprenticed at sea.

As Marlow's reflections develop, however, it becomes increasingly clear that this cannot be the final meaning borne by this assertion. There are a number of figures who received training at sea but who remain notably different from Marlow and whom Marlow does not regard as "one of us." The German captain of the *Patna* is described as "monstrous" and "unnatural" in size, "inanimate" in gaze, "grotesque," and as displaying a "blind brutality" in action (25, 29). He is an object of Marlow's contempt and disgust, not his identification. Although he may in some original sense or state possess moral personhood—indeed, part of Marlow's disgust is readable as an inarticulate reaction to his betrayal or sullying of that personhood, to the dereliction of the capacities distinctive of it—the German ship captain is clearly not in his present form a vehicle for Marlow's recognition of that personhood's character. Marlow similarly finds himself distanced from Captain O'Brien, whose veiled jibing at Jim, unthinkingly seconded by Egstrom in an effort to soothe him, drives Jim from Egstrom and Blake's (117–19). Marlow is likewise ill at ease with Captain Brierly, whose prideful rigidity of behavior and subsequent suicide interest Marlow by contrast with Jim's behavior and deportment, but whose request to aid him in arranging Jim's escape from inquiry Marlow declines, calling Brierly "poor," apparently in spirit and sympathy (40–41). And, most important, Marlow is estranged from the French lieutenant, with whom he in the end finds conversation impossible. Each of these persons is clearly of the sea in having received training at it—each in fact serves at sea better than Jim—but none of them is one of us. Apparently one certifies oneself as one of us, in Marlow's judgment, not simply by having been to sea, but through manifesting in one's behavior a certain quality of motivation, or at least the continuing capacity for it.

2. That overt right action, as well as training, is necessary and

sufficient for being one of us is encouraged by Marlow's initial thought that in being one of us, in standing for "all the parentage of his kind," Jim possesses an "honest faith," "the instinct of courage," the "inborn ability to look temptations in the face," and "belief in a few simple notions you must cling to if you want to live decently and would like to die easy!" (27). In this strand of Marlow's opening thought, to be one of us is to be concerned to prepare oneself for death through courageous and principled right action.

Yet courageous and principled right action cannot simply and directly be necessary and sufficient for being one of us and for being a vehicle for the recognition of moral personhood. If exceptionless right action were necessary (and possible), there could be no question about Jim; his dereliction of duty would amount to an unalterable lack of moral personhood, rather than something to be acknowledged and incorporated into it. And it cannot be simply sufficient, for there are figures of principled courage who, Marlow finds, do not engage his sympathy and self-recognition. There is Brierly, whose behavior is thoroughly principled and impeccable—"He had never in his life made a mistake, never had an accident, never a mishap, never a check in his steady rise, and he seemed to be one of those lucky fellows who know nothing of indecision, much less of self-mistrust" (35)—but who is guilty of rigidity, intolerance, pride, and moral exceptionalism. Similarly, the French lieutenant is "seamanlike" and "a reliable officer" (85). He carries "an old wound" (86) as a mark of his courage, and he remained, "because it was judged proper" (86), on the derelict *Patna* for thirty hours as it was towed into port, kept from sinking only by a rusted paper-thin bulkhead. His courage and the propriety of his behavior are beyond question. Yet, despite his honor and courage, he and Marlow, as a result of his insistence on his honor, "faced each other mutely," Marlow reports, "like two china dogs on a mantelpiece. Hang the fellow! he had pricked the bubble. The blight of futility that lies in wait for men's speeches had fallen upon our conversation, and made it a thing of empty sounds" (90).

In the cases of both Brierly and the French lieutenant, overt moral rectitude is marked by pridefulness and rigidity. This attitude and demeanor are rooted in a narcissistic exceptionalism. The French lieutenant, though admitting he shares fear with everyone, claims unlike the many to "know nothing" of dishonorable action, indeed claims never to have thought of doing anything other than what he ought. Brierly is described by Marlow with evident suspicious hyperbole as never having made a mistake and as knowing nothing of self-mistrust. Their pride and sense of special moral purity are in marked contrast to the humility and sense of ordinariness of Marlow, who remarks that others approach him, by implication mistakenly, "as though, for-sooth, I had no confidences to make to myself, as though—God help me!—I didn't have enough confidential information about myself to harrow my own soul till the end of my appointed time" (21). Marlow further implies, in telling his audience that he forbore to point out an exception to Jim's remark that he will run away from no one, that we all have in us something that inclines us to run away from ourselves (46). Where the French lieutenant and Brierly fail in self-recognition and self-forgiveness, failing to see that their moral lives require acknowl-edgment of their imperfect pasts, Marlow's acknowledgments of his own lapses—perhaps in action, perhaps in motivation—into occasion-al pride and exceptionalism are in the forefront of his reflections on Jim's case.

The French lieutenant's and Brierly's inability to recognize and acknowledge their pasts is mirrored in their relations to others, in particular to Jim. Each of them wants Jim out of the way and prefers not to think about him. Brierly puts to Marlow a scheme, which Marlow refuses, for effecting Jim's self-removal from the court of inquiry, and by implication from the realm of personhood (41). (Marlow later him-self puts this same scheme before Jim, who declines to be removed, but comments that in doing so he was himself "selfish" and guilty of "subtle intentions of immorality" [93].) Brierly cannot bear Jim's pres-ence as a person who has done something shameful; what is shameful must always be denied or hidden or refused any connection with personhood. Similarly, when asked by Marlow what one might do when removed from the gaze of others, so that the possibility of "hon-our is gone," the French lieutenant confesses that he "can offer no opinion," concluding, "This, monsieur, is too fine for me—much above me—I don't think about it" (90–91). Whatever there is in per-sons that makes morally right action both difficult and a matter of motivation as well as behavior is refused acknowledgment, and this refusal is manifested in an unwillingness to think about Jim's case and its implications. The failure of attention to and acknowledgment of the categorial demands on personhood is figured as a failure of attention to and acknowledgment of others as co-bearers of moral personhood.

For both Brierly and the French lieutenant, morality is a matter entirely of overt actions in conformity to a conventional code. This code is accepted by them a priori as self-evidently correct, largely, it seems, because they regard whatever is accepted—by those who count, that is, those who accept what is accepted—as self-evidently correct. They are guilty of either pure a priorism or unthinking conven-tionalism (it is hard to tell which, and a Conradian charge against pure a priorism would be that it can amount to nothing but unthinking conventionalism) in moral philosophizing. For neither of them is the acknowledgment of moral principle an achievement in the interpretation of their personhood that requires the education and transfiguration of their own motivations. Morality is for them externally based and directed at overt action, not inner motivation.

Thus when Brierly is at last led by Jim's case to confront the question of his own deepest motivations and to imagine how he would act in the absence of conventions and external sanctions, he is forced to convict himself of unredeemable moral error. When an unthinkingly accepted convention around which one had structured one's life becomes no longer serviceable, one's sense of value as a person is likely to crumble, and this is what happens with Brierly. As a result of acquaintance with Jim's case, which makes actions not motivated by external sanctions, actions no one will ever know to reward or punish, of prime importance in the moral life, Brierly has had "start into life some thought with which a man unused to such companionship finds it impossible to live!" (36). His hardness and resoluteness in hewing absolutely to conventional moral standards, but without being genuinely motivated by or even concerned with respect for persons and the moral law, reveal themselves as a mask for moral brittleness and a lack of resourcefulness in moral self-struggle. In Brierly, conventions and external sanctions have replaced interpretive self-understanding and motivation by respect. Even when he has acted well overtly, his action has been prideful, sterile, and reward seeking, not an expression of the achievement of the fullest possibilities of the human, of the acknowledgment of the demand to be motivated by respect for persons and principle. Those who, like Brierly, are thus externally motivated fail to express in their actions, even when they are not overtly contrary to the moral law, the fullest achievement of human value. When they are forced by circumstance to confront their failure, they may crack. When they are not forced to do so, then, as Conrad elsewhere put it, they "go skimming over the years of existence to sink gently into a placid grave, ignorant of life to the last, without ever having been made to see all it may contain of perfidy, of violence, and of terror. There are on sea and land such men thus fortunate—or thus disdained by destiny or by the sea."[25]

Something of this sense that he has been disdained by destiny surfaces in Marlow's physical descriptions of the French lieutenant, who is said variously to be "imperturbable" (89), to have "submitted himself passively to a state of silence" (87), to display "immobility" (87), to have "heavy eyelids," to be "a quiet massive chap" (84), and to be "no longer very active" (85) and "not particularly talkative" (84). The dominant impression left by these descriptions is of one who has lost all onwardness in life and whom life has passed by. This impression is reinforced in Marlow's having come across him not in the business of life, but only "by the merest chance . . . one afternoon in Sydney" (84). In the finest and most significant of these descriptions, the one which is said to record "a moment of vision," Marlow remarks that "I saw him as though I had never seen him before. I saw his chin sunk on his breast, the clumsy folds of his coat, his clasped hands, his motionless pose, so curiously suggestive of his having been simply left there. Time had passed indeed: it had overtaken him and gone ahead" (87). Having struggled throughout his life to overcome his fear and do his duty, but being motivated externally rather than by respect for persons accepted as a motive of fundamental value in human life, the French lieutenant is now—now that the occasions for overcoming fear and winning honor have passed—left without motivation, sunk into moral torpor. Without a structure of motives regarded as fundamentally valuable for persons, as a continuously incarnatable value for persons, there can be no onwardness in one's life. In regarding morality externally, as a matter of actions and sanctions, the French lieutenant speaks "as though he had been the mouthpiece of abstract wisdom" (89), pointedly not as someone whose practical wisdom is a concretely shaped interpretive achievement of an understanding of value for persons. His wisdom is abstract in relation to issues about fundamental value, and hence hollow and exhaustible.

That the French lieutenant is more or less a Hobbesian in matters of morality, concerned with overt actions and external sanctions, as opposed to Marlow, who insistently raises questions about the structure of the soul and the nature of value for persons, almost in the manner of Plato or Kant, becomes clear as their conversation reaches its end, finding no place to go. In summing up the significance of Jim's case, the French lieutenant observes, "Man is born a coward (*L'homme est né poltron*). It is a difficulty—*parbleu!* It would be too easy otherwise. But habit—habit—necessity—do you see?—the eye of others—*voilà*. One puts up with it. And then the example of others who are no better than yourself, and yet make good countenance . . ." (90). Immediately Marlow is moved to oppose this emphasis on the eye of others and on making good countenance. His response—"That young man—you will observe—had none of these inducements—at least at the moment" (90)—suggests that morality is concerned with motivations of fundamental value for persons, motivations of which Jim, even while abandoning the *Patna*, may have had a partial and obscure presentiment, though he was unable to express this presentiment in action. Living well, bringing one's personhood to its proper expression in response to its requirements, is as Marlow would have it crucially a matter of one's motivations, of what one does or would do when honors and rewards are not in question. The contrast between Marlow and the French lieutenant is then marked again and deepened. The French lieutenant goes on to insist, "But the honour—the honour, monsieur! . . . The honour . . . that is real—that is! And what life may be worth when . . . when the honour is gone—*ah ça! par exemple*—I can offer no opinion. I can offer no opinion—because—monsieur—I know nothing of it" (90). To this declamation, Marlow's reply, the reply typical of a Platonist or Kantian concerned with the soul and value for persons, takes the form of a question, asking, about honor, "But couldn't it reduce itself to not being found out?" (90). When what is valuable is reduced to what is rewarded, and what is evil to what is found out and condemned, as the French lieutenant reduces them, then moral torpor threatens in the absence of the contingencies of reward, and we are left as moral persons buffeted about by the subjective considerations of those who surround us, just as the French lieutenant leaves Marlow, their relation having exhausted itself, driven "down wind with his hand to his head, his shoulders braced, and the tails of his coat blown hard against his legs" (91).

For both the French lieutenant and Brierly, then, respect for persons, even when they managed overtly to act in accordance with its requirements, (i) is not grounded in an interpretive achievement of an understanding of the grammatical necessity of respect as a fundamental value, but is rather a matter of convention, (ii) is not expressed in acknowledgments of their pasts and imperfections, (iii) is not expressed in sympathy for and attention to others, and (iv) is not part of the fundamental onwardness—which is hence likely to falter—of their lives as moral persons. Marlow, in reflecting on his own moral personhood, is seeking something more deeply and comprehensively valuable for persons than the ways of living and self-understanding they incarnate. They betray their personhood by subjectivizing judgments of moral value and hence by failing to live according to an interpretive understanding of personhood and its requirements. It is this that prevents each of them from being, with Marlow, one of us.

3. A further suggestion about what it means to be one of us appears in the remark by Marlow that immediately precedes his first assertion of this commonality. Jim, Marlow says, "came from the right place" (27). This remark takes on a distinct racial connotation as Jim's fairness is emphasized—". . . these blue, boyish eyes looking straight into mine, this young face, these capable shoulders, the open bronzed forehead with a white line under the roots of clustering fair hair. . . . He was of the right sort; he was one of us" (48)—and as Jim is conspicuously successful in winning authority and respect in Patusan. Jim in

Patusan is in fact compared by Marlow with Dain Waris, who is of the same rough age, intelligence, and courage, explicitly along racial lines. Dain Waris,

> that brave and intelligent youth ("who knew how to fight after the man-ner of white men") wished to settle the business [with Gentleman Brown] off-hand, but his people were too much for him. He had not Jim's racial prestige and the reputation of invincible, supernatural power. . . . Beloved, trusted, and admired as he was, he was still one of *them*, while Jim was one of *us*. Moreover, the white man, a tower of strength in himself, was invulnerable, while Dain Waris could be killed. (220)

A racial interpretation of moral personhood is also explicitly argued by the correspondent who receives Marlow's final written thoughts about Jim. Addressing this correspondent, Marlow writes,

> You said also—I call to mind—that "giving your life up to them" (*them* meaning all of mankind with skins brown, yellow, or black in colour) "was like selling your soul to a brute." You contended that "that kind of thing" was only endurable and enduring when based on a firm convic-tion in the truth of ideas racially our own, in whose name are established the order, the morality of an ethical progress. (206)

Apparently one of the meanings that "one of us" can bear is that of being white and committed to the universal imposition of European civilization. (Even Marlow, who is more ambivalent than his corre-spondent about European civilization, observes that Jim "was too much like one of us not to be dangerous" [65], thus suggesting, when these other remarks are considered, a connection between being white and being prone to tyrannical violence.)

Yet that one is a white European cannot be the final meaning borne by the phrase "one of us." Some white Westerners—notably the German captain of the *Patna* and Gentleman Brown, who, Marlow notes, displays enormous, though unprincipled, psychological acuity and attentiveness, and who incarnates a form "of evil . . . akin to madness, derived from intense egotism" (209)—are evident objects of Marlow's contempt, not figures with whom he identifies. A commit-ment to acting rightly and well, even when one could get away with doing otherwise, clearly has something to do with Marlow's sense of who he is, as the scenes with Brierly and the French lieutenant indi-cate. The German captain and Brown, though white and European, overtly have no commitment to acting rightly at all. They simply use others, and their lack of principle makes them objects of revulsion, not vehicles of self-recognition of our best possibilities. At the same time, the nonwhite, non-European Jewel (whose father is white [169] and whose mother is a "Dutch-Malay girl" [134]), Dain Waris, and Tamb 'Itam clearly display virtues of faithfulness, courage, and sympathy that all elicit Marlow's approval and moral solidarity. To be white and European, it becomes clear to Marlow, is less important to what is proper to moral personhood and to being one of us than is a certain commitment to principle.

Marlow's late characterization of Jim as white actually does nothing to undermine a thoroughly nonracial account of moral personhood and its proper end. While Jim is notably described as white in comparison with Dain Waris, Marlow is offering that comparison less from his own point of view than from that of the Bugis, attempting to explain how *they* see Jim and why he had authority over them. Marlow does not himself endorse the idea that being white is a crucial aspect of the moral personhood he is on the verge of regarding himself as sharing. Unlike some other white Europeans—again, notably the captain of the *Patna* and Gentleman Brown—Jim in Patusan treats non-Europeans attentively and with respect, not as means to be used. Even in exercising authority, Jim is less a tyrant and more one who encourages mutual respect and community within the prevailing forms of social life. He assumes no formal powers, attempting to oust neither Doramin nor Rajah Allang. He hears the complaints of impoverished fishermen against the Rajah and then at some risk to himself puts these complaints before the Rajah, asking for justice. And, crucially, Jim enters into relations of reciprocal respect and friendship with Dain Waris and, especially, Jewel. Marlow remarks that Jewel and Jim take "marital evening walks" (171), and Jim speaks her name "with a marital homelike peaceful effect" (169). Thus Jim conspicuously displays a capacity to enter into an existing community of non-Europeans, respecting them rather than tyrannizing them. He continues to feel himself to be a bit apart—one's birthplace and prior attachments are not given up so easily—but he is not prevented by his past from expressing his personhood in expressing respect in a non-European community. Thinking through all this, reflecting on Jim's behavior and motivations in comparison with those of the other figures in his story, Marlow finds he has an explicit argument with the correspondent whose racial conception of moral personhood and its proper end he is in fact attacking. After characterizing his correspondent's views and in introducing the account of Jim's end, Marlow remarks against his correspondent that "the point, however, is that of all mankind Jim had no dealings but with himself, and the question is whether at the last he

had not confessed to a faith mightier than the laws of order and progress" (206). This faith is something like a commitment to respect for
persons as a motive of fundamental value in human life.

4. Thus in the end Marlow is committed to regarding Jim as one of
us in the sense that he has understood the character of his moral
personhood, responded to its requirements, and expressed in his actions respect for persons regarded as a motive of fundamental and
comprehensive value in the life of a person. Jim has shown himself
capable of realizing our common capacity for leading the life of a moral
person. It is this meaning to the assertion that Jim is one of us that
finally takes shape in Marlow's consciousness through his consideration of the full course of Jim's career and through his encounters with
others. It emerges out of the confused welter of physical, craft-based,
conventionalist, and racial conceptions of personhood and its requirements on the basis of which Marlow had first obscurely sensed Jim's
likeness to himself. Jim stands in the end for our capability as persons
of being moved by an aspiration to inaugurate a kingdom of ends in
which human action is thoroughly motivated by respectful attention to
personhood in both others and oneself. In his death, Jim, Marlow tells
us, "goes away from a living woman to celebrate his pitiless wedding
with a shadowy ideal of conduct. Is he satisfied—quite, now, I wonder. We ought to know. He is one of us—and have I not stood up once,
like an evoked ghost, to answer for his eternal constancy? Was I so very
wrong after all?" (253).

A crucial question for the character of Marlow's understanding is
just *how* Jim has managed to act under the legislation of a kingdom of
ends, or to act so as to express respect for persons, or to act in a way
that celebrates his "wedding with a shadowy ideal of conduct." The
case for Jim's having so acted is, of course, not perfectly clear; judgments about motives are always interpretive and problematic. (Jim is
always seen "in a mist.") But the case must be made out interpretively
if the novel is to make sense as the record of Marlow's progress toward
moral self-understanding. Objectively—that is, considering first of all
Jim's actions, and only second Marlow's descriptions of his psychological states—the case rests principally on Jim's death, or, more
accurately, on his presenting himself to Doramin (after the massacre of
Dain Waris and his party by Gentleman Brown and his band), in order
to take responsibility for having failed to bring about the removal of
Brown and his pirates without harm to anyone. But though this incident is crucial, it must also, if the case is to be made plausible, be seen
as the culmination of an already well-incarnated commitment on Jim's
part to respecting persons. Unless it is so seen, Jim's presenting himself to Doramin for what he more or less knows will be his execution

will seem an act reflecting either a narcissistic desire for notoriety or a despairing withdrawal from life, or perhaps both. If, alternatively, Jim's life in Patusan reveals a well-embodied commitment on his part to respecting persons (a commitment also partially revealed to us in his death), then his death will appear to confirm this commitment. Thus, insofar as Marlow's understandings of Jim and of moral personhood are at issue, Jim's death must be considered against the background of his full life in Patusan.

If any acknowledgment of the fundamental value of respect for persons as a motive breaks through in Jim's character and comes to be expressed in his actions, it is clear that it happens almost entirely in Patusan, though also to a lesser extent through the development of his friendship with Marlow and of his appreciation of it. When we are first introduced to him, Jim suffers enormously from a combination of pridefulness, self-love, exceptionalism, and a refusal of his past of the sort that later appears more moderately, though more ineradicably, in Brierly and the French lieutenant. He habitually disdains the ordinary. The unnamed narrator tells us that, as a young recruit on a training ship, Jim's "station was in the fore-top, and often from there he looked down, with the contempt of a man destined to shine in the midst of dangers, at the peaceful multitude of roofs cut in two by the brown tide of the stream" (5). Having literally removed himself aloft to a position of both epistemic and moral isolation from his fellows, his country and its commerce, and his past, he imagines himself performing acts of unprecedented heroism:

> He saw himself saving people from sinking ships, cutting away masts in a hurricane, swimming through a surf with a line; or as a lonely cast-away, barefooted and half naked, walking on uncovered reefs in search of shellfish to stave off starvation. He confronted savages on tropical shores, quelled mutinies on the high seas, and in a small boat upon the ocean kept up the hearts of despairing men—always an example of devotion to duty, and as unflinching as a hero in a book. (5)

Even after he has conspicuously failed to join his fellow recruits in manning a small boat in order to save two men who had lost their ship during a heavy gale, he continues to congratulate himself for his exceptional courage and resolve. In distinct contrast to Marlow ("I don't like to feel exceptional in any way" [21]), the young Jim is eager to think of himself as able and ready to do what no one else can:

> Jim thought [talk of the rescue] a pitiful display of vanity. The gale had ministered to a heroism as specious as its own pretence of terror. . . . When all men flinched, then—he felt sure—he alone would know how

> to deal with the spurious menace of wind and seas. . . . He could detect
> no trace of emotion in himself, and the final effect of a staggering event
> was that, unnoticed and apart from the noisy crowd of boys, he exulted
> with fresh certitude in his avidity for adventure, and in a sense of many-
> sided courage. (6–7)

His exceptionalism—his inability to see either courage or moral worth in what others do and his inability to see himself in others—is further expressed in a distinct inability to see himself in his daily work, in a readiness to regard it as extrinsic to himself and as a burden: "He made many voyages. He knew the magic monotony of existence between sky and water: he had to bear the criticism of men, the exactions of the sea, and the prosaic severity of the daily task that gives bread—but whose only reward is the perfect love of the work. This reward eluded him" (7). That his pride, self-love, and exceptionalism are horrible misconceptions is to be made all too clear by his abandonment of the *Patna* after its accident, one of "those events of the sea that show in the light of day the inner worth of a man, the edge of his temper, and the fibre of his stuff; that reveal the quality of his resistance and the secret truth of his pretences, not only to others, but also to himself" (7).

Jim's pride, self-love, and exceptionalism have been nourished principally by popular romances of heroism and by the youthfulness that finds such romances engaging. It is "after a course of light holiday literature [that] his vocation for the sea . . . declared itself" (4). While below decks at sea, "he would forget himself, and beforehand live in his mind the sea-life of light literature" (5). Seeing oneself in heroic tales quite typically makes for, as Kant put it, not correct observers of duty, but "fantastic romancers."[26] Kant complains about precisely the literary diet on which Jim has nourished his imagination and self-conception:

> I wish [moral educators] would spare [the young] examples of so-called
> noble (super-meritorious) actions, which so fill our sentimental writ-
> ings, . . . since whatever runs up into empty wishes and longings for
> unattainable perfection produces mere heroes of romance, who, while
> priding themselves on their feeling of transcendent greatness, release
> themselves from observing the common and everyday responsibility as
> petty and insignificant.[27]

Having taken his conception of worth from popular romances and fallen into exceptionalism, Jim, in explaining to himself that his failure to participate in the rescue is a sign of his being destined for greater things, easily falls victim to "a type of sophistication to which self-love gives rise. Our inner advocate becomes a pettifogger, expounding the [moral] law sophistically to our advantage."[28] Or, in Hegel's formulation, once conformity to the moral law is no longer seen to be often exemplified by ordinary persons in ordinary situations, and moral worth is instead located only in the realm of the fantastic, then "my consciously ironical attitude [toward the ordinary] lets the highest perish and I merely hug myself at the thought."[29] Even in staying to face his punishment, unlike his fellow deserters of the *Patna*, Jim acts from a kind of insolent pride in himself. His staying is an effort to separate himself from his fellow deserters, who, he says, "'went away . . . went into hospitals. . . . Not one of them would face it. . . . They . . .' He moved his hand slightly to imply disdain" (94). In explaining to Marlow why he has decided to stay for the inquiry and in noting that he can never again go home, Jim, Marlow tells us, "discovered at once a desire that I should not confound him with his partners in—in crime, let us call it. He was not one of them; he was altogether of another sort" (49). He stays not out of a sense of responsibility and respect for his personhood, but out of a sense of his own special self-love: "I may have jumped, but I don't run away" (94).

Exceptionalism, disdain for the ordinary, self-deluding self-love, hero-worship—these are the dominant elements of the youthful Jim's character. They are, Marlow conjectures, dominant elements of the character of youth in general. Developing an independent identity requires a certain break, temporary in some ways and enduring in others, with one's past and with what is ordinary. Jim's development is typical in this regard, and the psychology that informs it is not peculiar to him: "Youth *is* insolent; it is its right—its necessity; it has got to assert itself, and all assertion in this world of doubts is a defiance, is an insolence" (144).

This psychology of development clearly implies an earlier innocent pastoral stage of unselfconscious communion with things out of which self-assertion later emerges. This earlier stage is not described directly. The lives of those who are in it have an undifferentiated character that resists special description. The elusive and problematic character of self-remembrance of one's origins is a standard theme in Romantic psychology. (Compare Wordsworth's "I cannot paint / What then I was," and related lines.[30]) Descriptions of individuals who are particular must locate them as already within the second stage of development. Thus, as Weinstein observes, "The people Conrad chooses to explore in both his land and sea novels have ventured away from a sustaining turf. . . . They are already immersed in the 'destructive element,'"[31] given over to self-assertion and particularity. The stage of primitive personhood prior to self-assertion is hence not described as a stage in the life of a distinct personality, since before self-assertion distinct personality is not yet evident. Rather the character of this first stage of undifferentiated personhood is implied through an account of the timelessly pastoral character of the landscape from which Jim emerges. The church and rectory of Jim's father are naturalized, are made to appear more as natural features of the landscape than as artifacts reflecting human self-assertion and striving. The church resembles a mossy grey rock, the trees have memory, and the various parts of the landscape, natural and man-made, seem to be in essential harmonious and mysterious interaction:

> Originally he came from a parsonage. Many commanders of fine merchant-ships come from these abodes of piety and peace. . . . The little church on a hill had the mossy greyness of a rock seen through a ragged screen of leaves. It had stood there for centuries, but the trees around probably remembered the laying of the first stone. Below, the red front of the rectory gleamed with a warm tint in the midst of grass-plots, flower-beds, and fir-trees, with an orchard at the back, a paved stable-yard to the left, and the sloping glass of greenhouses tacked along a wall of bricks. (4)

Marlow, in remarking explicitly the importance of one's home in structuring one's life as a person, similarly notes that one's home landscape will appear to be comprehensively informed by spirit, in such a way that differentiation among its parts tends to disappear, so that at home one will feel oneself to be at one with what naturally is. In returning home, we "meet the spirit that dwells within the land, under its sky, in its air, in its valley, and on its rises, in its fields, in its water and its trees—a mute friend, judge, and inspirer" (136). In leaving such an undifferentiated and spiritualized landscape—that is, in running away to sea from his sustaining yet static past—Jim falls into the stage of self-assertion and exceptionalism that is typical of youth.

Once fallen into, moreover, self-love, exceptionalism, the denial of one's past, and the refusal of relatedness are not easily overcome. Both in taking up his initial succession of jobs after the *Patna* and in entering Patusan, Jim seeks a "clean slate" (113), seeks to "forget everything, everybody" (144), to "slam the door" (144) as though "the outside world had never existed" (142), to have "a chance" (141) again for greatness and heroism. ("This," Marlow comments concerning the entry into Patusan, "was not a proper frame of mind to approach any undertaking; an improper frame of mind not only for him . . . but for any man" [144].) Self-assertiveness thus involves an active escapism and moral exceptionalism

But yet, later, somehow, in Patusan, Jim—Marlow's description of his end suggests—manages to recover from his self-love, exceptionalism, and moral escapism, and in this recovery to enter a further stage of self-understanding and self-responsibility. Self-assertiveness and a desire for fame are supplanted as motives in Jim by a respect for persons that is an achievement on Jim's part of the dignity and value of which persons are capable. Apart from his final reference to a shadowy ideal of conduct, Marlow implies that Jim in the end acts artfully and respectfully of what is, rather than tyrannically, assertively, and manipulatively. In the course of describing Jim's life in Patusan, Marlow asks us whether we "notice how, three hundred miles beyond the end of telegraph cables and mail-boat lines, the haggard utilitarian lies of our civilization wither and die, to be replaced by pure exercises of imagination, that have the futility, often the charm, and sometimes the deep hidden truthfulness, of works of art" (172). Apparently Jim in Patusan manages not to use people as means either to his glorification—the role he had once allotted to others—or to the promotion of some abstract utilitarian good. He frees himself from domination by "the haggard utilitarian lies of our civilization" and from unrespectful self-assertion. How is this possible? How does one become in this sense one of us—one in whom we can recognize the incarnation of the fundamental value and dignity of persons?

Three newly emergent relations crucially distinguish Jim's life first as a water-clerk and then more deeply in Patusan from his prior life at sea: his relations to work, to nature, and to others. In contrast to his work at sea, from which he failed to win the reward of its love, Jim, Marlow notes, "tackled [his work as a water-clerk] with a stubborn serenity for which I must give him full credit," in a way that seemed "an expiation for his craving after more glamour than he could carry" (92). In Patusan he is yet more devoted to his daily business and more conscious of its importance. Marlow reports that, during his stay with Jim in Patusan, "now and then . . . a word, a sentence, would escape him that showed how deeply, how solemnly, he felt about that work which had given him certitude of rehabilitation" (152).

Partly through having found there work to which he is able to devote himself, Jim comes to sense the very landscape of Patusan to be informed by a mysterious purposiveness that has come to shape his own life. He is, in Patusan, "in complete accord with his surroundings—with the life of the forests and with the life of men" (107):

> He looked with an owner's eye at the peace of the evening, at the river, at the houses, at the everlasting life of the forests, at the life of the old mankind, at the secrets of the land, at the pride of his own heart; but it was they that possessed him and made him their own to the innermost thought, to the slightest stir of blood, to his last breath. (152)

Having found his work in that place, Jim finds his own development again to be intimately bound up with both the beauty of the landscape and the life of his community: "The land, the people, the friendship, the love, were like the jealous guardians of his body. Every day added a link to the fetters of that strange freedom" (160). His own purposiveness and onwardness are no longer sharply separable from either his place or the lives of those around him.

The persistent friendship and trust of others—partly simply given through Stein, partly won heroically, and partly slowly developed with Marlow—play perhaps the most important role in the transfiguration of his self-conception and his motives. In contrast both with his early pridefulness and moral exceptionalism and with the way in which his notorious abandonment of the *Patna* makes him always someone apart from others, Jim is both given friendship by Stein and prepared to value it in entering Patusan. Jim explicitly comments upon the importance of the ring Stein has given him in order to identify himself to Doramin as Stein's particularly valued representative. Marlow reports Jim's comment to us: "I probably didn't realize, he said with a naive gravity, how much importance he attached to that token. It meant a friend; and it is a good thing to have a friend. He knew something about that" (143). In saying this to Marlow, Jim is also clearly acknowledging, as he is about to depart for Patusan, the friendship that has developed between them since the board of inquiry ("He nodded at me expressively . . ." [143]). As he leaves Jim on the boat about to set out for Patusan, Marlow reports that "there was a moment of real and profound intimacy, unexpected and short-lived like a glimpse of some everlasting, of some saving truth" (147). Once in Patusan, the trust of people in general becomes a central element in Jim's recovery of self-respect and in his commitment to stay: "I must feel—every day, every time I open my eyes—that I am trusted—that nobody has a right—don't you know? Leave! For where? What for? To get what?" (151). A special friendship springs up between Jim and Dain Waris. In them, Marlow "seemed to behold the very origin of friendship" (160). And then there is Jewel, with whom Jim accomplishes something very like a marriage, and by whom Jim is "*made* to understand every day that [his] existence is necessary—you see, absolutely necessary—to another person" (185). The structure of Jim's motives is fundamentally altered from pridefulness and a desire for fame to respect for persons and a kind of seriousness in honoring both their individuality and their likeness to him as moral persons, through his having become attached to others with whom his life is bound up: "There is in his espousal of memory and affection belonging to another human being something characteristic of his seriousness" (168). Having found himself—understood the dimensions of his personhood—through his work, his relation to the landscape, and his relations to others, Jim is plausibly seen by Marlow and by us as having moved beyond sheer particularity, exceptionalism, and self-assertiveness to the acknowledgment of respect for persons as a motive of fundamental value for persons, incarnated in ongoing communal life.

This transformation in Jim's character is in the end expressed and certified in his death, or so, at least, Marlow seems to suggest in referring to Jim's "wedding with a shadowy ideal of conduct." It becomes easier to see how Jim's going to Doramin may plausibly be interpreted (as it were, externally, since we cannot see directly into our hearts, but then also just interpreted, since there is no position we, or Jim, can occupy, against which our position might properly be called external) as expressing respect for persons when his alternatives to presenting himself to Doramin are considered. After the massacre of Dain Waris and his party has become known and has demonstrated that Jim is not infallible, then, as Watt has noted, Jim has three courses of action open to him: rallying his few remaining followers to fight Doramin and the Bugis who have turned against him, running away, and going to Doramin.[32] The first two alternatives seem wrong, inconsistent with the requirements of respect for persons. (This novel requires us to ask not only why Jim, in the end, does what he does, but also what, in the light of our emergent understanding of persons, it would be right for him to do.) To fight would be to treat others as mere inconvenient matter to be disposed of. Jim has no just cause to initiate violence against the Bugis. Whatever threat he faces from them must be met not by preemptive violence on his part, but by facing the surviving political and moral authority, Doramin, taking responsibility for what he has done and leaving it to Doramin and his understanding of justice to determine what will become of him. "There is," Jim explains to Jewel, "nothing to fight for" (250), and, while it has overtones of either despairing or prideful fatalism, this remark is also true: Jim has no just cause to fight.

To run away would be both to fail to respect others and to compromise his own personhood. It is neither simply, as critics have often noted, that running away would be a repetition of Jim's abandonment of the *Patna*, which is psychologically impossible, nor that there is no place in the world left for Jim to go. (Though there is truth in each of these remarks, the concepts of psychological impossibility and possibilities of life that they employ stand in need of analysis: flight is impossible in light of the moral development of his personality, not physically impossible.) Rather, the deepest reason for not running away is that, for Jim, to run away would be to deny the importance of his relations to these people in shaping his self-understanding and in structuring his daily activities expressive of respect for persons; hence it would be to cut off a part of his own developed and embodied moral personhood, and it would be to deny to others the roles of friends and co-bearers of moral personality that they had come to occupy with him. Even his relationship with Jewel, central though it is to who he now is, cannot be wrenched out of its location in the life of its sur-rounding community and survive unaltered. In not fleeing together with Jewel, Jim acknowledges the importance of public social life in shaping the texture and meaning of the most private relationships. Though Jewel, afraid of losing Jim, may not see the situation so sharp-ly, it is nonetheless true in large measure that for Jim to run would be to reject or deny the person he has been with her. And this in turn would also be to reject her, in failing to take seriously her commitment to that person. The idea that Jim and Jewel might simply leave together, with nothing between them altered and with their respect for themselves intact, is a piece of sheer escapism that denies the possibility of tragedy in human life. Considering where and how his moral personhood has been incarnated and given expression, and considering the fact that he has explicitly taken responsibility for the care of the community in dealing with Gentleman Brown, "there is," Jim tells Jewel, "no es-cape" (250); he must live up to his incarnated moral personhood and relations with others by facing Doramin. Were Jim to fail to do this, then, as he tells Jewel, he "should not be worth having" (251): he would be unable to respect himself and unworthy of the respect and love of Jewel.

In going to face Doramin, thus taking "upon his own head" (252) his failure to have protected those in his care, Jim senses that he is going to his death. This sense is recorded in the final and fatal tone of his "There is no escape" (250), in his request to Jewel for forgiveness (251) (a request which also further acknowledges his relatedness to her), in his "measured steps" (252) in approaching Doramin, in his attitude before Doramin of waiting (252), and in his words, "I am come in sorrow. . . . I am come ready and unarmed" (252). Yet it is impor-tant to remember that there are alternatives to execution that are open to Doramin. He might, for example, have chastised Jim for having imprudently promised something—the protection of all in giving Brown a way out—that was not in his power and then forgiven him. (It is not even clear that Jim's promise was either knowably imprudent or wrong. Jim could perhaps not be expected to know of the by-channel from which Brown's party attacks Dain Waris's, and Dain Waris could have positioned himself better. Further, Jim has no direct evidence of the evil of Brown, who, for all his rapacious intentions, was actually fired upon first by the Bugis in Jim's absence [218], and whose responses—even the murder of the Bugis villager [226]—might from Jim's point of view generally be considered defensive.) Or Doramin might have banished Jim, or simply refused him recognition. Hence one might conclude that in going to Doramin Jim is expressing respect for him (and for his own person) that is then not returned.

Or, better—and this accounts as much as anything, perhaps, for the air of inevitability about Doramin's execution that everyone senses—Doramin's action may be itself readable as an expression of respect. Having become the preeminent moral authority, source of justice, and object of esteem in the community, Jim cannot, having come initially as an outsider, realistically assume a lesser place within it, or even within its memory as someone who came and simply went away. (Had he stayed fifteen years before Brown's arrival, this might have become possible.) In shooting Jim, even while feeling "mad pain" and "rage" (253), Doramin may further be acknowledging that Jim had come in respect for others and himself and in commitment to his community of persons, but without any way to remain in it except by dying. "If," as Kant's thought runs, "I cannot preserve my life except by violating my duties toward myself," perhaps duties that have been socially embodied, then "I am bound to sacrifice my life rather than violate these duties."[33] This is not suicide, which is typically a withdrawal from personhood and its requirements, but honorable self-sacrifice, in which one has been a "victim of fate."[34] "There are duties which are far greater than life and which can often be fulfilled only by sacrificing life,"[35] and Jim, in going to face Doramin, knowing what it is open to Doramin to do in respecting personhood, going because "he should not be worth having otherwise," may well be acting from such an understanding of duty. And so Marlow, seeing this, comes to his fullest and final understanding of their shared moral personhood, of what it means to be one of us.

3. Ambiguity, Interpretation, Remembrance, Projection: Marlow's End

And yet, somehow, evidently, there remains a question open, for Marlow and for us. Marlow describes Jim, in leaving Jewel to go to Doramin, as saying "'Nothing can touch me,'" in "a last flicker of superb egoism" (251). Then, further, Jim's wedding to an ideal of conduct is said by Marlow to be "pitiless," and his determination to go to Doramin is said to be in response to "the call of his exalted egoism" (253). If Marlow's progress in coming to understand Jim, *his* progress, and their shared personhood is what it otherwise seems to be, then why is the issue of Jim's egoism raised at the end? Why is it suggested that his achievement in going to Doramin may express a desire for notoriety rather than respect for persons? What light does this qualifying suggestion shed on the character of Marlow's understanding of personhood, and on our own epistemic and metaphysical relation to such understandings?

A number of closely interrelated thoughts about the nature of knowledge of the moral character of personhood are brought into play by these references to egoism. A ready first thought is that they register once again the interpretive and problematic character of ascriptions of motives. While Jim's conduct in going to Doramin is plausibly construed as objectively right in that it conforms to the behavioral requirements of respecting persons or to the legislation under which alone a kingdom of ends is possible, it does not follow that his conduct is morally worthy, that it has actually been motivated by respect for persons grounded in respect for the moral law and an acknowledgment of the nature of value for persons. The final scenes of Jim's deciding to go to Doramin and then going are introduced by Marlow's asking himself, and us, "What thoughts passed through his head— what memories? Who can tell?" (248). The understandings and desires and acknowledgments that motivate particular actions are not directly open to our view; we cannot see into the hearts of persons, others' or our own. "The last word," Marlow's references to egoism remind us, "is not said—probably shall never be said" (137). Marlow is able to "affirm nothing" (206); his characterizations of Jim's motives have the character more of narrative-enabling and interpretive conjectures always open to reassessment than of experimentally grounded assertions. It is up to us to accept and continue them—to use them to make sense of others and ourselves—or to reject them: "Perhaps you may pronounce—after you've read. There is much truth—after all—in the common expression 'under a cloud' " (206).

In particular, given the fairly undeniable and universal appearance in human lives of a stage of self-assertiveness and of the sense of particular selfhood, any judgment that a particular person has come to be morally self-legislative, to acknowledge the character and requirements of personhood in community with others, to act according to the legislation of a kingdom of ends, must be especially problematic. Egoism is not easily overcome, especially when the situation is desperate and the stakes are high. As objectively right conduct or conduct overtly in accord with the requirements of morality becomes more difficult, as it seems likely to provoke violent responses directed at oneself and those to whom one is attached, perhaps even to bring about one's death, it becomes easier to be motivated in doing what is right not by respect for persons and the moral law, but by pride in one's own right conduct. Right conduct can itself be a mode of prideful self-assertiveness without moral worth. (This fact accounts for whatever uneasiness we may sometimes feel about the achievements of Socrates and Jesus—figures with whom Jim is often rightly compared—in giving up their lives.) It remains fully possible that Jim's going to Doramin is motivated by a continuing juvenile and theatrical sense of his own inner heroism, now to be ratified and glorified in his perverse self-sacrifice. All that we, and Marlow, have to set against this possibility are our senses of Jim's character as it has shown itself, obscurely, in his devotion to his work, in his relations with Jewel and Dain Waris, in his evident ease in Patusan, and above all in his friendship with Marlow. This may, or may not, be enough to enable us, and Marlow, to see Jim as in the end a figure of achieved capabilities of respect for persons. There is, in any case, nothing else on which to base an account of Jim's and our, capabilities. Although Marlow seems to see Jim predominantly as motivated by respect for persons and the moral law and in being so motivated as expressing a fundamental value of personhood, it is not clear and provable ("Who knows? He is gone, inscrutable at heart . . ." [253]) that he is not motivated otherwise.

Not only is it possible for right conduct to be prideful; it is also the case that none of our conduct stands unmarked by desire that remains in less than full harmony with reason and the moral law. Our wills are not holy; we are unable to desire only that to which we are directed by reason. Although desire can be shaped and redirected by reason, it is not perfectly educable by it. Particular attachments from our pasts continue to influence us, even as we have come to desire to do what reason commands us to do. We are unable to bring about in our lives the inauguration of a perfect kingdom of ends in which each person acts always out of respect for persons grounded in an acknowledgment of our nature and with passions fully directed toward the inauguration or maintenance of a kingdom of ends. Typically, even in being motivated by respect for persons and the law and by reason-transfigured desire, we are at the same time seeking to win the approval of others whom we have introjected and whose internalized voices continue to shape our self-understanding. It is for this reason that there is and can be no unambiguous, perfect, and genuinely full account of someone who is perfectly motivated by respect for persons and the law, with desires fully in harmony with reason. Close and full examination of motives always reveals our imperfections, reveals the presence in motivation of desires shaped in part by particulars, desires that are ready to assert themselves, to establish their autonomy and unruliness, and to direct us to the pursuit of ends that are not set for us by our rational nature. In coming to know—or, better, to acknowledge—our nature, its end, and our possibilities for the education of desire, the best we can hope for are not examples of human wills that are holy, but rather a range of cases, a perspicuous representation, in which various aspects of desire are educated and transfigured in ways that are seen to be valuable, thus suggesting that the education of desire by reason in general, though always imperfect, is what we are led to aspire to by our shared nature as persons, as beings who are both rational and embodied. Our universal nature and our particular attachments and desires can be brought only into a harmony that is incomplete, but also—as various cases, Jim's among them, may show us—into harmonies that, though imperfect, severally reveal to us our nature and its end. Through such cases, human life emerges for us as the place of the incarnation of reason and its commands in a body it properly guides but cannot perfectly subdue.

Marlow's understanding of personhood and its end do not remain untouched by either our inscrutability or our imperfection. His claim that the expression of respect is fundamentally valuable for persons is staked to his progress in understanding Jim's character as revelatory of our nature and its possibilities. The claims that Jim, in his life and death in Patusan, was motivated by and expressed respect for persons, that Jim came to have desires informed by an acknowledgment of our nature and its end, and that Jim acted well, incarnated value for persons so far as possible, are Marlow's route to an acknowledgment of the fundamental value for persons of acting out of respect, while that emerging acknowledgment simultaneously shapes Marlow's understanding of Jim. The interpretation of particulars and the acknowledgment of a universal principle are conceptually welded, are two aspects of the same understanding. Only as we can interpret various lives as expressive of imperfect achievements and incomplete failures in the embodiment of value for persons can we acknowledge a fundamental moral law; only as we come to acknowledge a fundamental moral law can we treat particular lives as more than local achievements and failures in the realm of value. Principles without interpretations are hollow; interpretations without principles are wild. Nor, given the historicity and imperfectness of human life, can associated principles and interpretations be secured once and for all. New kinds of actions will arise and call for new interpretations, in which principles will be both employed and tested. And no full interpretation of the life of a person can show it to be free of evil and perfectly good. Acknowledging the moral character of our personhood and the bindingness of the principle of respect for persons will be ongoing interpretive achievements of understanding of which persons *must* be capable—if Marlow's understanding of Jim is correct—but which will be embodied in new reflections on new examples. Thinking as the effort to acknowledge our personhood cannot be completed.

The truth of associated interpretations and principles is something that cannot be settled within an individual consciousness alone. That the expression of respect for persons is fundamentally valuable for persons emerges as a criterion of personhood; that is, it is one of the criteria for being a person that respect for persons is fundamentally valuable as a motive for the action of a person. Claims about criteria are not entailed by purely a priori knowable or intellectually knowable epistemic rules. They are not derived inductively from the presentation of an object to consciousness. There are no autonomous third entities—concepts, ideas, thoughts, forms, principles—such that acquaintance with them issues in certain knowledge of criteria. It is rather that the criterion of truth for a claim about criteria is that it enables recognition for persons. Its acceptance enables persons to make sense of themselves in their activities and to go on from pasts they can acknowledge as theirs into a future they will be able to accept.[36] Making sense of the expression of one's personhood in this way is fundamentally not an individual achievement. The activities that are distinctive and characteristic of persons—using language, assuming self-responsibility, evaluating desires and interests as fitting and worthy or not, responding to waywardness, seeing various lives as achievements and failures in the incarnation of value—are fundamentally communal in character (though developed out of individual *capacities* themselves identifiable not physically, but only functionally, by reference to the activities they enable). In this sense, a community is the locus of the life of personhood, as Hegel and Wittgenstein variously taught, though particular communities can be creatively reshaped by individuals, and a background to particular communities is always provided by the shared nature of persons, which is at it were the condition of their possibility. A claim about criteria is correct—that is, is recognition-enabling for persons—just to the extent that it brings the members of a community to self-recognition of their shared personhood as it is expressed, well or badly, in their activities.

Alone, Marlow cannot know he has voiced a correct claim about the criteria of personhood and value. Even to put forward a claim about the criteria of personhood and of value for persons is to have a kind of presumption, in that it is to see the members of one's community as at present failing in the recognition of personhood and as threatening themselves in so failing with the dissipation of community and the exhaustion or betrayal of their personhood. Marlow, in awareness of this, tells us that "all assertion in this world of doubts is a defiance, is an insolence" (144). His understandings of Jim, person-hood, and value may stem more from "the secret sensibility of [his] egoism" (93) that he shares with Jim than from genuine understand-ing. Marlow's claims about the criteria of personhood and value will be redeemed from sheer insolence and self-assertiveness only insofar as they are accepted, ultimately, by others as having the force simul-taneously of a remembrance of personhood and a projection of its future. It is for us to judge by our words and deeds the correctness of Marlow's understandings of Jim and personhood. Perhaps Jim re-mained motivated by egoism, perhaps Marlow in inquiring into Jim's character was also—or perhaps Marlow is right ("The proverb has it that the onlookers see most of the game" [137]).

None of us is, however, simply an onlooker. We are given over as persons to the expression of our personhood in activity—to either its acknowledgment or its avoidance, alike modes of its expression—and to either the articulation and employment of claims about value as persons or to the refusal of them. Without criteria of value for per-sons—voiced when necessary as remembrances and projections, simply lived out in community otherwise—we do not embody in our lives the value of persons, in that sense do not as it were lead the lives of moral persons. Our possibilities of value, possibilities distinctive of us, go unexpressed, and our communities become groundless and fragmented ("We exist only in so far as we hang together" [136]). And there will be no claims about the criteria of value that succeed as remembrances and projections except insofar as we jointly test our understandings of the natures of things, especially our own, in artic-ulations and in action: "I affirm nothing. Perhaps you may pro-nounce—after you've read. There will be no message, unless such as each of us can interpret from the language of facts, that are so often more enigmatic than the craftiest arrangement of words" (206).

When one has fallen out of articulation of one's personhood to-gether with one's community—perhaps the community is wayward and inauthentic; perhaps one's self-assertions have become extreme—what is then in order is the joint work of the interpretation of particu-lars and of the achievement of acknowledgments of principles. This work, yoked to the interpretation of the particular, and not driven by a priori intellectual intuition, will naturally take the form of a narrative one's emerging achievements in interpretation and acknowledgment. This narrative will be tested in its presentation to others, who will accept its achievements and live against them, or not: "And later on, many times, in distant parts of the world, Marlow showed himself willing to remember Jim, to remember him at length, in detail and audibly" (21). If these achievements of interpretation and acknowledgment are genuine, then they will have the force for those who encounter them of remembrances and projections of personhood in activity in community. Such remembrances and projections are articulations of personhood and claims to personhood, community, and onwardness. They are true or false as we, in full attention and in the effort to articulate and acknowledge our own personhood, do or do not accept them. How full were Jim's achievements in understanding and expressing value for persons, especially at his death, a moment that seems to stop time? To what extent do these achievements remain marked by desire and moral escapism? How full, and how stable, is Marlow's understanding, as he tells and retells his story, "many times, in distant parts of the world"? "Was I," Marlow asks us, "so very wrong after all?"

SELF-UNDERSTANDING
AND COMMUNITY
IN WORDSWORTH'S POETRY

1. Wordsworth and the Problem of Expressive Activity

How can there be an achieved understanding of personhood and its value that can be expressed not only, or centrally, in a moment of blinding self-sacrifice against the world, but also in ongoing activity in the world? We are unlikely to find actual motivation by respect for persons and for the moral law to embody a fundamental value for persons if it typically ends in a death that can itself be read in part as a prideful withdrawal from the world. How then can we fully and fitly express our personhood in ongoing activity?

Even the possibility of self-understanding is problematic whenever events in nature are conceived, as physics since the seventeenth century has urged, to be only materially caused, not purposive. Given that human actions are events in nature, physical explanations then seem to be both necessary and sufficient for understanding them. It becomes difficult to see how to understand and explain one's actions as grounded in a partial grasp of an intelligible order of things. The person, it seems, isn't real; bits of matter are, and their motions are mechanical, not plotted in a divinely ordered book of nature. Thus the person as a locus of autonomous agency and understanding comes to be regarded as a fiction, not a physical something and not effective in the occurrence of events, so not a something at all. Human actions are no longer seen as stemming from persons who can alter and are responsible for them, but instead as complex events falling under physical laws.

Yet, despite the revolutionary revisions in the explanation of human action and the account of personhood seemingly forced by the new physics, self-understanding is not something easily abandoned in favor of knowledge of matter. It is not easy to conceive of one's actions as nonpurposive and of oneself as an unreal plaything of fortune. Determinism seems incompatible with individual responsibility and hence with morality. Determinists make claims, investigate things, and regard these activities as significant and under their control, yet it is hard to see how this could be if physicalist determinism were true. Even within modern scientific understanding, autonomous creativity and human understanding are generally allotted roles in experimentation as well as in the rest of life. Yet this acknowledgment of human autonomy is seemingly in fundamental conflict with the commitment to the explanation of all events under physical laws that is characteristic of the modern scientific attitude.[1]

In the absence, however, of a well worked out description of how we can autonomously generate partial understandings of our proper ends as persons, understandings to which we then give ongoing expression in action, these objections will seem hollow, and the sense that it *must* be possible to explain our actions fully under physical laws will press upon us. If we cannot say how we can understand ourselves and our end in ways that inform our actions, then it will seem wise to abandon trying to understand agentive persons and to try instead to formulate the physical explanations of the motions of our bodies that are seemingly in order. Only material desire, with its causal antecedents, will be found at the roots of human action generally, and the idea that we can understand and express a personhood with a peculiar autonomy and dignity will be called into question.

Here Wordsworth's poetry can be of special value, for one of Wordsworth's chief poetic concerns was to diagnose and locate skepticism about the possibility of self-understanding as a natural but temporary stage in the lives of persons who *can* grasp their nature and the modes of ongoing activity that are appropriate to it. Skepticism about action-guiding self-understanding, on his showing, is a plight of mind to which self-conscious beings succumb just as they most fully assert their particularity and separateness from others. Recovery from this plight occurs naturally when they come both to see that genuine autonomy requires community with others in expressive activity and to find themselves already so engaged. Further self-conscious and effective engagement in this expressive activity then emerges as an end of central value for persons and as an end that is to be achieved communally. The scandal of philosophy, as Wordsworth would have it, is that this natural development of the mind, a development Wordsworth traces throughout his own career, should be ignored in favor of the pursuit of overly abstract, narrow, and impoverishing causal explanations of our behavior.

Wordsworth thus offers us a detailed and comprehensive illustration of how there can be action-guiding self-understanding of our nature and its possibilities of full and appropriate expression. If his account of his career is convincing, so that we can see our own natural plights of mind and possibilities of recovery reflected in it, then we will be able after following it out to say a good deal about how we are able to understand persons and value. The investigation of causal relations will itself then appear to be not the sole route to understanding anything in nature, but one activity among many in the lives of self-conscious moral beings naturally directed and directing themselves to the embodiment in activity of value for persons. Rehearsing Wordsworth's account of his development and checking its plausibility are hence ways for us to test our own possibilities of self-understanding and activity.

2. The Aims of Poetry and Wordsworth's Understanding of Personhood

In characterizing his poetic project in the preface to the *Lyrical Ballads*, Wordsworth remarks that he has attempted, by following certain principles, to produce "a class of Poetry . . . well adapted to interest mankind permanently, and not unimportant in the quality, and in the multiplicity of its moral relations."[2] That is, it is the aim of his poetry to reveal to us how our nature leads us both to act and to be bound to act in certain ways, to come to stand in certain moral relations. To know that our nature so leads us would be both to possess self-understanding of permanent interest and to come to be at home in certain activities of value.

This poetic project is to be accomplished "by tracing [in various 'incidents and situations from common life'] . . . the primary laws of our nature: chiefly, as regards the manner in which we associate ideas in a state of excitement" (Pref., 447). The poet seeks to reveal how and what, given our shared nature, we think and feel in various circumstances and furthermore what forms of life are appropriate for beings who think and feel in these ways. Poetic power consists in the ability to speak as an immediately responsive human being, not as an essentially particular person, and possession of this power is tested in the responses of others to the poet's speech. Cultivation of this power for affective and normative speaking is the sole route to self-understanding and engaged activity, so that cultivation of this power is necessary for leading the life of a person who lives well according to a partial conception of objective value.

Wordsworth's poetry is thus fundamentally shaped by his sense that self-characterizations are necessary for leading a stable, coherent life expressive of who one is and by his sense that empirical observation alone yields no self-characterizations that are both morally informative and believable. In contrast with the putatively empirically grounded, but in fact unfounded and useless, claims about the operations of the mind put forward by scientists, Wordsworth offers us only his *"best conjectures* [of] Our Being's earthly progress,"[3] and he insists that such conjectures must suffice, if anything does, in enabling adequate and morally significant self-understanding. Conjectures are explicitly the sorts of claims that are tested for plausibility through such things as conversation with others (both imaginary and real), rehearsals of past evidence of a talent for conjecturing, and their acceptance or rejection by others. Moreover, to issue conjectures about oneself is as much a mode of self-creation as it is of self-observation. When we turn to conjecturing about the unities or drifts of our personalities in the past and about the appropriateness for us of various vocations or ways of life, then, as Hegel put it, "consciousness no longer aims to *find* itself *immediately,* but to produce itself by its own activity. It is *itself* the End at which its action aims, whereas in the role of observer it was concerned only with things."[4] We continuously recreate ourselves out of who we already are by positing ends for ourselves and articulating conceptions of objective value. It is this ongoing activity of persons that is both described and displayed in Wordsworth's poetry in its complex interlocking of self-example and theoretical formulation.

The specific occasion of Wordsworth's display and description of his ongoing self-re-creation is an overdetermined problem all at once of artistic discipline, political judgment, happiness in activity, and the burden of personhood. As W. B. Gallie has characterized it, Wordsworth's immediate problem as a poet was to blend his primitive responsiveness and memories, the impulses of his poetry, on the one hand, with his maturity and craft, on the other, in such a way that poetry of genuine value would result:

> There appeared to be two opposing elements in poetic inspiration; on the one hand the spontaneous receptivity and response characteristic of childhood and on the other hand the self-mastery, the calm of mind, the conscientiousness of the mature artist. How could these be brought together into a satisfying and productive harmony?[5]

Impulse without craft can issue only in incoherence; craft without impulse can issue only in the sort of sterility and academicism that Wordsworth scorned in the Augustans. Only if impulse and craft are blended can the mind engage in genuinely poetic activity. Book 1, lines

1–269, of the *Prelude* describe Wordsworth's anxiety about his inability
to fit craft to impulse, as his major poetic work lies, to his mind, before
him unaccomplished, until in line 269 the problem of entering into the
state of mind productive of poetry becomes itself the subject of the
Prelude.

The problem of entering into this state of mind is not, however,
the poet's alone. Echoing Plato's analogy between the structures of the
soul and the state, Wordsworth finds the problem of the direction of
our capacities and experiences into poetic activity reflected in the problem of the proper direction of the state. As James Chandler has noted,
"The crisis we see enacted in book 1 with respect to the psychology of
poetic composition is congruent or homologous with the crisis we see
narrated in book 11 with respect to the psychology of political morality."[6] And beyond analogy there may even be a causal interrelation
between the problem of the poetic mind and the problem of political
judgment. The poet is under an obligation as poet to win an audience,
is under "the necessity of giving immediate pleasure to a human being
possessed of that information which may be expected from him . . . as
a Man" (Pref., 454). But if the state, which provides the public space for
human action and development, is badly directed, then the poet may
find this obligation nearly impossible to satisfy. Conversely, without
the guidance of a poetic vision of the human, of its place in nature, and
of value, the public life of the state may become hollow and dominated
by empty formalisms and false pieties.

Finally, the problem of engaging our capacities and experiences
in productive activity in such a way that ongoing self-direction and
self-recognition are possible is neither the poet's nor the politician's
alone. It is, as Gallie has noted, "the wider problem . . . of the active
happiness, responsive and responsible, of every good man."[7] How
can one engage in coherent, self-expressive, fulfilling, and recognition-
enabling activity, especially when this question is raised from a position of reflective nonactivity? This is what one might call the moral
burden of personhood, for in the absence of character-expressive, recognition-enabling action there is, one might say, only physical motion,
or nothing left that is distinctive of persons and valuable for them.

All these worries—the poetic, the political, and the moral—are
fused in the 269 lines that open the *Prelude* into a general problem of
waywardness or recreance of mind, an inability to invest oneself in any
particular activity, inasmuch as the routes to self-recognition through
activity seem closed. Wordsworth's anxieties about waywardness of
mind and the inexpressibility of personhood culminate in the summary passage of the opening.

> Thus my days are past
> In contradiction; with no skill to part
> Vague longing, haply bred by want of power,
> From paramount impulse not to be withstood,
> A timorous capacity from prudence,
> From circumspection, infinite delay.
> Humility and modest awe themselves
> Betray me, serving often for a cloak
> To a more subtle selfishness; that now
> Locks every function up in blank reserve,
> Now dupes me, trusting to an anxious eye
> That with intrusive restlessness beats off
> Simplicity and self-presented truth.
> Ah! better far than this, to stray about
> Voluptuously through fields and rural walks,
> And ask no record of the hours, resigned
> To vacant musing, unreproved neglect
> Of all things, and deliberate holiday.
> Far better never to have heard the name
> Of zeal and just ambition, than to live
> Baffled and plagued by a mind that every hour
> Turns recreant to her task; takes heart again,
> Then feels immediately some hollow thought
> Hang like an interdict upon her hopes.
> This is my lot; for either still I find
> Some imperfection in the chosen theme,
> Or see of absolute accomplishment
> Much wanting, so much wanting, in myself,
> That I recoil and droop, and seek repose
> In listlessness from vain perplexity,
> Unprofitably travelling toward the grave,
> Like a false steward who hath much received
> And renders nothing back.
> (1.237–69)

Here the image of false stewardship in recreance of mind captures the sense that recreance threatens the sustenance and very existence of personhood. To have a mind so baffled and perplexed is to verge on failing to exercise the capacities of agency, responsibility, and expressive activity that are definitive of personhood. The affective mark of such a mind, in Romantic poetry, is melancholy, a burdensome sense of lassitude in feeling oneself to be unable to go on expressively.

Wordsworth's characteristic way out of this recurrent situation is to throw himself into the activity of investigating its occurrence and cure. Thinking about his melancholic condition and transforming it are fused in writing about and out of it, beginning with the question "Was it for this?" in line 269 that sets the *Prelude* on its course. Wordsworth's desperate interest in the conditions of occurrence and the cure of way-wardness and melancholy is similarly reflected in the backward-looking lines that open so many of his most important self-diagnostic poems: "Five years have passed; five summers with the length / Of five long winters," in "Tintern Abbey"; "There was a time . . . ," in the "Intimations Ode"; "Six changeful years have vanished . . . ," in book 7, as Wordsworth resumes in 1804 the poem he had begun in 1798 and abandoned in 1799; "There was a roaring in the wind all night," in "Resolution and Independence." In each case, the effort is to ask, "What brought me to this condition, and what way on or out is there?" The "this" of book 1, line 269, thus refers, as James Chandler has put it, to the nearly inexpressible "situation" of waywardness and self-dissolution "over which poetry triumphs to come into being"[8] and beyond that to the situation we all must overcome through the exercise of something like poetic judgment in order to go on living expressively as persons at all. To ask "Was it for this?" is, in Wordsworth, to ask "Why am I unable to go on, and how could I now go on, with my life as a person?"

In responding to this question, Wordsworth is concerned less with a priori proofs about either the nature of personhood or the nature of human happiness than he is concerned to discover, as Gallie has it, "the *way* of happiness (to use a religious phrase) or (if the phrase be preferred) the *art* of it."[9] In other words, Wordsworth does not consider personhood or happiness abstractly or as having transcendent essences, the route to the exemplification of which would always remain a further problem even after they had been understood. Instead, he looks for a way of expressive activity and human happiness that is immanent in human life, in particular in his own.

> His answer to [the problem of "the true end of man"] is at once nor-
> mative and interpretative; it is an attempt to show the reality of certain
> "may-bes" in human experience with a view to convincing us that these
> are, in the ethical sense, "must-bes." . . . [Wordsworth] makes the es-
> sential moment of morality one of recognition. . . . And he believed that
> to *show* [the way of happiness] was the only way to make men better.[10]

Wordsworth's strategy then is to consider how he has so far lived, thence to reinterpret his present condition as a merely temporary or apparent disengagement from both a discipline or activity and connections to others. Under scrutiny, waywardness of mind gives way to already established habits of activity and response: "One's present discipline resides in the habitual contemplation of how one supposes oneself to have been disciplined in the past."[11]

Wordsworth's normative-interpretive or conjectural approach to the problem of how to express personhood in activity is thus radically opposed to any naturalist subsumption of psychological states under material causal laws. Wordsworth continually scorned those engineers of human souls who would seek to analyze away self-sustaining moments of self-interpretation and self-recognition in favor of causally law-governed psychic events, those "Sages who in their prescience would control / All accidents, and to the very road / Which they have fashioned would confine us down / Like engines" (5.355–58). Persons are essentially self-interpreting beings, simultaneously looking backward to see how they have already been disciplined and looking forward to see how they can go on, and in this looking encountering not unambiguous data, but always already interpreting what they see. What has happened to make one who one is—a being with certain habits, capacities of activity, and social relations—is not sharply separable from who one now, in the effort to go on, imagines oneself to be. Retrospective self-recognition cannot be wholly parted from prospective self-creation.

> Of these and other kindred notions
> I cannot say what portion is in truth
> The naked recollection of that time
> And what may rather have been called to life
> By after meditation.[12]
> (3.612–16)

To ignore or dismiss our moments of self-interpretation in favor of the explanation of events under causal laws is not only to make a mistake about the situation and interpretive character of consciousness— "Hard task, vain hope, to analyse the mind, / If each most obvious and particular thought, / Not in a mystical and idle sense, / But in the words of Reason deeply weighed, / Hath no beginning" (2.228–32)— it is to impoverish us, to "confine us down" by directing us away from the exercise of our interpretive capacities.

In seeing ourselves as self-interpreting beings and in forging new self-interpretations, it is important to recognize that, while they are not unambiguous, our specific pasts do nonetheless constrain our self-shaping self-interpreting. Chandler emphasizes that the interpretive conception of persons at which Wordsworth arrives, according to which conjectures about one's past habits and experiences point the way to further expressive activity, is a specifically English way of thinking about who one is. Wordsworth's deepest moments of self-confrontation, the so-called spots of time through which he interpretively recovers his discipline and habits of activity and commitments, "must be understood as representing the triumph not only of mental discipline, but also of discipline as tradition, a discipline grounded on what Burke calls prejudice. In Burke's description, . . . this conception of discipline is specifically English."[13] In recovering himself interpretively and thus emerging from melancholy, Wordsworth accomplishes "a reunion not only with the English countryside but also with the English mind and character, with a way of thinking and feeling."[14]

This is, in a deep sense, true, in that one emerges as a particular person as already a part of a specific culture and community against which one will take one's bearings and out of whose standard evaluations one will shape one's own, which then express and sustain one's specific personhood. England is, as it were, the place of Wordsworth's emergence, and the English respect for English tradition and culture bespeaks a strong sense of the importance of place and lineage to specific personhood.

Yet in a deeper sense, Wordsworth's rediscovery of his Englishness can also be read as metaphorical for his acknowledgment of the social and historical roots of self-consciousness, responsibility, and agency in persons in general. Our evaluative and interpretive capacities, definitive of us as persons, do not originate, Wordsworth shows us, in us as individuals. Not only does he, in his crisis of waywardness, recapture his Englishness; he also recaptures what anyone who is to live expressively as a person must capture. There is a "flaw" or "incoherence" in the individualist conception of personhood and value, and this shows in Wordsworth's progress; one episode of his crisis of waywardness occurs precisely when he attempts, under the temporary sway of French rationalism and individualism, to live as a person and as a moral agent on "his private stock of reason."[15] The fruits of individualism are self-dissipation and melancholy.

Importantly, however, none of this is to say that one is completely bound in articulating one's conceptions of value by whatever is locally current. Rather, what goes on as we as evaluators take our points of departure from our culture is that we look, in attempting to extend our evaluations to new situations, to the ideals of flourishing they were meant to serve, as it were to their essence. Wordsworth does not recover himself by beginning to do whatever the English were doing at the moment; he deplored the "degrading thirst after outrageous stimulation" (Pref., 449) displayed by his urban countrymen in particular. Instead he attempted to recover and live according to the deep and hidden values of being English—where being English means, again, being attached to specific others and places and reflecting these attachments in conversation, concern, and poetic activity. Thus, Wordsworth shows us, our situation as persons emergent in specific places and cultures is to find ourselves confronted with the task of aligning ourselves and our projects with our culture, which may mean, among other things, radically transforming a culture that had disciplined one in the past but that has now lost touch with the ideals that once gave it shape. In going on, with my life, from my culture, in my culture, and on its behalf,

> What I require is a convening of my culture's criteria, in order to confront them with my words and life as I pursue them and as I may imagine them; and at the same time to confront my words and life as I pursue them with the life my culture's words may imagine for me: to confront the culture with itself, along the lines in which it meets in me.[16]

Thus, in taking up a normative-interpretive approach to the situation and problems of personhood, one comes to define oneself and to act not simply according to prevailing custom, but according to what one takes to be best or best served by a complex history of customs and values itself in need of interpretation. Persons are seen through interpretation as in their pasts and cultures already on the way, imperfectly and not always progressively, to the appropriate expression of our shared nature. Wordsworth offers us his account of this appropriate expression, putting it before us as objective and his achievement of it as proleptic, as he describes the understanding of personhood and value he has arrived at on Snowden and will henceforth attempt to live by. A certain power of higher minds

> . . . is the very spirit in which they deal
> With the whole compass of the universe:
> They from their native selves can send abroad
> Kindred mutations; for themselves create
> A like existence; and, whene'er it dawns
> Created for them, catch it, or are caught
> By its inevitable mastery,
> Like angels stopped upon the wing by sound
> Of harmony from Heaven's remotest spheres.

Them the enduring and the transient both
Serve to exalt; they build up greatest things
From least suggestions; ever on the watch,
Willing to work and to be wrought upon,
They need not extraordinary calls
To rouse them; in a world of life they live,
By sensible impressions not enthralled,
But by their quickening impulse made more prompt
To hold fit converse with the spiritual world,
And with the generations of mankind
Spread over time, past, present, and to come,
Age after age, till Time shall be no more.
Such minds are truly from the Deity,
For they are Powers; and hence the highest bliss
That flesh can know is theirs—the consciousness
Of Whom they are, habitually infused
Through every image and through every thought,
And all affections by communion raised
From earth to heaven, from human to divine;
Hence endless occupation for the Soul,
Whether discursive or intuitive;
Hence cheerfulness for acts of daily life,
Emotions which best foresight need not fear,
Most worthy then of trust when most intense.
Hence, amid ills that vex and wrongs that crush
Our hearts—if here the words of Holy Writ
May with fit reverence be applied—that peace
Which passeth understanding, that repose
In moral judgments which from this pure source
Must come, or will by man be sought in vain.
                    (14.91–129)

The expression these higher minds achieve and to which, Wordsworth is suggesting, his own past has led him inextricably combines an *activity* ("for themselves create," "build up greatest things," "willing to work"), a *capacity for response* ("are caught by," "willing . . . to be wrought upon," "need not extraordinary calls to rouse them"), a *mood* ("bliss," "cheerfulness"), a *consciousness of self* ("the consciousness / Of Whom they are"), a *relation to others* and a *power of affection* that defeat alienation ("a like existence," "fit converse . . . with all the generations of mankind"), a *capacity for agency, self-responsibility, and morality* ("repose in moral judgments"), and an *overcoming of waywardness and disengagement* ("Hence endless occupation for the Soul").

Persons are reflected to themselves in others' and their own recognitions of them in activity. Human happiness is neither a state of feeling alone nor a state of knowledge alone nor a social relation alone nor an activity alone, but all of these intermingled into joy, that contrary of melancholy that blends feeling, knowledge, and sociality in activity.

Both understanding the conditions of this expression of our nature and arriving at it—acts which are in any case not wholly separable—are inherently public phenomena requiring a community for their realization. Success in revealing others to themselves is a criterion of self-understanding of one's shared best possibilities as a person. But if this is so, and further if there are no others to endorse one's interpretations and share in the realization of these possibilities in expressive activity, then the self-interpreting poet will have failed to overcome the subjectivity of value and will have failed all at once in self-understanding, mood, agency, and activity. The confirmation of a self-interpretation is always deferred to new audience after new audience, any one of which may always understand itself and those it reads (or ignores) differently. Truthfulness or authenticity in self-interpreting is not a matter of describing what is unalterably there; it is a matter of articulating a self-shaping conception of value in such a way that one's living and personhood can be recognized and shared in through this articulation.[17] One's interpretation of personhood and value may always be found fantastic or hallucinatory or self-deluding. The threat of melancholy must always haunt joyful activity.

This fact accounts for the somewhat desperate or pleading tone evident in Wordsworth's addresses to his imagined audiences, from the prayer in the "Prospectus" ("Fit audience let me find though few!"[18]), to the addresses to Dorothy in "Tintern Abbey" ("Oh! yet a little while / May I behold in thee what I was once";[19] "Thy memory be as a dwelling place";[20] "Nor, perchance, wilt thou then forget"[21]), and above all to Coleridge in the *Prelude*—". . . thus should neither I be taught / To understand myself, nor thou to know / With better knowledge how the heart was framed / Of him thou lovest; need I dread from thee / Harsh judgments . . ." [1.626–31]; "And certain hopes are with me, that to thee / This labour will be welcome, honoured Friend!" [1.646–47]; "what we have loved, / Others will love, and we will teach them how . . ." [14.446–47]). One seeks one's confirmation and full achievement of personhood in the acceptance by others of the then objectively valuable activities in which one finds one's personhood to be fully and fitly expressed. We seek to be, for others, "joint labourers in the work / (Should Providence such grace to us vouchsafe) / Of their deliverance, surely yet to come" (14.441–43) by bringing them to self-knowledge, activity, and moral peace, delivering them from waywardness. One feels both that the value of the activities held out to persons is objective, that its acceptance is "surely yet to come," and that one cannot know with certainty that this is so, that whether acceptance will come is a matter of mysterious grace.

If certainty in self-interpretation always eludes us as we wait upon the responses of others, if, in the end, grace is always required for self-understanding, knowledge of value, and the overcoming of waywardness, then what closure can there be to the labor of poetic self-interpretation? What achievement of self-understanding can there be? What peace?

3. "Resolution and Independence"

In a canceled "Advertisement" to the 1807 edition *Poems, in Two Volumes,* Wordsworth remarks that the short poems of that work were composed "when I had not resolution to apply myself"[22] to *The Recluse,* the projected great philosophical poem on which he staked his ultimate value as a poet. As Kenneth Johnston has observed, this "use of the word *resolution* . . . suggests that the great 'Resolution and Independence,' which first appeared in 1807, may . . . be a poem about the difficulty of writing *The Recluse* [and] avoiding 'despondency and madness.'"[23] That is to say, this poem asks *how* the poet's work of the interpretation of personhood and its appropriate modes of activity can be accomplished. The argument of the poem is that the way of self-understanding is to be found not in a solution or answer, but only in a resolution which is, as Harold Bloom has noted,[24] both a way out, a resolving, of the problem of self-interpretation and an act of determination, a commitment to always ongoing activities of self-interpretation, remembrance, and conversation. These two senses of "resolution" are intimately linked; only through the activities to which the poet recommits himself, and not through the mere acceptance of certain propositions, can personhood be sustained and can it come to terms with itself. "Resolution and Independence" depicts Wordsworth's fall away from and reattachment to the activities essential to the life of personhood.

The poem opens with an expression of the poet's sense that nature is there to be comprehended through the use of the senses ("There was a roaring in the wind all night; / The rain came heavily and fell in floods"[25]). Now nature is intelligibly present to him. Where once there was a roaring, now there are singing, chattering, answering, and a sweet voice, and the poet is able quite precisely to name and know what speaks: doves, jays, and magpies.

But now the sun is rising calm and bright;
The birds are singing in the distant woods;
Over his own sweet voice the Stock-dove broods;
The Jay makes answer as the Magpie chatters;
And all the air is filled with the pleasant noise of waters.
                    (3–7)

After the first two lines, the first two stanzas are in the present tense, as though all that is described is taking place now, at the moment of writing, so that the protagonist's present is the author's present, the preceding night belonging to both of them. In the third stanza, however, the narrative abruptly shifts into the past tense ("I was a Traveller then upon the moor; / I saw . . . / I heard . . ." [15–18]), where it remains for the rest of the poem, save for the future tense of the quotation that appears in the last two lines. The daytime traveler-protagonist is now being remembered by the poet-narrator. The suggestion of this shift is that the poet is now remembering his earlier experience as a protagonist and drawing on his memory to solve a present problem in writing very like the past problem encountered and resolved by the protagonist. Whatever problem this is, it appears to be one whose resolution must always be reaccomplished. The closure of self-understanding that is to be achieved consists more in continuous re-engagement in an activity than in simply knowing certain truths about persons.

What is this problem once resolved and now recurring? It is described straightforwardly as a fall from joy in contemplation of the beautiful and intelligible natural scene into dejection.

But as it sometimes chanceth, from the might
Of joy in minds that can no further go,
As high as we have mounted in delight
In our dejection do we sink as low;
To me that morning did it happen so. . . .
                    (22–26)

There is undoubtedly a psychological dynamic here, reminiscent of the Boethian wheel of fortune, Chaucer's "joy after woe, woe after gladnesse," and Keats's view that melancholy "dwells with Beauty—Beauty that must die; / And Joy, whose hand is ever at his lips / Bidding adieu, and aching Pleasure nigh, / Turning to poison while the bee-mouth sips. . . ."[26] As Harold Bloom puts it, "the very strength of joy engenders its contrary. When delight reaches its limits, dejection replaces it."[27] But the simple postulation of a psychological dynamic leaves unexplained—especially in light of the general connection in Wordsworth's writing between melancholy and failures of self-understanding, responsibility, and agency—why the protagonist feels just the particular sort of dejection he comes to feel and why that dejection can subsequently be cured through an encounter with another. Why, there and then (in the protagonist's present), and now (in the poet's present), that dejection, with that cure?

This experience of dejection, like others, is plausibly occasioned by the protagonist's sudden sense of his inability as an isolated merely experiencing individual to know himself, his place in nature, and the activities appropriate to his nature as a person. Recall that the transition to dejection opens with the poet's recitation of his perceptions as protagonist ("I saw . . . I heard . . ." [16–17]). The protagonist had not been particularly concerned with the objectivity of his perceptions, with whether they accurately represent objects apart from him ("I heard the distant waters roar; / Or heard them not, as happy as a boy" [17–18]). Immersed in his subjective perceptual experience, the protagonist finds himself apart, not a member of a community:

> The pleasant season did my heart employ:
> My old remembrances went from me wholly;
> And all the ways of men, so vain and melancholy.
> (19–21)

And so he loses himself, as the fleeting pleasantness of the moment masks the self-dissolving character of the lack of remembrances. Without "the ways of men," without membership in a community, one is left only with the flux of one's experience. One becomes unable to go on to lead the life of a person, expressing one's personhood in action. There is no knowledge, either of nature or of oneself, no sense of one's freedom, purposiveness, or ability to grasp and achieve appropriate ends, no sense of either power over oneself or a power to apprehend and shape nature: only the inrush of unintelligible subjective experience is left: "And fears and fancies thick upon me came; / Dim sadness—and blind thoughts, I knew not, nor could name" (27–28). Without the words provided by the language one shares with others, one finds oneself unable even to characterize one's private experience. The protagonist finds himself unable to name what happens to him, unable to characterize even his own thoughts. The dominant feature of his dejection and his anxiety is his awareness of his apparent lack of autonomy. Things come upon him and to him unbidden. And if blind thoughts and fears and fancies can thus come unbidden, then why not yet worse things? "But there may come another day to me— / Solitude, pain of heart, distress, and poverty" (34–35).

What is the way out of this dejection and to a sense of one's power or ability to know and to act? It is pointedly not the way of waiting praised in Milton's claim "who best / Bear his milde yoak, they serve him best."[28] According to Wordsworth, in contrast, we must bring ourselves to act, take our lives and fates into our own hands: "But how can He expect that others should / Build for him, sow for him, and at his call / Love him, who for himself will take no heed at all?" (39–41). Wordsworth here joins forces with Hegel, who likewise criticized the quietist attitude of "lifeless indifference which steadfastly withdraws from the bustle of existence, alike from being active as passive, into the simple essentiality of thought."[29] Such an attitude enables only an empty, unreal freedom, not a sense of one's concrete, embodied autonomy and power as an agent and apprehender.

Still, as Hegel also knew, the mere determination to act, not wait, is not enough to enable freedom, self-knowledge, and self-realization. Alone, such determination remains a sign of distress. One must concretely find one's way out of absorption in subjective experience and to actual knowledge and rational and expressive action. How can this move be made?

Only through the experience of an other. Locked in his despondency, and seeking a way out, the protagonist suddenly finds himself to be not alone.

> Now whether it were by peculiar grace,
> A leading from above, a something given,
> Yet it befel that, in this lonely place,
> When I with these untoward thoughts had striven,
> Beside a pool bare to the eye of heaven
> I saw a Man before me unawares:
> The oldest man he seemed that ever wore grey hairs.
> (50–56)

Despite the language suggestive of divine Providence ("grace," "from above," "something given"), the subordinating conjunction "whether" makes it clear that the protagonist was unaware of exactly how the other had come to be there, and that this does not matter: it simply befell him to find himself in another's presence. So, it will then seem, do persons in general find themselves.

The resulting encounter is enabling for the protagonist not so much in virtue of what the old man says—the protagonist pays little attention to that ("his voice to me was like a stream / Scarce heard; nor word from word could I divide" [107–8])—but more through the old man's serving as an emblem of both rootedness in nature and community with others. In the first place, the old man is there, so that sheer aloneness, and consequent derangement and dejection, clearly need not be permanent conditions. Second, the old man's speech retains a manifest power indicative of autonomy, at least to the protagonist, who, in experiencing the speech as an undivided stream of sound, receives it under a traditional figure of the sublime. Yet this sublimity is not unhinged from the world. The old man remains rooted in the natural world, not subject to fits of solipsistic disconnectedness. His body is nearly made a part of the natural scene, as he is compared to a stone and to a sea beast reposing in the sun (57, 62). But perhaps the most important fact about the old man is that he is, despite his appearance in this isolated spot, in his essence neither a man apart nor a victim of melancholy. The form of his speech makes it clear that he is a member of a community and that he has carried with him in his wanderings the capacities and powers enabled by his personhood in relation to a community.

> His words came feebly from a feeble chest,
> But each in solemn order followed each,
> With something of a lofty utterance drest—
> Choice word and measured phrase, above the reach
> Of ordinary men; a stately speech;
> Such as grave Livers do in Scotland use,
> Religious men, who give to God and man their dues.
> (92–98)

This man's life is informed by his engagement with others—he is one of those "who give to God and man *their* dues"—and his participation in this common project has preserved in him what the protagonist alone had seemed to lack: the power to speak, to name things, and the power to act expressively, to grasp and move toward appropriate ends.

Realizing that the old man has sustained these powers by being connected with others and realizing that the old man and he are alike—they are in this spot together, and, like the old man, he also in fact comes from a community—the protagonist finds his mood immediately lightened. The old man's natural powers, which survive his reduced circumstances through his participation in a communal project, make the protagonist aware of his own powers. If the old man, a figure of consciousness reduced to its minimal essential conditions, retains his natural powers throughout his solitary wanderings in virtue of his community with others, then the protagonist must likewise retain his powers and his connectedness to others, even in *his* most dejected, passively subjective moments, both in the past and now in their recurrence. What the poet says of the old man in conclusion provides an apt characterization of himself as well: "I could have laughed myself to scorn to find / In that decrepit man so firm a mind" (137–38). The dejection that had appeared to be unavoidable and possibly permanent has emerged as a transient mood grounded in a temporary, natural, and yet naturally overcome forgetting of one's community with others in personhood and the work of its fit expression in activity.

What the backward-looking poet then learns through his present memory of this enabling encounter is that characteristically human nature, or human capacities for self-understanding and freedom, are realized, or only fully exist, as Hegel observed, "in an achieved community of minds,"[30] in which alone their exercise is possible. This is the poetry not of nature and not of the visionary imagination's solitude, but of the exemplary discovery of the social nature and the possibilities of life of persons.

Not only is community necessary for self-understanding, agency, and the overcoming of waywardness, but a certain way of acting and interpreting is necessary for community. Our communities will provide sustenance for our capacities of action and interpretation only as long as we exercise those capacities to sustain the community. Thus the protagonist resolves, "I'll think of the Leech-gatherer on the lonely moor!" (140) in order to commit himself, by remembering their locus and home in a community the leech gatherer symbolizes, to the activities of public self-interpretation and conversation. Only through autonomous resolution to engage in these activities is it possible to maintain a community in expressive activity that enables the overcoming of dejection and the emergence, out of blind nature, of the human.

And beyond the protagonist's resolution, there is the poet's actual remembrance of the protagonist's encounter and his own echoing resolution in the present tense. Here, in the poet's echo of resolution, there is in fact ongoing activity of self-interpretation. Wordsworth simultaneously displays in recall and enacts in interpretive activity a self-sustaining commitment to go on with the project of understanding personhood through its public activities. Self-understanding consists not in abstract knowledge, but in engagement in cooperative interpretation of the end of persons and its contextual requirements. Closure is continuation, the acceptance of the ongoing revelation of ourselves to ourselves that occurs only through our interpretations of what we do and that enables the overcoming of waywardness. Resolution is reengagement in this interpretive activity.

4. The Generalization of Expressive Activity: Wordsworth as Egoist and Exemplar

To be a person at all, Wordsworth's example shows us, is to be engaged with others, well or badly, in a continuous interpretation of oneself as objectively directed to certain ends. In the absence of such activity, there is no scope for talk about what *we* do in acting. Interpretive activity continuously sustains our personhood. Even quietism, stoicism, and skepticism—conscious withdrawals from the ongoing rearticulation of and effort to engage in fit modes of activity—are themselves genuine, but defective, modes of interpretive activity.

This interpretive activity is inherently public, in two important senses. It begins from the shared conception of value in a community into which one has been initiated, and it is carried out in the language of a community. This might be called the fact of the sociality of personhood: persons exist as interpreters of their objective ends only insofar as they live in society.

But beyond that, the interpretations of value for persons that one produces are objective for persons in general only insofar as they enable cooperative and authentic community, itself necessary for anyone to lead a life fully expressive of personhood. The appropriate end for persons, posited by Wordsworth, of activity, responsiveness, bliss, consciousness, power, agency, and engagement is not, in his conception, peculiar to him. It is only in arriving at a conception of activities objectively expressive of personhood and its value, activities by design to be pursued cooperatively by persons in general, that Wordsworth's personhood is expressed and sustained. These activities may, and must, take various forms: poetry for some, or politics, or experimental inquiry, or teaching, or child-rearing, or farming. But, no matter how various, the objectively expressive activities to which we are directed nonetheless set objective constraints on us; any achievement of an authentic expression of our nature must display the seven or so features Wordsworth notes. Individuals are not left free to pursue whatever projects they wish. The pursuit of the expression of personhood through activity is essential to the maintenance of personhood, to going on as a person, and its pursuit and achievement necessarily involve one in a community of similarly directed persons. Together, these might be called the facts of the objectivity of the expression of personhood: persons live in authentic and cooperative society only insofar as they are similarly engaged in objectively expressive activities.

What defects there are in Wordsworth's interpretation of personhood lie in his occasional failure to acknowledge the ongoing difficulty in uniting persons in objectively expressive activities. Wordsworth did a great deal through his writing to cure himself and us by putting forward a new interpretation of personhood that ran contrary to the Humean naturalist background. Yet he tended sometimes to live out this interpretation by withdrawing into the role of the recluse or the isolated sage of Grasmere, abandoning cooperative interaction with others. While it remained his aim always to speak for us all "from the necessities of [our] nature" (Pref., 445) and further to write the great poem on social theory that would set out the conditions for the cooperative development of variant exemplifications of appropriate expressive activity, his retirement too readily suggests that the achievement of this aim can be accomplished by educated and isolated elites. Any suggestion of this tends to collapse our common and objective directedness as persons toward certain activities into mere sociality and to ignore the impoverishings of human possibilities that stem from present social structures. While it is true that only an interpretation of the directedness of persons to certain objectively expressive activities can save us from melancholy and waywardness, it is also true that articulating such an interpretation alone is not enough: one must also find oneself recognized as living in light of it by others who cooperate in so living. Whether one's audience can accomplish this recognition— whether an audience for one's interpretation even exists—will depend in part upon the material and cultural circumstances of persons, circumstances which one may hence be obliged to reform in the interest of having one's own interpretation of personhood upheld and in the interest of one's own recovery from melancholy. Subtle awareness of this problem is omnipresent in Wordsworth's writing. It is registered in "Resolution and Independence" in the suggestion that the poetic power of autonomous expressiveness, of voicing, itself leads (in contrast to the old man's dimmer but more natural power) to a sort of alienation and melancholy that require continual curing in the reattachment of autonomous expressiveness to community.

Against this awareness, it is surely Wordsworth's occasional individual self-certainty about the incarnation in his own life and activities of the best possibilities of expression for persons that has led readers to a sense of his egoism, or of what Keats famously stigmatized as "the wordsworthian or egotistical sublime" in his poetry.[31] Wordsworth seems in certain moments to regard the achievement on his part of an *interpretation* of the activities that are fully and fitly expressive of our personhood as complete in itself, and sometimes even as a satisfactory substitute for the fully general acknowledgment and social manifestation of the value of these activities. Thus Wordsworth is capable of such remarks as "I am myself one of the happiest of men; and no man who does not partake of that happiness . . . can possibly comprehend the best of my poems."[32] This remark suggests an unattractive and implausible confidence in the achievement on one's own of a full understanding and expression of value for persons, precisely where no such achievement can be fully individual.

Yet, despite these moments of overweening egoism and self-confidence, Wordsworth remains above all else a poet of anxiety, aware of the partiality of his understanding and continually uneasy about the reception and authenticity of his own achievements. There is, again, the desperate or pleading character of Wordsworth's addresses to his imagined audiences.[33] And the very writing of "Resolution and Independence," in the evident need of the present poet to recover and reachieve the cure for melancholy and waywardness previously achieved by the past traveler on the moor, belies the idea that self-understanding can be fully and permanently achieved.[34] As Geoffrey Hartman has repeatedly urged, we see in Wordsworth not so much moments of full self-completion as a kind of brooding alternation between experiences of beauty, or "the calm that composes, but may end life," and of the sublime, of a "fear or terrible beauty" that sets us over against nature.[35] It is essentially through these alternating experiences that Wordsworth's self-understanding and understanding of persons are at best anxiously and partially achieved.

For all the anxiety and partiality of his achieved understanding, however, it remained Wordsworth's deepest aim to display our community in personhood and in certain possibilities of objectively expressive activity and further to work to see this community and these possibilities acknowledged. That aim is evident in his ambition to produce a social philosophy and in the character of his overcoming of melancholy. His discovery of his own possibilities of expressive activity is one we are all to repeat, and the effort to make these possibilities actual is to become evident as already a common project of which we will henceforth become self-conscious. As the poet remembers the protagonist's encounter with the leech gatherer, in this remembrance finding himself engaged with others in expressive activity, so are we to uncover the activities and engagements that are appropriate for us through Wordsworth's poetry of remembrance.

Despite his resistance to Wordsworth's egoism, Keats marked out the possibility of this kind of reception of Wordsworth's poetry. "It seems to me," Keats wrote, "that [Wordsworth's] genius is explorative of those dark Passages [where "we see not the ballance of good and evil"]. Now if we live, and go on thinking, we too shall explore them. he is a Genius and superior [to] us, in so far as he can, more than we, make discoveries, and shed a light in them—."[36] What then remains for us to work through is whether Wordsworth's anxious explorations and understandings foreshadow ours—only if they do will they be objective—and how, if at all, these explorations and understandings of expressive activity that befits our nature can be given embodiment, not only privately, but further in actual (not only imaginary) and general human relationship. Can Wordsworth's exemplary achievement of understanding be parted from his egoism? How far, if at all, can Wordsworth's understanding of our personhood and the expressive activities appropriate to it be accepted, and genuinely and generally lived?

DEJECTION, RECOLLECTION, AND TEMPORALITY: COLERIDGE'S "FROST AT MIDNIGHT"

1. Naturalism and Romanticism

A serious objection to any morality of aspiration is that it is unlivable, in that the ideals of justice, of human fulfillment, and of the expression of our human dignity that it sets before us simply cannot be effectively pursued in any sustained way. Any attempts to pursue these ideals will end, it may be objected, either in failure or in radical compromise, and any denial that these attempts will have these outcomes will itself encourage a fantastically misplaced and narcissistic false pride in our capabilities. The inevitable way of the natural world, and of human beings within that world, is, it is argued, just too strong on its own for ideals to have a place in it. Attempts to live according to ideals must then end in a withdrawal from the natural expressed in self-sacrifice, alienation, and the refusal of ordinary human relationships. With such a sense of the inevitable way of the natural world in mind, it then becomes easy to read Jim's self-sacrifice as the archetypal failure of moralities of aspiration to be livable and to regard Wordsworth's mixed withdrawals from the public world and reductions of his early ideals of unleashed poetic power to religious conservatism as typical of the more relaxed, yet still alienating, compromises at which ideal-obsessed moralists must inevitably arrive if they are to live at all. What is then needed, the objection continues, is not more moralizing about ideals, but more relaxation and more simple and ordinary commitment to what we already naturally do. As though to ratify this objection, the phrase "morally worthy" now sounds almost like a term of criticism, as though it could not really be good to do whatever, according to some priggish theorist, it is morally worthwhile to do. Even to think se-riously about moral ideals is seen by some as a refusal of our naturalness and of our ordinary commitments and choices. Thus Richard Rorty has observed that "the attempt to answer . . . the moral agent's request for justifications [of answers to questions such as "What ought we to do with ourselves?" and "How ought we to live?"] with descriptions of a privileged domain [of ideals, wherein such justifications can be discovered] is the philosopher's special form of bad faith—his way of substituting pseudocognition for a moral choice."[1]

But is there anything that anyone just naturally does, as long as one is not distracted or misinflated by so-called artificial moral ideals? Naturalism itself puts before us an ideal of gracefulness and naturalness in engagement with the way of the world, asking us to choose to pursue this ideal as a way out of our fall into excessive theorizing. The fact that naturalism typically arises as a reaction against what it takes to be excessive theorizing suggests that we *do* naturally question the coherence and meaningfulness of our lives. We seem to be, in Heidegger's famous phrase, the kind of beings who call their own being into question. And if this is the case, then the ideal of graceful engagement that naturalism puts before us may itself seem to be urging a self-denying betrayal or refusal of our equally natural capacities for the reflective articulation of ideals and for sustaining lives that are expressive of them. That naturalism issues in a betrayal of our capacities for autonomy is the heart of the accusation laid by Wordsworth and Coleridge against the naturalist associationism of Hume and Hartley. As Harold Bloom characterizes this accusation,

> Essentially, associationism put the emphasis on what we might call the topics of *ethos* [that is, of "fate, necessity, powerlessness, experience, and nature"], leading to reductive tropes of *ethos* [that scant our capacities], and rather less upon topics and figures of *pathos* [that is, of "power, potential, will, greatness, inspiration, and salvation"]. It could even be said that the advance beyond associationism taken by Wordsworth and Coleridge was to attempt to reconcile or balance a Romantic rhetoric of *pathos* with the associationist rhetoric of *ethos*.[2]

Thus, it is charged, associationists and naturalists fail to see that a sense of dignity and power in being able to articulate ideals is itself natural, and they fail to see that an effective and sustained pursuit of ideals can take place within the natural way of the world: *ethos* can be blended with *pathos*, autonomy can be reconciled with embeddedness.

If this is right—if the articulation of ideals takes place within the frame of our natural human life, and if well-articulated ideals can sustain and even deepen one's attachments to the natural—then thought about ideals will itself naturally take the form not of disengagement from the world, but of alertness to our own moves in and out of reflection. These moves will be bound up with certain moods, dejection or melancholy as we are forced by the frustrations of the world back into rearticulating our ideals and rethinking their possibilities of expression, joy and assurance as we complete this rearticulation and succeed in reengaging with the world. That this rearticulation can be completed so as to inform and sustain our attachments to the world, in activities and in relationships, is the burden of the Romantic response to naturalism. Within its conception of the person, acquaintance with and movement through cycles of thoughts and moods itself may serve to sustain us in our ideals and our attachments, in our autonomy and our embeddedness.[3] Acquaintance with what one might call general subjunctive features of human temporal existence may enable us to find our ways, repeatedly, to the articulation and expression in action and relationship of ideals that are livable.

Coleridge's poem "Frost at Midnight" is near enough to the historical beginning of the Romantic reaction to Humean naturalism and skepticism about ideals to be worth considering on historical grounds alone. It also presents in a compressed and accessible form a picture of how one might go about mediating on one's moods in the hope of uncovering general subjunctive features of human life. Tracing out its progress can help us to appreciate the character of the enterprise and to test the possibilities it offers for resisting moral skepticism and for discovering the conditions of the authentic expression of our personhood and its ideals in activities and relationships within the world.

2. Humean Skepticism and Romantic Autobiography

Coleridge absorbs and even endorses the skeptic's attitude toward the attempt to justify moral rules universally by deducing them from self-evident truths. The emptiness and unlivability of moral ideals generated in pure reflection are taken for granted. But that does not lead Coleridge to conclude that no moral rules are universally justifiable and that no moral ideals are natural and livable. Coleridge is able to envision another way besides a priori demonstration to articulate ideals and to uphold rules of conduct. He enters into this way with the result that he becomes able to justify—he finds himself living out—the rule "Devote yourself to reflection on the conditions of melancholia and joy and to teaching your understandings to others."

Just what is Coleridge's progress, and is his justification of this moral rule a good one? To answer these questions, it is useful first of all to see Coleridge as responding to Hume's versions of skepticism and naturalism.

Hume observes in the first *Enquiry* that "morals and criticism are not so properly objects of the understanding as of taste and sentiment."[4] In the *Treatise,* he comments more pointedly on our inability to dispute rationally about questions of conduct.

> But what have I here said, that reflections very refin'd and metaphysical have little or no influence upon us? . . . The intense view of the manifold contradictions and imperfections in human reason has so wrought upon me, and heated my brain, that I am ready to reject all belief and reasoning, and can look upon no opinion even as more probable or likely than another. Where am I, or what? From what causes do I derive my existence, and to what condition shall I return? Whose favour shall I court, and whose anger must I dread? What beings surround me? and on whom have I any influence, or who have any influence on me? I am confounded with all these questions, and begin to fancy myself in the most deplorable condition imaginable, inviron'd with the deepest darkness, and utterly depriv'd of the use of every member and faculty.[5]

The only way out of this darkness which Hume is able to imagine is not to discover a *vocation* which banishes and redeems the darkness, but rather to put aside questions of conduct and take up an *avocation.*

> Most fortunately it happens, that since reason is incapable of dispelling these clouds, nature herself suffices in that purpose, and cures me of this philosophical melancholy and delirium, either by relaxing this bent of mind, or by some avocation, and lively impression of my senses, which obliterate all these chimeras. I dine, I play a game of back-gammon, I converse, and am merry with my friends; and when after three or four hours' amusement, I wou'd return to these speculations, they appear so cold, and strain'd, and ridiculous, that I cannot find in my heart to enter into them any farther.[6]

This is not a happy solution to the problem of how to emerge from the darkness of moral despair, for some three or four hours still later one's interest in reasonings about conduct is likely to reawaken and to bring in its train the very despair that one had sought to escape, now redoubled by the thought that its occurrence is inevitable even when one willfully flees it. Whatever interests and worries first gave rise to refined and metaphysical reflections are, it seems, not so easily quieted by "blind submission" to "follies . . . natural and agreeable."[7]

One may wish to escape the despair attending the realization that one cannot rationally justify any claims about the propriety of certain pursuits. One may wish to know how to live. But how could these wishes be realized? Is it not true that, as Hume argues, we cannot know what pursuits are proper for us? Is it not the case that we will inevitably, like Hume, become dejected periodically, and is it not the case that all we can do when dejected is wait either for our avocations to distract us or for our bodies' chemistries to change? If not, why not?

In seeking answers to these questions, we may do well to attend to the accounts of the travails of their lives produced by the major writers of the Romantic periods in England and America and by later writers who inherited their preoccupations. Such writers as Coleridge, Wordsworth, Carlyle, Emerson, and John Stuart Mill suffered through mental crises very like Hume's fall into darkness. The state of mind Coleridge and Wordsworth called dejection is precisely the subjective state accompanying the realization that one does not know, and may well be unable to know, how to live. Wordsworth, in book 11 of the *Prelude*, describes this state of mind in very nearly the same terms Hume used in the *Treatise* to describe his own mental crisis.

> This was the crisis of that strong disease,
> This the soul's last and lowest ebb; I drooped,
> Deeming our blessed reason of least use
> Where wanted most: "The lordly attributes
> Of will and choice," I bitterly exclaimed,
> "What are they but a mockery of a Being
> Who hath in no concerns of his a test
> Of good and evil; knows not what to fear
> Or hope for, what to covet or shun."[8]

Unlike Hume, however, Wordsworth did not take refuge from his dejection in avocations, and he did not resign himself to the necessity of learning how to live with skepticism.

> Depressed, bewildered thus, I did not walk
> With scoffers, seeking light and gay revenge
> From indiscriminate laughter, nor sate down
> In reconcilement with an utter waste
> Of intellect; such sloth I could not brook.[9]

Wordsworth's unwillingness to accept the notion that there is either no particular vocation for which he is suited or no way to know what it is and to adopt instead a policy of self-amusement is typical of the writers named above. As M. H. Abrams notes, "The distinctive Romantic genre of the *Bildungsgeschichte* describes a painful process of self-formation, crisis, and self-recognition, which culminates in a stage of self-coherence, self-awareness, and assured power that is its own reward."[10] How one might successfully pass through this painful process is generally taken to be discernible not through abstract philosophical reflection and not through scientific investigation, but through meditation on the events of one's life. As Abrams describes Wordsworth's account in the *Prelude* of his achievement of self-understanding and self-integration, the "ultimate goodness governing the course of his life is brought into question by his suffering and crisis of spirit, then is established by the outcome of his experience, which is then represented as prototypical for the men to whom he addresses himself."[11]

That Coleridge, like Wordsworth, was continuously occupied with attempting to understand his place in nature as a thinking being and with establishing, despite the failure of introspectionist foundationalism, what pursuits are appropriate to that nature is evident in his correspondence. In February 1801, Coleridge wrote to Davy, "I have been *thinking* vigorously during my illness, so that I cannot say that my long, long wakeful nights have been all lost to me. The subject of my meditations has been the relations of thoughts to things; in the language of Hume, of ideas to impressions."[12] A month and a half later, he announced to Poole that these meditations had borne fruit: "I have overthrown the doctrine of association, as taught by Hartley, and with it all the irreligious metaphysics of modern infidels—especially the doctrine of necessity."[13] Thus Coleridge claims to have discovered both that he is free and that he has a place in a meaningful, divinely ordained scheme of things.

This discovery, held in place at least for a time, stands further as a discovery of objectively valuable possibilities of human activity and relationship. Through it, one is returned all at once to a sense of oneself as an active being, to a natural world that is no longer alien and threatening, and to social life as an arena for human fulfillment. Our autonomy and our embeddedness are reconciled in activity within the frame of natural and social relationships. How is this discovery accomplished?

3. Recollective Reflection and Onwardness with Others

Coleridge's discoveries of his own freedom and of a vocation in the world fit for a free being are described most fully and carefully in "Frost at Midnight," written in February 1798.[14] The poem opens with the poet's calm, recollective recording of his sense that he is both somehow within nature and human society and somehow outside them or sealed off from them by his lack of an understanding of exactly

how and for what purposes natural and social phenomena are produced. The poet feels himself to be at once within and distinct from
nature.

> The Frost performs its secret ministry,
> Unhelped by any wind. The owlet's cry
> Came loud—and hark, again! loud as before.
> The inmates of my cottage, all at rest,
> Have left me to that solitude, which suits
> Abstruser musings: save that at my side
> My cradled infant slumbers peacefully.
>
>   (1–7)

His attention skips from event to event in nature, from the formation of
the frost to the lack of wind to the owlet, until he is startled by the
repetition of the owlet's cry. That nature is capable of startling him
reminds him that he does not live in continuous harmony with nature,
that he does not know, and has not accepted, his place in nature, that
nature's ministrations, to him and within herself, are secret. He takes
others to be alike inmates in nature, sealed off from knowledge of her
actions, yet, unlike him, to be at rest, free of worry about their situation. (One way to understand the poem is to take it as recording the
poet's attempt to establish that the gap between himself and others is
temporary.) The poet revoices his sense of being both surrounded by
and sealed off from nature and from others who are mysteriously less
restless and better adapted to life in nature than he is as he thinks of

>   . . . Sea, hill, and wood,
> This populous village! Sea, and hill, and wood,
> With all the numberless goings-on of life,
> Inaudible as dreams.
>
>   (10–13)

Unnumbered and inaudible, the workings of nature and social life pass
by his understanding.

Thus the problems the poet is reflecting on are those of how to
still his restlessness, how to alter his sense of being surrounded by
nature and society ("Sea, hill, and wood, / This populous village! Sea,
and hill, and wood") yet somehow sealed off from them, and how to
come to terms with his desire to know his place in nature and society.
Nature, in her hiddenness ("'Tis calm indeed! so calm, that it dis-
turbs / And vexes meditation with its strange / And extreme silent-
ness" [8–10]), calls forth the desire to know one's place in nature but

withholds its full satisfaction. Recognizing this, the poet is forced to contemplate his desire to know and to query its motives, the possibility of its being satisfied, and the likelihood of its persisting.

Wondering then whether the numberless goings-on of life can be made to reveal their significance, and, if so, how, the poet finds himself drawn to the only other restless thing within his notice: a piece of sooty film fluttering on the stove grate.

> Only that film, which fluttered on the grate,
> Still flutters there, the sole unquiet thing.
> Methinks, its motion in this hush of nature
> Gives it dim sympathies with me who live,
> Making it a companionable form.
> (15–19)

That is to say, the poet finds, in looking at the film on the grate, an image of himself at home in nature. The film and his spirit both flutter, yet the film's flutterings are altogether natural, not sealed off from nature, but produced as part of nature's secret self-ministrations. The film thus represents for the poet the union or integration of his own restlessness with the fullness and internal connectedness of nature, of, one might say, being for itself with being in itself. The film is both natural and alive; it "still flutters"—that is, its fluttering or restlessness is persistent, part of its nature, and yet not unsettling, but rather for it what it is to be still.

The poet, however, is unable to sustain his identification of himself with the film. It is not only a companionable form, but one

> Whose puny flaps and freaks the idling Spirit
> By its own mood interprets, everywhere
> Echo or mirror seeking of itself,
> And makes a toy of thought.
> (20–23)

Such pieces of fluttering film were commonly known as *strangers* and were thought to indicate the imminent arrival of a friend. The poet catches himself suddenly looking at the fluttering film not merely as a thing in itself, but as something to be interpreted. Now restrospectively, contemplating his act of identifying himself with the stranger, he is moved first to recognize the difference between his own activity in interpreting and the stranger's causally induced motions and then to reconfront his own restlessness and desire to know his place in nature.

This reconfrontation with his desire to know leads the poet to recollect similar confrontations with that desire, similarly brought about by its disappointment, in the past. He recalls that he had, when young and at school, similarly looked at the film on the grate and invested it with meaning.

> But O! how oft,
> How oft, at school, with most believing mind,
> Presageful, have I gazed upon the bars,
> To watch that fluttering *stranger!*
>   (23–26)

This memory in turn leads him to recall that, just as in the present he for a moment regarded the film on the grate as a natural phenomenon with manifest significance, he had in childhood regarded natural and social phenomena as obscurely significant, as imminently revelatory of his place in nature and of how to live happily in nature with a stilled consciousness, knowing his place in it and the pursuits appropriate to that place.

> and as oft
> With unclosed lids, already had I dreamt
> Of my sweet birth-place, and the old church-tower,
> Whose bells, the poor man's only music, rang
> From morning to evening, all the hot Fair-day,
> So sweetly, that they stirred and haunted me
> With a wild pleasure, falling on mine ear
> Most like articulate sounds of things to come!
>   (26–33)

Thus human works (the bells) and nature (the hot air and his ear) conspired to speak to him; that is, they possessed significance in themselves, were in harmony with one another, and thus suggested that, by grasping their message, the child could enter into a like state of harmony with and within nature and bring significance to his life. Or, rather, human works and nature only seemed to be significant. Their sounds never became fully significant but remained only "most like articulate sounds of things to come."

The promise of these sounds is not realized; the child, after hearing them throughout the hot Fair-day, falls asleep, and the poet's memory returns to his experiences of gazing in school at the film on the grate. The child at school, however, together with the poet recollecting the experiences of the child, has carried away with him from the Fair-days of his birthplace a latent sense that satisfaction of his desire to know how to live has not been and may not be forthcoming. This latent sense of dissatisfaction is then reinforced by the similar experience of gazing in school at the stranger, remembering the sound of the bells. In school, the child takes the stranger to be evidence of the possibility of being transplanted into a world where he is at home and no longer restless.

> And so I brooded all the following morn,
> Awed by the stern preceptor's face, mine eye
> Fixed with mock study on my swimming book:
> Save if the door half opened, and I snatched
> A hasty glance, and still my heart leaped up,
> For still I hoped to see the *stranger's* face,
> Townsman, or aunt, or sister more beloved,
> My play-mate when we both were clothed alike!
> (36–43)

Thus the child's desire for nature to speak to him and care for him is literalized, as the child takes the film on the grate, a natural phenomenon, to have, or portend, a particular face, namely that of the person who will remove him from school into another world where he will be more at home. The phrase "the stranger's face" fuses the idea that phenomena in nature are obscurely significant and are preparing a place for him with the idea that there are others (townsmen, aunt, or sister—familiars, yet strangers having knowledge he lacks) who already know the significance of nature, who carry that knowledge on their faces, which in some sense then belong to nature, and who might lead the child into a new world, stilling his restlessness and making him joyful in his pursuits, as he is not in school. Yet the child's desire to be led into a new world is similarly disappointed. The poet's memory breaks off, the poet returns to the present, and the child is left in school.

Thus, what unites the three scenes described in the poem—the poet's present contemplation of the film on the grate, the child's hearing, or remembered hearing, of his town's church-tower bells, and the older child's inspection in school of the film on the grate—are the themes of the occurrence, frustration, and persistence of the desire to know how to live and of the consciousness of oneself as a restless interpreting being, a consciousness which accompanies the frustration and persistence of that desire. The recurrence of this desire, its frustration, and the accompanying consciousness of self have not brought about the satisfaction of the poet's desire to know how to live, but only the knowledge that it is possible to survive the frustration of that desire, even while surmising that it, its frustration, and the associated state of restless self-consciousness will recur.

Yet one last time, the poet imagines that he has, and might come to know and glory in, a place in nature, not in his life but in his life transplanted, that is, in the life of his son. He conjectures that his own continuing restlessness stems not from the nature of consciousness as such, but from the circumstances of his upbringing.

> For I was reared
> In the great city, pent 'mid cloisters dim,
> And saw nought lovely but the sky and stars.
> But *thou*, my babe! shalt wander like a breeze
> By lakes and sandy shores, beneath the crags
> Of ancient mountain, and beneath the clouds,
> Which image in their bulk both lakes and shores
> And mountain crags: so shalt thou see and hear
> The lovely shapes and sounds intelligible
> Of that eternal language, which thy God
> Utters, who from eternity doth teach
> Himself in all, and all things in himself.
> Great universal Teacher! he shall mould
> Thy spirit, and by giving make it ask.
> (51–64)

Here Coleridge, having reflected on the persistence—and persistent frustration—of his desire to know how to live by knowing his place in nature, seems to have satisfied his desire. He has apparently uncovered the cause of his dejection—life in London—and he foresees that his son, having been freed from the influence of this cause, will be free of dejection. The poet himself again surmises that events in nature, including the phenomena of human life, are significant, even providentially determined; God reveals Himself to Himself through them. Although understanding of the exact character of this divine self-revelation eludes the poet, he is nonetheless able, by diagnosing the cause of his dejection, to assign a meaning to his life and to envision passing that meaning on to his son. Thus, just as God, somewhat like Hegel's Absolute Spirit, through His work of creating all things teaches Himself the meaning of His own original yet undeveloped nature, so the poet, through his diagnostic recollections of his experience, teaches himself how to be a teacher to his son and how to understand the significance of his experiences as preparatory for his activity as a teacher. His proper vocation, he now surmises on the basis of his reflection on his experiences, is that of teacher to his son.

Yet, despite the poet's sense of triumph in this passage at having understood and redeemed his existence, something remains not quite right. The poet perhaps realizes that, in identifying with his son and anticipating his son's joyful, meaningful life, he is once again anticipating, and failing to achieve, his own transplantation into a world where he will not be troubled by restlessness. Once again, it is the poet who is imaginatively assigning a meaning to events—this time not to the fluttering of the film on the grate or to the sound of the bells, but to the repeated welling up and frustration of his desire to know how to live—and anticipating, as a result, both further evidence in the future, in his son's happy life, of the correctness of his assignment of meaning and, through the appearance of that future evidence, the ultimate confirmation of his vocation as teacher. The poet has, again, imagined his present situation to be the first scene in a play whose progress will inexorably reveal its meaning. Here, as in Wordsworth, the achievement of an individual interpretation of the conditions of human fulfillment masks the lack of the satisfaction, general or particular, of these conditions. In the articulation of this interpretation, actual and general activity and relationship that are fulfilling for persons are not yet achieved.

Perhaps then the poet begins to suspect that his present assignment of meaning to his life and anticipation of his son's happiness are the result of yet one more welling up of his own desire to know how to live, a desire that may well be destined again to be frustrated. Unable to puzzle out God's self-instruction, he is again forced to confront the fact that his vision of what his son's life will be like is imaginatively constructed and not fully grounded. The triumphant prophesies of lines 51–64 are abandoned in favor of something more nearly resembling unknowing hope, and perhaps faith, that his understanding of his vocation and his son's future happiness is correct. He concludes both his address to his son and the poem by redescribing events in nature not as full of providential significance, but as having purposes mysteriously beyond human understanding.

> Therefore all seasons shall be sweet to thee,
> Whether the summer clothe the general earth
> With greenness, or the redbreast sit and sing
> Betwixt the tufts of snow on the bare branch
> Of mossy apple-tree, while the nigh thatch
> Smokes in the sun-thaw; whether the eave-drops fall

Heard only in the trances of the blast,
Or if the secret ministry of frost
Shall hang them up in silent icicles,
Quietly shining to the quiet Moon.
                    (65–74)

Here the poet's sense of the incomprehensibility of natural phenomena has reemerged. Nature's works do not speak to him, but are
instead again secret and silent. The wind, in its silence, entrances itself
and does not include the poet; he feels himself once again to be left
behind. The recitation of the changing appearances nature assumes
from season to season and the suggestion that these appearances are
continuously evolving into one another without being sharply distinct
combine to make one in following the images feel oneself, together
with the poet, to be surrounded by nature spatially as nature's temporal self-development surrounds or passes one by. The repeated
whether-or formulations leave the poet's summary in the register of
surmise,[15] indicating that the poet lacks confidence in his ability to
know what will happen when, and why. The idea that nature will be
sweet to or favor his son represents a withdrawal on the poet's part
from the idea that his son will grasp God's providential plan. His son is
now represented more as passively affected by nature than as wander-
ing and knowing. The poet himself is unable with any assurance to
predict the course of events in nature; nature continuously and fluidly
develops herself, beyond the poet's grasp. Yet, despite all this, the
poet's tone remains calm and optimistic. What, then, can be the source
of this calm and optimism, if it is not an achievement in knowing?

What is distinctively achieved in this last qualified imagining of
himself as his son's teacher—an achievement that is not evident in the
earlier moments of repeated recollection—is a sense of futurity with
another. Now the poet finds himself speaking not only to himself, but
also to his son. He can only conjecture about, but not know, the sweet-
ness of his son's future. But what is more important than the knowing,
and what accounts for the persistence of the tone of recovery, is that
the future will be a future of continuing relationship between father
and son.

This sense of continuing relationship, embodied in the sustained
mode of address to his son of the last twenty lines ("But *thou*, my
babe! . . . so shalt thou see and hear . . . thy God . . . thy spirit . . . to
thee"), is then further deepened and extended in the concluding image of the hanging icicles, which may be read as a figure for the poet's
presence to his child and to us. As Harold Bloom reads the concluding
lines, "The secret ministry of frost is analogous to the secret ministry of

memory, for both bind together apparently disparate phenomena in an imaginative unity. The frost creates a surface both to receive and reflect the shining of the winter moon. Memory, moving by its overtly arbitrary but deeply designed associations, creates an identity between the mature poet and the child who is his ancestor as well as with his own child."[16] The poet is represented in this image as achieving more than unity and identity alone, however. The icicles are different from, and yet reflect for and to, those who apprehend them, so that the poet is to be understood as being different from, yet present in his words for and to, certain others: his child and his audience. It is this sense of achieved and continuing relationship that brings the poem its closure and the poet his peace.

4. Actuality, Imagination, and the Sustenance of Relationship

That the poet's peace is achieved through the anticipation of a continued reception by either a months-old infant or an unidentified audience must raise worries about the genuineness and depth of this reception. How fully actual is the poet's presence to his son or to us? The child is there in his care, and we have the poem before us, to be sure. But is the poet actually attentive to and received as attentive by either his son or his audience? Can any relationship that lacks reciprocity, as these projected relations of continuing reception do, be taken to be deeply objectively fulfilling for persons in general?

It is possible to regard the image of presence and reflection to others that concludes "Frost at Midnight" as itself a mode of escape into imagination from the demands of authentic and reciprocal human relationship. The image of the shining icicles involves no sense of action or mobility on the part of the poet, hence perhaps no sense of the demands of active care for and responsiveness to another. What will happen to this image of the reception of the reflecting poet—will it hold up?—when the child needs food, or a bath, or patient play, or someone against whom to test and assert independence? It is as though the poet has alone once again scripted in imagination an end to dejection that freezes time and overcomes otherness in favor of a guaranteed reception and relationship. The other, whether child or imagined audience, is not allowed a full share in the shaping of the relationship; the poet's imagination alone has done all the work.

Yet the child *is* there, in the poet's care, and we have these words before us. And these actual relations between poet and child and poet and audience are sustained and found to be of value for the poet through his imagining their continuation. It is not then that the poet is wrong to imagine the continuation of relationship: worthwhile relations may call for such imaginings and make them natural. Relations so sustained may further be essential to overcoming our dejection and to leading lives fitly expressive of our personhood. In showing us this, the closing mode of address and imagery of "Frost at Midnight" display an authentic achievement of partial understanding of our possibilities of expressive life as persons. The partiality of this achievement will then be that it remains a further task—one from which "Frost at Midnight" in particular and perhaps the lyric in general may in their compactness shrink—to discover how imagining the sustenance of actual yet bare relationship may be extended to the actual sustenance of a fully reciprocal relationship. Can another be given a full share in the work of imagining a relation's development while nonetheless retaining the sense of the relation's enduring value and stability that brings the poet his peace? Thinking through this will require yet further investigation, interpretation, or reading of how ideals may both inform and be developed and transformed through a reciprocal relationship, wherein each party is fully present and responsive to the other.

IDEALITY, MATERIALITY, AND VALUE: *PRIDE AND PREJUDICE* AND MARRIAGE

1. The Difficulty and Interest of *Pride and Prejudice*

Perhaps no other novel that has been widely read and taught for generations has gained a reception that is not only as mixed, but as explicitly contradictory, as that accorded *Pride and Prejudice*. This contradictory reception—which has persisted without resolution, sometimes even within the responses of acute individual critics—directly reflects the preformed understandings of human motivations, social institutions, actual and possible relationships, and values that shape our readings, for the history of reception is the product not only of what the novel says, but also of what we bring to it. The history of this contradictory reception is thus a rich resource for coming to terms with our complex and opposed pre-understandings. Not only that, but in uncovering how the novel directly invites such contradictory responses and then subjects the pre-understandings on which they rest to criticism, we may hope to isolate and retain what is best in each opposed response, reduce their contradictoriness, and achieve a juster understanding of our motivations, institutions, and possible achievements of value in relationship than those with which we began. We may come to be able to see just how a sense of human dignity may naturally arise and may then, despite persistent difficulties, be given sustained expression in an achieved relation with another. We may hope to be able to test in the progress of this novel's protagonists to what extent the ideal may find a sustaining home within the natural, to what extent our senses of our autonomy and our embeddedness may be expressed coherently together. In order then ultimately to trace the novel's invitation and criticism of our contrasting responses and pre-understandings, of our senses of our autonomy and our embeddedness in nature, it will be helpful to begin by rehearsing the histories of our responses and of the controlling senses of ourselves that lie behind them.

Early critical appreciations of Jane Austen's work praised above all else the accuracy and penetration of her depictions of characters and actions. This praise typically contrasted the believable turns of her plots and the plausible motivations of her characters with the outlandish coincidences and simplistic passions of the popular romances of such writers as Maria Edgeworth and Fanny Burney, whose example Austen herself had both criticized and drawn upon. Sir Walter Scott began this line of appreciation in 1815 in a review of *Emma*, two years after the publication of *Pride and Prejudice* in 1813. Scott remarks that

> a new style of novel has arisen, within the last fifteen or twenty years, differing from the former in the points upon which the interest hinges; neither alarming our credulity nor amusing our imagination by wild variety of incident, or by those pictures of romantic affection and sensibility, which were formerly as certain attributes of fictitious characters as they are of rare occurrence among those who actually live and die. The substitute for these excitements, which had lost much of their poignancy by the repeated and injudicious use of them, was the art of copying from nature as she really exists in the common walks of life, and presenting to the reader, instead of the splendid scenes of an imaginary world, a correct and striking representation of that which is daily taking place around him.[1]

In 1820, Richard Whately continued this line, observing that "certainly no author has ever conformed more closely to real life, as well in the incidents, as in the character and descriptions."[2] An essayist in the *Edinburgh Review* of 1830 informed his audience that Austen's readers found that "her characters act and talk so exactly like the people whom they saw around them every day."[3] George Henry Lewes remarked in 1859 that "if ever living beings can be said to have moved across the page of fiction, as they lived, speaking as they spoke, and feeling as they felt, they do so in *Pride and Prejudice, Emma,* and *Mansfield Park.*"[4] In one of the subtlest and most ambivalent responses to her work, Richard Simpson in 1870 took care to honor Austen's realism. Her characters, he wrote, "are all natural, all more or less commonplace, but all discriminated from one another beyond the possibility of confusion, by touches so delicate that they defy analysis, and so true that they elude observation, and only produce the effect by their accumulation."[5] Reginald Farrer commented in 1917 that "of all writers, she it is who pursues truth with most utter and undeviable devotion. The real thing is her only object always."[6] Even in post–Second World War

New Criticism, where direct attention to complexities of plot, language, and imagery generally displaces assessments of accuracy of depiction, Austen's realism remains a guiding subtext that occasionally comes to the surface. The interest of the critic's investigations of Austen's complexities, it is assumed at bottom, lies in the fact that these complexities are penetratingly faithful to how we live, form attachments, reveal our characters in conduct, and so forth, in all our ambivalence and incompleteness, and under social pressures. Thus Marvin Mudrick observes that Austen in *Pride and Prejudice* employs her irony as "an instrument of discrimination between the people who are simple reproductions of their social types and the people with individuality and will, between the unaware and the aware."[7] That is to say, *Pride and Prejudice* accurately and exhaustively distinguishes and illustrates two types of characters to be found, according to Mudrick, in real life, and it moreover goes on, as Mudrick assumes life does, to reward awareness with riches and happiness. Similarly A. Walton Litz takes the interactions between Elizabeth and Darcy to "dramatize the persistent conflict between social restraint and the individual will, between tradition and self-expression,"[8] thus implying that Austen has accurately and in fine detail discerned a conflict that runs through our lives generally. The overwhelming drift of this line of appreciation is that Jane Austen got something—whether character, motivation, coherence of plot, or social conflict—thoroughly right.

Typically Austen's realism is taken to be the ground of her greatest effects and of her standing as an artist, to lay the claim her writings have on our attention. Her novels, to repeat Scott's phrase, differ from others "in the point upon which the interest hinges." Whately, citing "the precepts of Aristotle" on the economy and probability of plots, finds Austen's "perfectly correct pictures of common life" to be "*instructive*" and to furnish us with "general rules of practical wisdom."[9] Lewes remarks that through the truthfulness and economy of her dramatic representations "Miss Austen has carried the art [of the novelist] to a point of excellence surpassing that reached by any of her rivals."[10] The realism these critics praise is thus regarded as the central distinguishing feature of the art of her writings and thus of their moral and practical significance.

Praise for the realism of *Pride and Prejudice* and for its moral significance is intimately bound up with a positive evaluation of the marriage of Elizabeth and Darcy that is its culmination. In the earliest critical responses, the idea that marriage, at least of the sort accomplished by this pair, brings into harmony reason and passion, society and individual, public responsibility and private behavior, was perhaps too commonplace to require iteration. Since then, however, we have become more suspicious of the value of marriage per se for all persons, and criticism has additionally turned toward the explicit articulation of the ideas and values adumbrated in plot and style. As a result, an enormous amount of attention has been focused, in the criticism of the twentieth century that praises Austen's realism, on the special praiseworthy characteristics of the marriage of Elizabeth and Darcy. These special characteristics are taken to distinguish their marriage from the range of rather poor marriages described in the novel—Lydia and Wickham's, Charlotte and Mr. Collins's, and above all Mr. and Mrs. Bennet's—and to make it appropriate to see it as a natural and good sanctification of their prior relationship. Samuel Kliger apparently began this line of attention in identifying "the art-nature antithesis as the ground of the book's action and its mode of organization."[11] Elizabeth, according to Kliger, stands for "man-in-nature," individuality, and the egalitarianism of the Levellers, while Darcy represents "man-in-society," artifice, and class hierarchy. In being educated and chastened by one another, and in coming consequently to appreciate one another's qualities, thence expressing their appreciation in marriage, Elizabeth and Darcy show us that as a result of reform or education a natural and coherent social existence is possible for us—as, one suspects, Kliger takes it to be. Litz directly endorses this reading.[12] Alistair M. Duckworth, Julia Prewitt Brown, and Mary Poovey continue and deepen it by connecting the naturalness and artificiality of Elizabeth and Darcy respectively with more basic qualities of character and opposed yet complementary needs of both the human spirit and social life that Elizabeth and Darcy display in their actions. Duckworth finds Elizabeth representative of "individual energy," "spontaneity," selfhood, and presentness, while Darcy typifies "discipline," the appeal to "inherited forms," the claims of society, and pastness. Their marriage exemplifies the goodness of "self-in-society, the vitalized reconstitution of a social totality, the dynamic compromise between past and present, the simultaneous reception of what is valuable in an inheritance and the liberation of the originality, energy and spontaneity in the living moment."[13] Julia Prewitt Brown similarly identifies Elizabeth with irrationality, anarchy, and chaotic energies and Darcy with rationality, order, and civilization. Their marriage is fitting in that "only through civilized forms does the chaos of human nature find meaning, and only through the inclusion of chaotic energies does civilization find meaning."[14] Mary Poovey nicely blends the social and psychological categories of Duckworth and Brown and deepens their readings by noting the existence of passion in Darcy and respect for the social order in Elizabeth, rather than taking each as a simple and unambiguous type. In the interactions of Elizabeth and

Darcy, she argues, "Austen brings individual desire into confrontation with social institutions in order first to discipline anarchic passion and then to expand the capacity of such institutions to accommodate educated needs and desires."[15] Upon the completion of the education of desires and the reform of society, "principled feeling"[16] will find itself at home in reformed institutions, as Elizabeth and Darcy apparently are to find themselves and their feelings at home in their marriage. Austen's artistic achievement is thus to have succeeded in developing "rhetorical strategies [that] harness the imaginative energy of her readers to a moral design; she thus manages to satisfy both the individual reader's desire for emotional gratification, and the program of education prescribed by traditional moral aestheticians."[17]

That energy and form, individual desire and developed social institutions, and innovation and tradition must be intermingled in the ways they are in this marriage in order for the lives of individuals, societies, or married pairs to avoid lapsing into either hollow repetitiveness or fragmentary waywardness is, on this line of reading, a truth *Pride and Prejudice* has to teach us and a truth embodied in its culminating marriage. The marriage of Elizabeth and Darcy is understood as symbolizing and accomplishing the conciliation of differences not only between individuals, but also within both social life at large and the individual psyche. Marriage in general is both the figure and scene of accomplishment of conciliation and healing.

As the critical talk of the education and discipline of energy suggests, associated with this line of reading is a tendency to see the marriage of Elizabeth and Darcy as a reflection and product of an achievement of self-consciousness or understanding on their parts. Elizabeth and Darcy are taken to have come to realize that for each of them the best chance for a creative and fulfilling life lies in ongoing relationship with this complementary other. Elizabeth's overcoming of prejudice and Darcy's overcoming of pride occur as they each come to understand their natural complementarity as individuals and the natural complementarity of the qualities and capacities they each embody. Having survived their misunderstandings and misappreciations of one another, they marry out of apt appreciation and genuine self-consciousness. *Pride and Prejudice* thus teaches us that a marriage founded on understanding of oneself and the other is both possible and good.

AGAINST THIS POSITIVE reading that emphasizes Austen's realism and accepts the conciliating possibilities of self-conscious marriage, there persists a considerably more troubling reading, according to which the plot of *Pride and Prejudice* is unrealistic and marriage is a basically discredited institution. According to this troubling reading, the positive reading is riddled with empty abstract symbolisms introduced by critics in order to give apparent weight to what is really a contrived and unrealistic plot. The plot is unrealistic in that persons generally are simply not motivated often, and especially not in marrying, by self-conscious reflection about how to conciliate spontaneity and discipline or energy and form. Motivation in general, this latter reading suggests, is a matter of passions and needs that demand satisfaction. In men generally, and in Darcy in particular, the real passion motivating marriage is that for sexual and economic possession on the part of the materially dominant; for relatively materially self-sufficient men, women are adornments and objects for gratification and domination. In contrast, in women generally and in Elizabeth in particular, the real passion motivating marriage is economic; only by marrying can women escape a life of material misery. Early on in *Pride and Prejudice*— for example in the worries of Mrs. Bennet about the futures of her daughters, in the Charlotte Lucas plot, and in the general interest of the neighborhood, including Elizabeth and Jane, in the arrival of Bingley and Darcy at Netherfield—both Elizabeth and Jane Austen seem to be aware of this hard material fact. Yet the novel shrinks from pursuing it, as Austen shapes *Pride and Prejudice* in accordance with the convention of the popular romance that a marriage of love can solve all social and individual problems. But this popular convention is radically false, is in fact a fantasy that women consume and that encourages their subservience. A marriage of love to a wealthy man is in fact available only to a very few women, and even when it is accomplished it only perpetuates relations of domination that ought to be undone. As Duckworth, who opposes this dark reading, puts it, "Elizabeth's final entry into the estate of Pemberley is . . . , as some critics would have it, a conventional escape (for Elizabeth) from a life of penury and mediocrity, or (for Jane Austen) from troubling insights into the nature of society."[18] It is these escapes that are then seen as desperately unrealistic in light of the less materially advantageous marriages most women will contract and in light of the domination women will suffer in any marriage. The real motivating forces shaping relationships are economic fear, in women, and sexual-possessive passion, in men, and if either the economic situation of women were made more equal or perhaps, virtually *per impossibile*, men were educated out of their possessiveness, then marriage would clearly be outmoded as an institution. In light of Austen's unrealistic scanting of these facts about relations between the sexes, the only real value of *Pride and Prejudice* lies in its initial exhibition of Elizabeth as a woman with energy, individuality, and judgment. The subsequent chastening of these qualities

of Elizabeth through the use of the marriage plot makes the last third of
the novel stale and conventional. It is far more likely that Elizabeth
would have married someone else, been forced to repress her individuality while secretly retaining it, and become ultimately embit-
tered and resentful than it is that she would achieve the marriage
she does.

Fed by the currents of Marxism and feminism since the 1950s, this
latter reading shows signs of becoming ascendant over the more
positive one. Its seeds were planted, however, as early as 1870 in
Richard Simpson's criticism of Austen's "Platonism" and suggestion
that the actual plot of *Pride and Prejudice* is inconsistent with Austen's
"Platonic" conception of human motivation and ideal relationships.
According to Simpson,

> Miss Austen has a most Platonic inclination to explain away knavishness
> into folly. Wickedness in her characters is neither unmixed with good-
> ness, nor is it merely a defect of will; she prefers to exhibit it as a
> weakness of intelligence, an inability of the common-sense to rule the
> passions which it neither comprehends nor commands.[19]

This idea that folly and wickedness can be explained as resulting from
weakness of intelligence leads Austen to denigrate sheer passion and
to offer an intellectualistic picture of ideal relationships. She "seems,"
Simpson writes,

> to be saturated with the Platonic idea that the giving and receiving of
> knowledge, the active formation of another's character or the more pas-
> sive growth under another's guidance, is the truest and strongest
> foundation of love. . . . Her favourite ideal was to exhibit this intelligent
> love in its germ, to eclipse it for a season by the blaze of a great passion, to
> quench this glare, and to exhibit the gentle light of the first love reviving
> and waxing till it perfects itself in marriage. . . . [Her aim was] to make
> true love rather an adjunct of the sober common-sense than of the impet-
> uous and passionate side of the soul.[20]

There is, Simpson finds, something desperately detached and unrealistic in this downgrading of the role of passion in relationships, both
actual and ideal, and in human motivation generally. Austen writes as
someone who "sat apart on her rocky tower, and watched the poor
souls struggling in the waves beneath . . . [with] her sympathies not
too painfully engaged."[21] As a result, the relationship she really ap-
proves is that of friendship, not love. She regarded "friendship [as]
being the true light of life, while love was often only a troublesome and
flickering blaze which interrupted its equable and soothing influ-

ence."[22] Worse yet, apart from any questions about the realism or plausibility of her pictures of motivation and ideal relationship, Austen's practice as a novelist is inconsistent with her ideals. While she

> treated as mere moonshine . . . that predestination of love, that preordained fitness, which decreed that one and one only should be the complement and fulfillment of another's being, . . . she at the same time founded her novels on the assumption of it as a hypothesis.[23]

Thus the plot of *Pride and Prejudice* incorporates an implicit acknowledgment that particular passion is strong enough to make Platonic intellectualized love less than fully satisfying for human beings as they are genuinely motivated. If this insight were consistently pursued, then "the exhibition of intelligent love" as an ideal would have to give way to a more concrete investigation of the roots and vagaries of particular passion; absent this investigation, the plot is incoherent.

Marvin Mudrick locates a similar failure of realism that underwrites the conventional marriage plot in the handling of Darcy, where Austen "is so uncharacteristically clumsy as to rely on inconsistencies of personality to move her story along."[24] The plot requires Darcy to be "a proud man with a strong sense of at least external propriety and dignity," yet at the initial ball he is made to speak "with a vulgarity indistinguishable from his aunt's."[25] Similarly, "in spite of his rigid and principled reserve," Darcy sends "a thoroughly frank and unreserved letter" of explanation to Elizabeth after she has refused his first proposal.[26] Ultimately Darcy "emerges into flatness" and is "ironed out into the conventionally generous and altruistic hero."[27] The only explanation there can be for this inconsistent and flat treatment of Darcy is that Austen is awkwardly forcing the development of her characters to conform to the requirements of the conventional marriage plot. The result, Mudrick observes, is that

> we get outbursts of irrelevantly directed moral judgment, and a general simplification of the problems of motive and will down to the level of the Burneyan novel. Jane Austen herself, routed by the sexual question she has raised, is concealed behind a fogbank of bourgeois morality; and the characters, most conspicuously Darcy . . . fall automatically into the grooves prepared for them by hundreds of novels of sentiment and sensibility.[28]

The real value of *Pride and Prejudice*, and a value partially betrayed by its plot, lies in its portrait of Elizabeth as a "complex individual . . . aware and capable of choice" who manages, partially but only partially, notably in refusing Mr. Collins, to resist the demands of "an acquisitive society" that would "standardize and absorb her."[29]

Mary Poovey similarly reads the marriage plot in *Pride and Prejudice* as a conventional refusal of initial insights into the nature of human motivation, into the social structures of bourgeois society, and into their interconnections. Poovey convincingly shows that Elizabeth's initial wit and cleverness function as defenses against both emotional involvement and the acknowledgment of her hopes for rescue through marriage from her desperate material situation.[30] Darcy's rejection of her at the initial ball wounds her in that it "defeats not only her romantic fantasies of marriage to a handsome aristocrat but, more important, the image of herself upon which such fantasies are based."[31] Her response is then to tease Darcy and cultivate a dislike for him in order to keep her romantic fantasies and self-image intact by showing herself that Darcy was not her proper rescuer anyway. The subsequent development of the marriage plot then counteracts and undermines this initial insight on Austen's part into how social causes, here Elizabeth's desperate material situation and institutionalized dependence, can bring about psychological effects, here Elizabeth's fantasies of marriage and self-protective defensiveness. Thus, Poovey writes,

> The romantic conclusion of *Pride and Prejudice* effectively dismisses the social and psychological realism with which the novel began. . . . [W]hen marriage with Darcy cancels all the gloomy forecasts about Elizabeth's future, Austen no longer suggests a possible relationship between social causes and psychological effects.[32]

Elizabeth's initial attraction to Darcy, or to any wealthy potential suitor, is rooted in her institutionalized material dependence. Yet the fact that psychological responses have social roots runs directly counter to the conventions of romance that shape the plot: "The fundamental assumption of romantic love—and the reason it is so compatible with bourgeois society—is that the personal can be kept separate from the social, that one's 'self' can be fulfilled in spite of—and in isolation from—the demands of the marketplace."[33] Here again, as in Simpson's and Mudrick's readings, the forces of passion, now understood as having social roots, are taken to be implicitly recognized by Austen, but then refused analysis as the conventional marriage plot is developed. In *Pride and Prejudice*, Austen "foreground[s] romance convention in order to displace complexities raised by the introduction of realistic social and psychological details."[34] Furthermore, as Rachel Blau DuPlessis puts it, developing this line of reading, not only are insights into the interrelations of the social and psychological refused, the very energies of the plot, crystallized in the energies and quest for self-realization of Elizabeth, are undermined through the use of the conventional marriage ending. Here "the resolution subordinating quest to love reveals much tension . . . , for . . . the nature of the resolution, obeying as it does social and economic limits for middle-class women as a group, is in conflict with the trajectory of the book as a whole."[35] What really capture our attention and interest are Elizabeth's energy and questing, and it is precisely these qualities that are denied development and satisfaction in the marriage plot. Realism and the construction of just and plausible ideals of fulfillment for strong and distinctive women are sacrificed to implausible convention and the rationalization of the bourgeois social order.

HOW COULD THERE be such opposed lines of reading—the positive line emphasizing Austen's realism and moral wisdom, and the more troubling line emphasizing her conventionality and rationalization of social injustice—that both possess such considerable plausibility and interest? The tension here lies not only between critics of different tastes and temperaments. One finds oneself tempted by both lines of reading, and torn between them. In the best, most interesting critics— Simpson, Mudrick, and Poovey—one finds a certain ambivalence, as Austen is seen both as a consummate realist in depicting fundamentally social individuals and as something of an unrealistic moralist. And here it will not quite do to say, with Mudrick and Poovey, that Austen initially depicts Elizabeth's complex character in society realistically but fails to do so later on, for our experience of Elizabeth is that she remains a coherent, exemplary individual. Those who favor the more troubling reading often say something like "In marrying Darcy, Elizabeth did the best she could do in the circumstances." Mudrick more or less says this overtly in taking her to find in Darcy a complexity that answers to her own.[36] When we say something like this, we endorse at least part of the more positive reading; we reveal that we experience the marriage of Elizabeth and Darcy as not merely the product of economic necessity and direct sexual passion, but as a more generally fitting and desirable relationship. We do not, after all, think Elizabeth's character would have been more naturally and appropriately developed had she become a minor governess making her way marginally through the marketplace, or had she become the wife of some other, possibly more liberated, wealthy man, or had she become a more or less badly used provincial wife in the manner of her mother or Charlotte Lucas. For most readers, even those alert to the material and social circumstances, marriage with Darcy somehow seems right. And yet it is impossible not to appreciate the constraints imposed on Elizabeth by her material situation and to suspect that marriages of her sort, and our acceptance of them, have a role in perpetuating these very constraints.

The explanation of our ambivalence must lie in our prior ambivalence about the nature and value of marriage as a form of human community. Is marriage, at least when it is accomplished by certain people in a certain way, the natural and ideal home for the blending of individuality and society, energy and discipline, innovation and tradition? Or is it inevitably or predominantly the arena for the perpetuation of exploitation and possessiveness?

Austen's aim and achievement in *Pride and Prejudice* are to lead us to think of marriage in both of these ways. This is evident first of all in the considerable range of marriages she shows us, emphasizing especially the exploitativeness and the sterility of the mature ones while simultaneously engaging us in the courtship of Elizabeth and Darcy. More important, her aim and achievement are to lead us beyond these initial conceptualizations of marriage to an account of marriage as a potentially valuable and genuinely realizable form of relationship for persons. Where the positive reading relies on a conceptualization of marriage as an escape from embodiment, temporality, society, and materiality into a static ideal balance of forces, and where the negative reading relies on a conceptualization of marriage as both epiphenomenal upon and reinforcing of the ceaseless temporal development of material passions for economic or psychological gratification, Austen puts before us a conceptualization of marriage as a productive, stable, yet adaptive form of ongoing relationship for partially autonomous and embodied beings. In doing this, she would educate us to a sense of our best real possibilities. What prevents us from receiving this education, and what keeps us locked in our ambivalence, is the strength of the prior conceptualizations of marriage that we bring to the work. In order to see how we might be educated by *Pride and Prejudice* away from these prior conceptualizations and toward an appreciation of marriage of a certain sort as a materially realizable ideal, we need first to articulate and acknowledge these prior conceptualizations.

2. Two Conceptualizations of Marriage

In the traditional religious understanding, marriage is an exemplary form of human community in that through it enslavement to one's brute passions and consequent manipulativeness of others are displaced by personal dignity and relations of reciprocity and responsiveness. As Paul enjoined the Corinthians, in order to avoid the self-enslavement and manipulativeness involved in fornication,

> . . . let every man have his own wife, and let every woman have her own husband.
>   Let the husband render unto the wife due benevolence: and likewise also the wife unto the husband.
>   The wife hath not power of her own body, but the husband: and likewise also the husband hath not power of his own body, but the wife.[37]

Here, through marriage, sexual relations are expressive not of bodily urges alone, but of responsiveness to the other as a person; it is in this sense that each "hath power" of the body of the other. In thus embodying responsiveness in their relations, each will render the other the benevolence that befits a person, rather than merely using the other instrumentally, so that, in Augustine's words, "in a good marriage . . . the order of charity . . . flourishes between husband and wife."[38]

Marriage is thus regarded as a natural vehicle for the embodiment of our dignity as persons and for our recognition of one another that is also a recognition of ourselves. Milton explicitly connects the achievement of our dignity and humanity with the achievement of full human relationship.

> . . . God in the first ordaining of marriage, taught us to what end he did it, in words expresly implying the apt and cheerfull conversation of man with woman, to comfort and refresh him against the evill of solitary life, not mentioning the purpose of generation until afterwards, as being but a secondary end in dignity, though not in necessity; . . . in Gods intention a meet and happy conversation is the chiefest and the noblest end of marriage. . . .[39]

As wife and husband respond to one another, they exercise their distinctive capacities as persons, therein finding in the other and incarnating in their activity the full dimensions of their personhood. In this relationship, as Hegel urged, "consciousness immediately recognizes itself in another, . . . and there is knowledge of this mutual recognition."[40] Marriage enables us to act in awareness of the other as a person, and hence in awareness of our own capacities for this awareness.

This awareness of the other and oneself as persons is embedded in daily life, not concluded once and for all. Awareness and relatedness are to be, in Cavell's phrase, "something that is always happening, day by day," as "the acceptance of human relatedness" takes the form of "the acceptance of repetition."[41] Through marriage, experience itself is transfigured from the individual's punctual receipt and pursuit of goods and satisfactions into a cooperative embodiment of purposiveness. Experience comes to be expressive of our personalities, rather than something simply consumed. As Hegel would have it, in "love, trust, and common sharing of their entire existence as individuals," wife and husband will achieve in daily life liberation from banal and empty repetitiveness into a repetitiveness that is expressive of will and choice and acceptance and development, so that in this transfigured repetitiveness "they attain their substantive self-consciousness."[42]

In enabling what might be called ongoing purposiveness without the final completion of a specific purpose, marriage is fundamentally "not a contractual relation . . . ; it is precisely a contract to transcend the standpoint of contract, the standpoint from which persons are regarded in their individuality as self-subsistent units."[43] Contracts have a specific end or purpose. Their establishment and fulfillment are instrumental to an individual's happiness, which he or she will also pursue through actions not required by any contract. To be a contractor is to undertake to make use as an individual of goods or services for which one exchanges goods or services. The purposes that individuals bring to contracting are established by them on their own and are extrinsic to the contract; they do not require the contract for their very existence, and they could always be fulfilled, though perhaps more awkwardly, through different means. Hence contractual relations, with their terms and limits negotiated by individuals, cannot transfigure the experience of individuals from the punctual receipt and pursuit of goods and satisfactions into the embodiment of cooperative purposiveness. Each contractor remains instrumental to the other.

To regard one's marriage as a contract arising out of private passion is thus both to ensure its failure to accomplish our transfiguration into freedom and relatedness and to promote its likely dissolution. Contracts, after all, may be fulfilled or breached; a better deal may always come along. They bind only conditionally. As Denis de Rougemont has argued, where marriage is regarded as a contract for pleasure, and

> a couple have married in obedience to a romance, it is natural that the first time a conflict of temperament or of taste becomes manifest the parties should each ask themselves: "Why did I marry?" And it is no less natural that, obsessed by the universal propaganda in favor of romance,

each should seize the first occasion to fall in love with somebody else. And thereupon it is perfectly logical to decide to divorce, so as to obtain from the new love, which demands a fresh marriage, a new promise of happiness. . . . Thus, remedying boredom with a passing fever, "he for the second time, she for the fourth," . . . men and women go in quest of "adjustment." They do not seek it, however, in the old situation, the one guaranteed—"for better, for worse"—by a vow. They seek it, on the contrary, in a fresh "experience" regarded as such, and affected from the start by the same potentialities of failure as those which preceded it.[44]

Dissolutions and repeated failures of relatedness are not the only threats attendant upon a contractualist-instrumentalist conception of marriage. Experience itself becomes something that is suffered and fled, as its consumption becomes unsatisfyingly repetitive. If we misunderstand marriage as contractual and instrumental, and so refuse its possibilities for the transfiguration of experience, then we will, as individuals pursuing happiness as something to be acquired or experienced or consumed, always find ourselves demanding more: "Every wish to experience happiness, to have it at one's beck and call—instead of *being* in a *state* of happiness, as though by grace—must instantly produce an intolerable sense of want."[45] For many, there are other modes of relatedness—friendship or politics or service or parenthood—through which happiness may be accepted and lived rather than sought, consumed, and resought. But for most the dailiness of marriage offers the most natural and complete mode of the achievement of relatedness and the transfiguration of experience.

With its transfiguration of experience out of successive moments of production and consumption and into something we accept and live within, marriage—at least as it is understood by writers of more or less religious sensibility: Paul, Augustine, Milton, Hegel, de Rougemont, and Cavell—is inimical to comprehensive capitalism and utilitarianism. Persons are not homogenized and made exclusively into generally intersubstitutable producers and consumers of bits of experience. Rather, in and through marriage they become creative in their work and faithful to both one another and the work jointly undertaken.

Not all modes of work will express and support joint creativity and faithfulness. Those that will—education, or politics, or science, or art, or, above all, for most, child-rearing—must have objects, such as justice, or understanding, or children, that are not commodities repetitively manufactured for consumption, but instead develop independently without a specific and perfectly achievable final end. Relatedness, intimacy, and creativity may be expressed and sustained through the nurturance of these objects, and they will very likely prove evanescent if such objects are lacking. When our work is creatively directed toward particular objects of these kinds, rather than being the repetitive manufacture of commodities to be consumed, then our lives together come to possess a dignity and value that it is difficult to reconcile with the rationalizations and efficiencies of production of comprehensive capitalism and utilitarianism. When our personhood demands that we embody dignity and value in our lives, then public institutions and activities such as markets and consumption will properly have to be adapted to the domestic institutions and activities, such as marriage and child-rearing, that nurture our personhood.

And the reason for this is that the embodiment of the dignity and value of our person, as it may be expressed and sustained through these institutions and activities, makes an overriding claim on us, is that alone which redeems our lives and experience from boredom and into meaningfulness. Daily relatedness in incompletable, creative activity, and fidelity to this relatedness and activity, rather than the pursuit of individual satisfaction, most meaningfully express our nature as persons.

> Fidelity thus understood sets up the person. For the person is manifested like something made, in the widest sense of making. It is built up as a thing is made, thanks to a making, and in the same conditions as we make things, its first condition being a fidelity to something that before was not, but now is in process of being created. Person, made thing, fidelity—the three terms are neither separable nor separately intelligible. All three presuppose that a stand has been taken, and that we have adopted what is fundamentally the attitude of creators. Hence in the humblest lives the plighting of a troth introduces the opportunity of making and of rising to the plane of the person—on condition, of course, that the pledge has not been for "reasons" in the giving of which there is a reservation which will allow those reasons to be repudiated some day when they have ceased to appear "reasonable"! The pledge exchanged in marriage is the very type of a *serious* act.[46]

THE SERIOUSNESS, relatedness, and transfiguration of experience that are furthered in marriage have all the attractions of high ideals—and perhaps many of the worst features of ideologies. Once one begins to turn one's eyes away from largely masculine and religious rhapsodizing about marriage and to the specific material history of marriage, then one may begin to see the religious conception of marriage as a rationalizing fantasy, propagated by men who self-servingly exploit the labor of women and suppress female desire and autonomy. The vow of marriage begins to appear not as the type of a serious act, but as the scene of the perpetuation of relations of domination. As

Durkheim, noting the material realities of marriage, already observed in 1897, in comparison with the man, the woman "loses more and gains less from the institution."[47] According to recent American sociological studies, married women as a group have greater incidences of depression, phobic tendencies, anxiety, and neuroses, as measured on standard personality tests, than either single women or married men.[48] Women report less satisfaction with family life than do men.[49] Anecdotally, women report having to curb their natural talents in order to win the attention and affection of men so that they may then have a chance of living out the marriage fantasy: "To be a success in the dorms one must date, to date one must not win too many ping pong games. At first I resented this bitterly. But now I am more or less used to it and live in hope of one day meeting a man who is my superior so that I may be my natural self."[50] Subscription to the marriage fantasy thus compromises women's possibilities of achievement and development. Actual wifehood, sought by women in part out of illusions nurtured by the marriage fantasy, is apparently experienced by women as what de Tocqueville called a continuous "voluntary surrender of their own will,"[51] with devastating psychological and material consequences. Or, as Nietzsche has it, "Woman gives herself away, man acquires more."[52]

Once these social phenomena are noted, actual marriages seem to have their roots not so much in self-conscious understandings of how autonomy in relatedness may be achieved as in economic necessity and infantile experience. As Shulamith Firestone has argued, the mother's rejection of the child creates a fractural self driven to possess, destroy, or incorporate a fantasized integrated, masterful Other who is envied, resented, and experienced as a challenge.[53]

In women, the fractural self's envy and resentment are reinforced by material dependence. Men control most jobs and most property, and that control is experienced by women as an enviable mastery. Given the real inequalities of economic power, the only strategy for acquiring control and mastery of the Other that is open to most women is mystification. Through her expertise in matters of fashion, style, and flattery, the woman may present to the man an image—albeit a false one—of lost maternal self-presence and approval, and so become for him something he must possess: "Thus 'falling in love' [which happens to men, not women] is no more than the process of alteration of male vision—through idealization, mystification, glorification—that renders void the woman's class inferiority."[54] Meanwhile, for the woman who manages so to bedazzle a man, "life is a hell, vacillating between an all-consuming need [forged through infantile rejection and reinforced by economic dependence] for male love and approval to raise her from her class subjection [and] persistent feelings of inauthenticity when she does achieve his love."[55] Thus marriage between men and women, driven by the needs of their fractural selfhood, becomes, in a phrase Firestone borrows from de Rougemont's criticism of marriages of passion, nothing more than "a false reciprocity which disguises a twin narcissism,"[56] itself shaped by material inequalities.

After a marriage has been accomplished, then, given the continuing fact of male economic power, the woman comes to play the role of a thing possessed and brought home, while the man is generally more able to play a public role and to seek, find, and become dissatisfied with yet again the approval and affection of a maternal Other, who artfully conceals a fractural self. The inequalities and unhappinesses that attend the roles of husband and wife so wedded are evident in the very words "matrimony" and "patrimony." Matrimony is a state or relation to be entered into, as a thing can enter into states or relations; a patrimony is a store of inheritable wealth that public honor requires a male inheritor to increase for his successors. What pertains to the mother is stasis; what pertains to the father is acquisitive activity without natural shape or limit.

An argument against the worth of marriage as an institution immediately emerges from these social facts. (1) Grounded in infantile needs and economic necessities, most marriages are matches of male power, wealth, and status with female attractiveness and artfulness. (2) In such marriages, neither party flourishes; women become objectified and men become emptily acquisitive. (3) Since most marriages are of this kind, to be married *means* entering this kind of relation; such marriages are generally regarded as appropriate and fitting, and married pairs will be expected to act accordingly. One cannot make one's acts of subscribing to a public institution and taking up public roles eccentric and privately meaningful. (4) Therefore, at least by and large, there cannot be good marriages. Marriage is an institution that inhibits human flourishing.

As arguments like this have been found forceful, women in particular have begun to articulate alternative ideals. Thus de Beauvoir writes, against marriage, that "the ideal, on the contrary, would be for entirely self-sufficient human beings to form unions with one another only in accordance with the untrammeled dictates of their mutual love."[57] Embodying this ideal will require new economic and social relations, as women must become less materially dependent and live more as active individuals. The facts that new relations are emerging and that women are becoming somewhat more independent materially—facts noted in this context as early as 1929 by Russell[58] and 1949 by de Beauvoir[59]—both promote the articulation of new individualist ideals and are a sign of their attractiveness. As Rachel Blau DuPlessis has argued, women writers in the twentieth century have imaginatively explored the possibility of "new paths of oedipalization" and have produced "narratives that offer . . . an alternative to individual quests [resolved by the plot of romance into] couple formation."[60] Narratives of development that move away from the presuppositions of traditional infantile experience and abandon the marriage resolution employ "strategies [that] involve reparenting in invented families, fraternal-sororal ties temporarily reducing romance, and emotional attachments to women in bisexual love plots, female bonding, and lesbianism."[61] Once they have begun to be liberated economically and imaginatively, women have, it seems, increasingly abandoned marriage both in fact and as an ideal. What women—and perhaps men too, if they could but free themselves of the acquisitiveness forced upon them oedipally and economically—require for their flourishing are not the narcissism and struggle for domination that inhabit most marriages, but rather liberation from marriage and the forces that have made it the repressive institution it is.

YET NOW ONE may once again begin to worry. Is the case against marriage as an institution fully compelling? Granting that most marriages are in part motivated by infantile fantasies of completion by the other and by economic necessity, and granting that they are in part nurtured by illusions, are they thoroughly and inevitably so motivated and nurtured? Do these motivations and illusions really *ground* marriages in general and establish their meaning? Is the course of development of a marriage basically shaped by the expectations of those not party to it, and are these expectations so unequivocal? Or do some marriages—some of the ones that last—promote instead the kind of autonomy in relatedness put before us by the religious-masculine ideal? Most of those who have divorced—even most materially independent divorced women—remarry,[62] perhaps seeking some form of relatedness that they continue to value, despite painful experience. Are we so driven in our actions by material and infantile-psychological forces that we cannot rationally hope to transcend the standpoint of contract and the pursuit of the satisfaction of individual needs, to live with one another in creative fidelity to an ongoing project? Do not hopes of this kind continue to move us, dimly and inarticulately? Do they not play some role, beyond those played by material economic and psychological forces, in motivating most marriages and in shaping the expectations of marriage of most people? Are such hopes nothing more than narcissistic infantile fantasies? Compared with such hopes, the alternatives offered by those who reject marriage seem sometimes to embrace the very individualist pursuit of satisfaction that makes our lives detached and hollow. Thus de Beauvoir calls for us to become "entirely self-sufficient human beings"[63] and for "the individual alone to determine"[64] whether to continue or end a relationship. Or, if not individualism, then we are offered revolutionary-apocalyptic fantasies of bonding without conflict and of merged "collective identities." No wonder then that the ideals of seriousness and autonomy in relatedness traditionally associated with marriage continue to move us in some dim region of our being.

And yet the material facts that trouble the embodiments of these ideals persist and prevent us from taking marriage as something to be aspired to without qualification. A compelling but more or less empty ideal of transfigured existence and autonomy in relatedness, an ideal whose actual embodiments are in many ways oppressive, is counterposed in our imaginations to a more or less vulgar materialism of psychological and economic forces, a materialism that cannot see its way clear to compelling ideals. Is there any way to bring ideality and materiality together? What ideals of human life admit of full and fulfilling embodiment?

It is our difficulty with these questions that divides our readings of *Pride and Prejudice,* pushing us back and forth between idealizing readings of Elizabeth and Darcy's accomplishment and materialist dismissals of the novel as an unrealistic fantasy. But it is also about these questions that *Pride and Prejudice* would itself educate us, would help us to reconcile our conflicting imaginations and aspirations—if we can read it alertly and in awareness of our fundamental concern to reconcile the demands of our autonomy and our material embeddedness in lived and embodied ideality.

3. Courtship, Criticism, and the Transfiguration of Experience

Although its action is resolved in a marriage, the opening sentences of *Pride and Prejudice* concisely and summarily enter the materialist case against marriage. At the outset, it is clear that this novel will not simply and unequivocally perpetuate oppressive romantic illusions. We learn that

> It is a truth universally acknowledged, that a single man in possession of a good fortune, must be in want of a wife.
> However little known the feelings or views of such a man may be on his first entering a neighbourhood, this truth is so well fixed in the minds of the surrounding families, that he is considered as the rightful property of some one or other of their daughters. (1)[65]

As we are told here not that a man is in want of a wife, but rather only that one "in possession of a good fortune" is, and as we are told that parents both believe this truth and for their daughters' sakes communicate it to wealthy young male newcomers, it becomes clear that, as Dorothy Van Ghent puts it, "a decorous convention of love (which holds the man to be the pursuer) embraces a savage economic compulsion (the compulsion of the insolvent female to run down male 'property')."[66] Just as the materialist criticism urges, marriage is both a partial solution for a few women to the problem of female dependence and, since the solution is only partial and is limited to a few, also part of the perpetuation of the problem.

The action of the novel then partially qualifies this initial charge against marriage. While many marriages, it remains clear, are principally motivated economically and are both rooted in and perpetuate domination, some marriages—those like Elizabeth and Darcy's, those accomplished under certain conditions, where experience is transfigured through courtship and where marriage is the sanctification and continuation of this transfiguration—are vehicles of worth for those who enter them, are relations through which the dignity and value of persons are nurtured. Such marriages are motivated for both parties not only by economic need or infantile-psychological passion, but also by respect for oneself and the other blended with love. Each party comes to be motivated by respect and love, and to be aware of this motivation, through courtship, particularly through the giving and taking of criticism. The kind of criticism that is at work at the heart of courtship is not, for these parties, ordinary or conventional. It is less a matter of judgment of the other than it is of coming through interaction with the other to appreciate for the first time one's own capacities for an authentic human relationship that expresses one's dignity in the world. Once begun, this kind of interaction becomes self-sustaining, as the parties to it each come to find activity, mood, sense of self, and relationship purposively and fulfillingly intermingled. The process of living responsibly and in responsiveness with one another, blending one another's talk and perception, that is begun in the giving and taking of criticism is what is then sanctified in the marriage. Austen's aim in *Pride and Prejudice* is to show us both how such a marriage is possible and that it is deeply valuable, against an acknowledgment of the depth and power of economic and infantile-psychological needs in human motivation generally. That aim is accomplished as we are shown the education of Elizabeth and Darcy to understanding and appreciation of one another and of themselves as persons capable of respect and responsible love. The marriage they achieve, in impressing us with its value and the difficult transfigurations it requires, then serves as a model for human education and the transfiguration of social relations generally. Their marriage enacts possibilities for the flourishing and fulfillment of persons in community.

Austen emphasizes the distinctiveness, difficulty, and value of the courtship and marriage, of the education and developed characters and relationship, of Elizabeth and Darcy by setting them into juxtaposition with the actions, characters, and marriages of a number of other figures that she deploys in order to deepen the initial case against marriage, against which the marriage of Elizabeth and Darcy stands as argument. A range of generally compromised and less than completely fulfilling marriages, in which characters and perceptions are not transformed, but are rather left painfully if amusingly one-sided, are put before us. These marriages typically match figures of excessive materiality, generally but not exclusively women, dominated by economic needs and by brute passions, with figures of empty ideality, generally but not exclusively men, dominated by an ideal of relationship, yet unable to achieve it, and behaving as withdrawn tyrants in relation to those around them. In these matches, neither party is able to learn from the other, and each becomes an object of both our amusement and our pity.

Among the figures of excessive materiality, the most obvious immediate counterpart to Elizabeth is Charlotte Lucas. Where Elizabeth refuses the pompous Mr. Collins, Charlotte is quick to accept him on wholly economic grounds. As the narrator acquaints us with Charlotte's reflections,

> Mr. Collins to be sure was neither sensible nor agreeable; his society was irksome, and his attachment to her must be imaginary. But still he would be her husband.—Without thinking highly either of men or of matrimony, marriage had always been her object; it was the only honourable provision for well-educated young women of small fortune, and however uncertain of giving happiness, must be their pleasantest preservative from want. This preservative she had now obtained. . . . (86)

Charlotte similarly avows the character of her motives directly to Elizabeth.

> "I am not romantic you know. I never was. I ask only a comfortable home; and considering Mr. Collins's character, connections, and situation in life, I am convinced that my chance of happiness with him is as fair, as most people can boast on entering the marriage state." (88)

In defense of her views and actions, Charlotte urges two central claims: deep and fulfilling attunement between persons is impossible ("Happiness in marriage," Charlotte claims, "is entirely a matter of chance. If the dispositions of the parties are ever so well known to each other, or ever so similar beforehand, it does not advance their felicity in the least. They always continue to grow sufficiently unlike afterwards to have their share of vexation . . ." [15]); and, given our embodiment and the perils of the world, money matters. The second claim is not challenged. And it is part of Austen's charity to find both the truth in the first claim and sympathy for Charlotte. Charlotte's prospects in the world are not good, in light of her unprepossessing appearance, her lack of means, and the unavailability of a public career to her. It is far from extraordinary that such a young woman, in such a situation, should come to think that money matters rather than love, since she lacks the attractiveness and independence that frequently serve as the basis of initial relationship and subsequent attunement. It is no real fault of Charlotte's that she lacks them. Society is rather to be condemned for denying her the means of winning her independence and of displaying her attractiveness of spirit. Thus Charlotte is presented to us as a sensible woman who achieves through her marriage some measure of contentment and independence in her drawing room (116).

Yet, for all her unjust treatment by the world, Charlotte's compromise and denial of the possibility of deep attunement are subjected to criticism. Genuine happiness and fulfillment in marriage, as both Elizabeth and the plot tell us, are not matters of compromise and material comfort, but are rather matters of attunement and intimacy, which are possible, and of the reasonable, principled, cooperative development of persons with integrity. This cooperative development is begun, tested, and sustained in courtship. Any life that lacks it will embody repression of a dimension of our being that is essential to fulfillment. Any marriage accomplished on the basis of a denial of the importance of this dimension of our being may be materially convenient, and may even be preferable to the alternatives plausibly, albeit unjustly, available to some, but cannot be fully in the interest of the person in general. As Elizabeth replies to Jane's defense of Charlotte's prudence in accepting Mr. Collins,

> "My dear Jane, Mr. Collins is a conceited, pompous, narrow-minded, silly man; you know he is, as well as I do; and you must feel, as well as I do, that the woman who marries him, cannot have a proper way of thinking. You shall not defend her, though it is Charlotte Lucas. You shall not, for the sake of one individual, change the meaning of principle and integrity, nor endeavor to persuade yourself or me, that selfishness is prudence, and insensibility of danger, security for happiness." (94)

The sort of marriage that Charlotte favors and accomplishes is *unreasonable*. It depends on a denial of the demands of our nature for fulfillment, and it requires the substitution of either fixed economic motives or fixed passions (in some ways, a similar case) in place of the discovery and development of relatedness and responsiveness to the other as a person. Accomplishing this sort of marriage requires both manipulating the other and compromising one's own integrity and possibilities of development. In full consistency with her views, Charlotte is quick to urge Jane to place herself in Bingley's way and to "shew *more* affection than she feels" (14) in order to make a quick and sure catch of him. Against this suggestion, Elizabeth insists on the possibility and importance of attunement and shared development, rather than material security, and on the importance of courtship as a means of testing for attunement and hence for the reasonableness of one's feelings. Reasonable, natural, nonmanipulative, and noncompromising attachment can proceed only from a proper courtship.

> "Your plan is a good one," replied Elizabeth, "where nothing is in question but the desire of being well married; and if I were determined to get a rich husband, or any husband, I dare say I should adopt it. But these are not Jane's feelings; she is not acting by design. As yet, she cannot even be certain of the degree of her own regard, nor of its reasonableness. She has known him only a fortnight. She danced four dances with him at Meryton; she saw him one morning at his own house, and has since dined in company with him four times. That is not quite enough to make her understand his character." (14)

To the extent that this criticism of Charlotte's views is in order, is accepted by us, it shows that what is in question for us, what we are determined to, is something more than personal satisfaction and manipulation of the other, is reasonable feeling and attunement, not use of the other.

In a somewhat different way, the other figures of excessive materiality—Lydia, Kitty, Mrs. Bennet, and Wickham—similarly fail to see our need for deep attunement and shared purposiveness, favor and (with the exception of Kitty) achieve marriages grounded in passion and accomplished without significant courtship, and act under the domination of unreasonable feeling in a way that compromises their integrity. Lack of integrity is perhaps the most obvious trait of these figures. A certain lability of judgment and attachment, guided by a passion for appearances and entertainments, resolves in their characters into a perpetual sameness, a failure to develop, as unreasonable feeling flits from object to object. This is most evident in the character of Lydia, in whom it is strongest. When she returns, after her unthinking flight with Wickham, with no marriage then in prospect, to her family to be received, thanks to Darcy's intercession. as Wickham's wife, we are told that

Lydia was Lydia still; untamed, unabashed, wild, noisy, and fearless. She turned from sister to sister, demanding their congratulations, and when at length they all sat down, looked eagerly round the room, took notice of some little alteration in it, and observed, with a laugh, that it was a great while since she had been there. (216)

Her very wildness and heedlessness are her constancy, a constancy of character that makes integrity and cooperative development impossible; underlying her wildness are manipulativeness and stasis.[67]

Lydia and Wickham together make "two persons . . . extravagant in their wants, and heedless of the future" (267), and Wickham further shares Lydia's concerns for appearances, personal pleasures, and money, so that continuing in serious and responsive relatedness to another, and in self-integrity, is likewise impossible for him: "His affection for her soon sunk into indifference; her's lasted a little longer" (267). Elizabeth comes to see Wickham's manners as "idle and frivolous gallantry" (160) masking a lack of seriousness and a persistent vanity: "She had even learnt to detect, in the very gentleness which had at first delighted her, an affectation and a sameness to disgust and weary" (160). He lacks the integrity and potential for cooperative development that must sustain a relationship, or a life.

Mrs. Bennet is similarly passionate, constantly inconstant in her judgment, and concerned with appearances and money. The lability of her judgment is evident in her initial "invectives against the villainous conduct of Wickham" (196) upon his running off with Lydia, followed by her delight in their ultimate marriage—"her joy burst forth. . . . She was now in an irritation as violent from delight, as she had ever been fidgety from alarm and vexation" (208)—and her favorable reception of Wickham: "[She] gave her hand with an affectionate smile to Wickham . . . , and wished them both joy, with an alacrity which showed no doubt of their happiness" (216). She is similarly moved by the announcements of the engagements of both Jane—"Wickham, Lydia, were all forgotten. Jane was beyond competition her favourite child" (240)—and Elizabeth.

"Good gracious! Lord bless me! only think! dear me! Mr. Darcy! Who would have thought it! And is it really true? Oh! my sweetest Lizzy! how rich and how great you will be! What pin-money, what jewels, what carriages you will have! Jane's is nothing to it—nothing at all. I am so pleased—so happy. Such a charming man!—so handsome! so tall!— Oh, my dear Lizzy! pray apologise for my having disliked him so much before. I hope he will overlook it. Dear, dear Lizzy. A house in town! Every thing that is charming! Three daughters married! Ten thousand a year! Oh, Lord! What will become of me. I shall go distracted." (261)

"What jewels . . . so handsome! so tall! . . . A house in town! . . . Ten thousand a year!" In these half-sentences, a distracted and disintegrated mind is circling through its persistent obsessions with money and appearances.

The general names in *Pride and Prejudice* for the sort of distractedness of mind, passion for pleasurable entertainments, and concern for appearances and money that Lydia, Wickham, and Mrs. Bennet exhibit are *silliness* and *thoughtlessness,* names that suggest a further connection with Charlotte's *unreasonableness* in suggesting a similar lack of concern for what really matters. As Mr. Bennet reproves Lydia and Kitty, after having suffered their "effusions" on the subject of officers, "From all that I can collect by your manner of talking, you must be two of the silliest girls in the country. I have suspected it some time, but I am now convinced" (19). Similarly, upon reading Lydia's letter describing her elopement, Elizabeth is moved to exclaim "Oh! thoughtless, thoughtless Lydia" (200), evidently assuming that it is this quality of character that has impelled Lydia into her unhappy career. Elizabeth develops this explanation of Lydia's conduct further, in assessing with Mr. and Mrs. Gardiner how likely it is that Lydia has run away with Wickham without marrying.

> "Perhaps I am not doing her justice. But she is very young; she has never been *taught to think* on serious subjects; and for the last half year, nay, for a twelvemonth, she has been given up to nothing but amusement and vanity. She has been allowed to dispose of her time in the most idle and frivolous manner, and to adopt any opinions that came in her way." (193; emphasis added)

Silliness, thoughtlessness, and frivolous use of one's time are generally matters of a taste for divertissements, of consuming one's experience by seeking pleasures in amusements. Lydia and Kitty are concerned daily to "amuse their morning hours" (19), while the "solace" of Mrs. Bennet's life is said to be "visiting and news" (3), and balls and gowns are the usual topics of conversation among the three of them. A concern for expensive clothes, hence for both appearances and money, is the principal mark of a thoughtless passion for amusements. Thus Mrs. Bennet praises Bingley, until she is interrupted, by remarking that "He is so excessively handsome! and his sisters are charming women. I never in my life saw any thing more elegant than their dresses. I dare say the lace upon Mrs. Hurst's gown—" (8). She advises her brother, as he sets off in pursuit of Wickham and Lydia, to "tell [her] not to give any directions about her clothes, till she has seen me, for she does not know which are the best warehouses" (197), and, after their marriage has been arranged, she is moved to exclaim "But the clothes, the wedding clothes! . . . My dear, dear Lydia!—How merry we shall be together when we meet!" (210). In being obsessed with money and appearances, and in individually consuming experience thoughtlessly, treating it as a storehouse of amusements, these figures are unaware of their possibilities of and needs for deep attunement and shared purposiveness. And in this unawareness they are silly, are incapable, in the absence of a transformation of character, of serious relationship and activity. Their excesses of material concern betray their very humanity.

The counterpoint to these figures of excessive materiality is provided in Mr. Collins, Mary, and, above all, Mr. Bennet, figures who think, but emptily, as a form of withdrawal from human relationship into hollow ideals. Their characters are dominated by a kind of heedlessness of others that is expressed in stiffness, abstraction, and inappropriate behavior. Mr. Collins, we discover, studies not for understanding but in order to flatter his patron in elegant phrases (47). Not only amusement, but also anything that might be called engagement with either others or topics of common concern, is far from his mind. Upon being invited to read aloud to the Misses Bennet, and then finding himself presented with a book already begun, Mr. Collins "protest[s] that he never read novels" and chooses instead Fordyce's *Sermons to Young Women* (47). In Elizabeth's judgment, "there is something very pompous in his stile" of writing, while Mr. Bennet finds in his letter "a mixture of servility and self-importance" that suggests he is "quite the reverse" of sensible (44). For Mr. Collins, books and stilted oratory are the means of self-protective flight into unresponsive high-mindedness. He is unable to be genuinely self-responsible and responsive to others, as his immersion in baroque abstractions blocks an awareness, which he might be unable to bear, of his own and others' needs.

Mary, though still young, shows every sign of replicating Mr. Collins's character. Upon being asked by her father for an opinion as "a young lady of deep reflection . . . [prone to] read great books and make extracts," Mary, we discover, "wished to say something very sensible, but knew not how" (4). Later, after the discovery of Lydia's flight, Mary's orotund and unfeeling "moral extractions from the evil before them" leave Elizabeth in silent "amazement," as Mary is unable to engage with either Lydia's plight or Elizabeth's response to it (198). Her moral extractions are for her flights from others and from herself.

Among these figures of empty ideality, interest in books plays virtually the same role in signaling distractedness of mind and disregard of others as that played by interest in clothes among the figures of excessive materiality. The extent of Mr. Bennet's engagement with others is thus open to question, as we discover that he is "regardless of time" (7) with a book and that he asks Mr. Collins to go out walking with his daughters because he is "anxious to get rid of him, and have his library to himself" so that he may be "sure of leisure and tranquility" (49). His withdrawals into his library bespeak an irresponsible and unresponsive failure of attention to others that amounts to a narcissistic aloofness. Elizabeth notes in particular "the mischief of neglect and mistaken indulgence" on her father's part toward Lydia (191) and "the little attention he has ever seemed to give to what was going forward in his family" (193). He acquires his wife for her beauty and his amusement, as one might with detachment acquire a bauble, and he treats her accordingly.

> . . . captivated by youth and beauty, and that appearance of good humour, which youth and beauty generally give, [he] had married a woman whose weak understanding and illiberal mind, had very early in their marriage put an end to all real affection for her. Respect, esteem, and confidence, had vanished for ever; and all his views of domestic happiness were overthrown. But Mr. Bennet was not of a disposition to seek comfort for the disappointment which his own imprudence had brought on, in any of those pleasures which too often console the unfortunate for their folly or their vice. He was fond of the country and of books; and from these tastes had arisen his principal enjoyments. To his wife he was very little otherwise indebted, than as her ignorance and folly had contributed to his amusements. This is not the sort of happiness which a man would in general wish to own to his wife; but where other powers of entertainment are wanting, the true philosopher will derive benefit from such as are given. (162–63)

With such altered views of domestic happiness, finding in his marriage not attunement and shared purposiveness, but rather finding in his wife, in his books, in, it seems, whatever experiences he values only amusements and entertainments, Mr. Bennet is led to a "continual breach of conjugal obligation and decorum, [thus] exposing his wife to the contempt of her own children" (163). He has become unable to find, either in his wife or in the books with which he occupies himself, anything other than entertainments, so that he is in the end "perhaps . . . lucky" in his wife's failing to become "a sensible, amiable, well-informed woman," since he "might not have relished domestic felicity in so unusual a form" (266). His life has become a series of disengaged entertainments, and he has lost the sense that anything else matters. It is thus no surprise that he should rhetorically, and no more than half ironically, ask Elizabeth, "For what do we live, but to make sport for our neighbours, and laugh at them in our turn?" (251). The amusing, and only the amusing, is what he has come to care about. His initial seriousness, exemplified in his concern for books, has been betrayed by his failure to engage with and respect his wife, so that even his books have now themselves become empty distractions. As is the case with Mr. Collins and Mary, he is now able only to flee from others, not engage with them.

Although excessive materiality, whether economic or passionate, and empty ideality are each subjected to criticism through the development of the characters of Charlotte and Mr. Collins, Lydia and Wickham and Mary, and Mr. and Mrs. Bennet, there is no single figure, against whom they might be measured, who perfectly blends ideality and materiality. Elizabeth and Darcy are more complex and mixed figures than these more simple types; each both maintains ideals and is motivated economically and passionately. Each both reads books and goes to balls. They both periodically distance themselves from others through their reading, using that reading to reflect on their situations and relations, and they both display economic and psychological passion: Elizabeth in her initial attractions to Wickham and to Darcy (where much of the attraction is economic and is masked by self-protective wit[68]), and Darcy in his continuing passion for Elizabeth and his pride in his situation. But neither is a figure who manages individually to blend reflective ideality and material passion in a wholly satisfactory way. Each makes significant errors of judgment, failing initially to see how ideals and passions may be blended and lived out with another: Elizabeth in accepting uncritically Wickham's account of his past history with Darcy, an error of defensive prejudice, and Darcy in presuming on the attractions of his station in proposing to Elizabeth, an error of pride. Only in relation with one another are they able to bring their passions and ideals into alignment and to satisfying fulfillment. In this way Austen makes it clear that our deep needs as persons can be satisfied only in a community of respect, where there are attunement and shared purposiveness.

The marriage of Elizabeth and Darcy is thus the embodiment of the positive interaction of material demands and ideal conceptions. But it is neither a direct balancing of opposed types nor a simple blending or merging of what already is. If the mere balancing of opposed characters were the achievement in question, then it is hard to see how the marriages of Charlotte and Mr. Collins or of Mr. and Mrs. Bennet would count as less than ideal. What is achieved is not the simple conciliation of given forces or characters in conflict. The narrative of the marriage of Elizabeth and Darcy is the story not only of the matching of prejudice and passion in Elizabeth with pride and stiffness in Darcy. It involves further the chastening, education, and trans-figuration of each by the other along multiple dimensions, as each comes to discover the possibility and value of deep attunement and shared purposiveness with the other. What is begun between them in courtship, and then sanctified in marriage, is a process of development in relatedness, not a state of balance. It is essential to the differences that divide Elizabeth and Darcy from the various other characters and to the value of their accomplished marriage that their courtship pro-ceeds through a growth in self-consciousness, a change in character, that amounts to a moral *Bildung* in our capabilities and possibilities as persons.

The virtues, or more particularly the *Bildungsqualitäten*, the capac-ities of moral education that are exhibited and furthered through their courtship, are themselves essentially qualities that are progressively acquired. As Richard Simpson observes, Austen

> contemplates virtues, not as fixed quantities, or as definable qualities, but as continual struggles and conquests, as progressive states of mind, advancing by repulsing their contraries, or losing ground by being over-come. . . . A character therefore unfolded itself to her, not in statuesque repose, not as a model without motion, but as a dramatic sketch, a living history, a composite force, which could only exhibit what it was by exhibiting what it did.[69]

If we are to honor the marriage of Elizabeth and Darcy, and accept it as an accomplishment, then these developing *Bildungsqualitäten* that lead to it must be both the ground and the consequence of their rela-tionship. They must both enable and require partial breaks from their pasts for each of them. They must emerge and develop essentially through Elizabeth and Darcy's interaction; they must not be assumed or attributed to a deus ex machina in order to prop up romantic fan-tasies. These *Bildungsqualitäten* must be possessed by the pair not simply as a result of material forces and past experience (in that case the marriage would not be their achievement), and not simply by fiat, out of nowhere (in that case the plot would be an illusion-nurturing set piece). Through the development of these qualities as ground and consequence of the relationship, throughout the courtship, Elizabeth and Darcy must come to a lived understanding of the capacities and possibilities of persons in relationship.

The discovery, exercise, and development of these crucial *Bild-ungsqualitäten* proceeds out of the initial complex characters and mixed ideal and material motivations of Darcy and Elizabeth. Darcy, we discover, is, in the words of Miss Bingley, "always buying books," and he confesses in reply that he "cannot comprehend the neglect of a family library" (25). Given the role in *Pride and Prejudice* of an interest in books as an indication of a narcissistic, withdrawing character, it is no surprise that at the initial Meryton assembly he is "discovered to be proud, to be above his company, and above being pleased" (6). His character evidently includes a tendency to refuse engagement and intimacy. He appears to be "inflexibly studious" (38). Yet at the same time he is open to being "caught by [the] easy playfulness" of Elizabeth's eyes (16), so that the abstractness and reflectiveness evidenced in his interest in books are already somewhat leavened, or can be, by his passion for a particular other. Elizabeth is lively, impertinent, and prone in the manner of Mrs. Bennet and Lydia to seek entertainments and amusements, in her case in teasing conversation. The defensiveness she displays in the course of her teasing is a sign of her material concerns,[70] which she likewise shares with her mother and youngest sister. Yet her character is also mixed, and her motivations are complex, in the manner of Darcy. Though she is quick to add qualifications, Elizabeth is said by Miss Bingley, in scorn, to be "a great reader," just after she has to the astonishment of Mr. Hurst chosen to "stay below with a book" in preference to a game of cards (25). Her reading, moreover, is not confined to libraries. As Bingley observes, Elizabeth is "a studier of character" (29), a reader of the manners and motives of others. Her real material concerns do not wholly inhibit her capacities for study and reflection. And her study of books has deepened her in, not distracted her from, her study of the world.

It is at the outset unclear, however, what will ensue from Elizabeth's and Darcy's respective mixed capacities for reflectiveness, passion, and material concern. The tragedy in *Pride and Prejudice* is that Mr. and Mrs. Bennet, it is suggested, might well at a certain time in their lives have had similarly mixed capacities that have fallen into desuetude through want of exercise and attention from the other. How can Elizabeth and Darcy manage to avoid this fate?

Their achievement begins in their first conversation, their first direct interaction, at the Lucas party. Motivated in part by defensive pride at the slighting of her by Darcy that she had overheard at the Meryton assembly, Elizabeth speaks to Darcy impertinently, asking for praise for a judgment and a manner of speech that from his stiff manner she knows him to scorn. "Did you not think, Mr. Darcy," Elizabeth asks, "that I expressed myself uncommonly well just now, when I was teazing Colonel Forster to give us a ball at Meryton?" (15). The sheer surprise to Darcy of this impertinent remark is breathtaking. In baiting him, hoping to lead him to show himself badly in the eyes of the others assembled, Elizabeth has, inadvertently, done what apparently no one else is able to do with Darcy: she has treated him as a subject, not an object; she has issued a challenge to his responsiveness, rather than pursued him as an object with flatteries and insinuations. It is just this treatment as a subject that Darcy has lacked, defined as he is for many by his wealth and eligibility for marriage, and surrounded by figures such as the transparently designing Miss Bingley, who herself confesses that she knows not how to tease him and laugh at him (39). It is, for him, exhilarating, and he is quick to return the treatment in observing—despite his having marked her "uncommonly intelligent" face (15), which sets her apart—that the subject of balls "always makes a lady energetic" (16). In this exchange, Elizabeth and Darcy have, however inadvertently, already begun to be subjects for one another, discovering all at once their attunement, their capacity for it, and its value.

Although their engagement is here begun, it is not more than begun. Their capacities for deep attunement and shared purposiveness must be further tested and developed—perhaps this first interaction was merely accidental—in order that their marriage may sanctify an achieved mode of relationship. Both Elizabeth and Darcy attest the importance of courtship as a vehicle for that growth in understanding and relatedness which alone can make an attachment reasonable and expressive of respect for oneself and the other. Elizabeth, in responding to Charlotte's view of courtship, notes the importance of coming to "understand [the] character" of the other (14), while Darcy similarly criticizes Miss Bingley's imagination for its "jumps from admiration to love, from love to matrimony in a moment" (18), so that the importance of courtship is overlooked.

And more even than as a test of what is given in the other, each understands courtship as a vehicle for the criticism and transformation of each party. This understanding comes out most clearly in their common rejection of the idea that cunning in the service of passion is our chief virtue. Darcy observes that "whatever bears affinity to cunning is despicable" (27), and Elizabeth rejects Charlotte's plan of "acting by design" (14). In thus criticizing cunning, they show that something more is in question for them than the satisfaction of passions and desires that are already given in them as individuals. If that were their chief end, then cunning would be altogether appropriate. Instead they seek in relationship what might be called mutual creative articulation or constructiveness, as though the setting up and continuance of something between them were to introduce its own imperatives and conditions of fulfillment, thus transforming the initial structure of ends of each. Each will have to acknowledge and learn to appreciate these new imperatives and conditions. They must come to understand the restructuring of their ends as already under way and as of value. And if each knows abstractly from the beginning that this is the proper work of courtship, each nonetheless fails in the beginning to live out this understanding. As their interactions begin, the chief motivations of both Elizabeth and Darcy are passionate and economic. They begin with one another, as the darker reading sees, in narrowly individual self-concern. And then, through their inadvertent interactions, they go on to discover the possibility and value of relatedness concretely, as something they live. Essential to the progress of their relationship through courtship is a sense of the continuous opening up of valuable possibilities for attunement and purposiveness with *this* other that have been dimly in preparation, that draw them forward, and that reshape their lived senses of what matters. Their abstract understandings must be brought to life. Courtship becomes a necessary animation of abstract possibilities, an adventure and education in what is concretely possible.

What sustain this courtship are notably the making and the acceptance of criticism, of both self and other, as each comes to share in the continuous and fulfilling realization of attunement and purposiveness. In this criticism of self and other, play and seriousness are blended to give seriousness a home in the world, rather than leave it isolated in stiffness. A sense of the importance of criticism, and of criticism as itself a mode of fulfilling relationship, is displayed by Elizabeth and Darcy early on in their interactions. In a conversation at Netherfield during Jane's brief illness there, they take up the topic of one another's vices, as Darcy remarks that

> "There is, I believe, in every disposition a tendency to some particular evil, a natural defect, which not even the best education can overcome."
> "And *your* defect is a propensity to hate every body."
> "And yours," he replied with a smile, "is wilfully to misunderstand them." (40)

The initial dark thought of Darcy's, which Elizabeth apparently accepts, should not obscure either the fact of agreement between them or the fact that they manage to go on from it, to specific criticism, in acknowledgment of it, or taking it into account. Our lives and communities do not admit of full perfection. Faced with death, and hence with the necessity of self-assertively shaping our lives within a finite time, we are prone both to manifest our individual energies excessively and irresponsibly, in the manner of Lydia or even of Elizabeth in certain moments, and to lapse into passive and mechanical acquiescence in empty relationships and activities, in the manner of Mr. Bennet or even of Darcy in certain moments. These are our various tendencies to particular evils. Against these tendencies, these natural ways of failing to achieve integrated humanity in community, there is all too little that education in doctrine or morals or manners can do. Such flourishings and fulfillments as there can be for beings situated under the necessity of self-assertiveness can proceed only from an acknowledgment of our finitude and of these tendencies. Flourishing and fulfillment are to be ongoing partial achievements managed in relatedness to another with whom one shares an understanding of our situation and our tendencies, and who is acute in uncovering our particular failures. To acknowledge the other as a co-critic is to come to terms constructively with our finitude, so that our lives are directed through attunement and shared purposiveness toward integrated humanity in community. Accepting Darcy's thought about the limits of education, it is this acknowledgment of the other and engagement in criticism that Elizabeth and Darcy achieve in their immediate remarks to one another. Here in the making and accepting of criticism, which is at the same time play, within the frame of a sense of the limits of education, are the *Bildungsqualitäten* that are essential to full human relationship and integrity.

The subsequent interactions between Elizabeth and Darcy then serve to deepen and develop these *Bildungsqualitäten*. In Elizabeth, the full exercise and appreciation of these *Bildungsqualitäten* are achieved initially as a result of her reading of Darcy's letter in explanation of his influence on Bingley and his treatment of Wickham. Upon thinking over Darcy's letter, Elizabeth is moved to self-criticism and to see connections between self-knowledge, ongoing criticism, humility, reason, and justice.

> "How despicably have I acted!" she cried.—"I, who have prided myself on my discernment!—I, who have valued myself on my abilities: who have often disdained the generous candour of my sister, and gratified my vanity, in useless or blameable distrust.—How humiliating is this discovery!—Yet how just a humiliation!—Had I been in love, I could not have been more wretchedly blind. But vanity, not love, has been my folly.—Pleased with the preference of one, and offended by the neglect of the other, on the very beginning of our acquaintance, I have courted prepossession and ignorance, and driven reason away, where either were concerned. Till this moment, I never knew myself." (143–44)

The criticism of her own vanity that Elizabeth here lodges depends essentially on her emerging understanding of the importance of criticism and community to reasonable judgment, just responsiveness, and self-responsibility. Her failure has been to suppose that she can achieve these things on her own. In pride in herself, she had denied to herself that they can be achieved only as one judges from a background of shared norms of judgment and response, taking these norms and the perceptions of others into account, and then going on. Rather than doing this, Elizabeth has, until now, attempted to go on in judgment and in relation to others only on her own, and prematurely. And hence she has failed to exercise her capacities for reasonable judgment, just responsiveness, and self-responsibility, and failed further to see that she has failed. Her judgments and responses had been both blind and inexpressive of her capacities. Now she has at last come to see that reasonable and just self-responsibility must be in part a gift of mutual criticism within social relationship. Alone one must flounder, as Elizabeth sees in continuing her criticism: "And yet I meant to be uncommonly clever in taking so decided a dislike to him, without any reason. It is such a spur to one's genius, such an opening for wit to have a dislike of that kind" (155). If full self-responsibility and human community in which our capacities are exercised require us to go forward on our own from given norms of judgment and response, going forward also has its risks. One can turn out to be only uncommonly clever, without any reason.

Darcy comes to the same understanding of criticism and humility as conditions of self-knowledge and self-responsibility as he comes to see and to criticize his own selfishness. Unlike Elizabeth's, however, Darcy's development in this direction occurs largely offstage, and we become aware of it only through Elizabeth's reading of it. There is no climactic scene of a change in self-understanding on Darcy's part. Instead, with Elizabeth, we first read his letter of explanation and then become aware of a change in his manner. We discover that Elizabeth, in meeting Darcy at Pemberley, saw in him

> an expression of general complaisance, and in all that he said, she heard an accent so far removed from hauteur or disdain of his companions, as convinced her that the improvement of manners which she had yesterday witnessed, however temporary its existence might prove, had at least outlived one day. . . . Never . . . had she seen him so desirous to please, so free from self-consequence, or unbending reserve as now, when no importance could result from the success of his endeavours. . . . (179)

Elizabeth is struck not only by his changed manners, but also by his estate. She confesses to Jane that she "must date [my love for Darcy] from my first seeing his beautiful grounds at Pemberley" (258). Here it is not simply, and not even primarily, that Elizabeth has been struck by Darcy's wealth, and hence his eligibility ("And of this place . . . I might have been mistress!" [167] she thinks as she first sees Pemberley): she had been all too aware of his wealth all along. Rather she has come, under the pressure already provided by the letter, to see the man in his estate. Darcy's full character, in both its fixed and changed aspects, is thus revealed, to Elizabeth and to us, not directly through confession, but through his letter, his manner, and his estate, which serve as the clothes and embodiments of his spirit.[71]

That Darcy's development in self-understanding occurs offstage and is evidenced in his writing, his manners, and his estate is crucial to the return of Elizabeth's confidence in herself as a reader of character, and, as we are shown the development of her skill and the return of her confidence, we further discover the conditions of positive critical understanding of the other. As she sets the letter, the manners, and the estate against one another, she begins to be able, as it were, to put the inner and the outer together again, seeing his character in its expressions. She becomes a reader of character who has overcome the rote habits of reading dominant in her past and in her family and who has resisted the temptations to ignore outer evidences and to flee into individual fantasy. She has managed to see things anew responsibly, to find, in reconnecting inner and outer, meaning that others can endorse. This achievement makes the healing and continuance of human relationship possible.

The self-understanding that Darcy acquires is virtually identical with Elizabeth's, as Darcy too connects self-knowledge, ongoing criticism, humility, reason, and justice with one another. The acknowledgment of these interconnections is here in Darcy, as in Elizabeth, the maturation of the *Bildungsqualitäten* that are essential to their relationship. The first direct characterization of the maturation of these *Bildungsqualitäten* in Darcy appears in Mrs. Gardiner's letter to Elizabeth in explanation of Darcy's role in effecting the marriage of Lydia and Wickham. As Mrs. Gardiner reports Darcy's first conversation with her husband concerning Lydia's flight with Wickham,

> He generously imputed the whole to his mistaken pride, and confessed that he had before thought it beneath him, to lay his private actions open to the world. His character was to speak for itself. He called it, therefore, his duty to step forward, and endeavour to remedy an evil, which had been brought on by himself. (220)

Evidently Darcy has begun to see that reserve and withdrawal can mask hollowness and irresponsibility. Openness to criticism from

others—accepting one's legibility to others, and its liabilities, no longer trying to speak only for oneself—may, Darcy implicitly
acknowledges, be essential to the recognition and removal of self-
stultifying masks. Darcy's understanding of the importance of criticism for self-knowledge, reasonableness, justice, and self-
responsibility is yet more explicit in the account of his past that he
offers to Elizabeth in the end.

> I have been a selfish being all my life, in practice, though not in principle.
> As a child I was taught what was *right*, but I was not taught to correct my
> temper. I was given good principles, but left to follow them in pride and
> conceit. Unfortunately an only son, (for many years an only *child*) I was
> spoilt by my parents, who though good themselves, (my father particu-
> larly, all that was benevolent and amiable,) allowed, encouraged, almost
> taught me to be selfish and overbearing, to care for none beyond my own
> family circle, to think meanly of all the rest of the world, to *wish* at least to
> think meanly of their sense and worth compared with my own. Such I
> was, from eight to eight and twenty; and such I might still have been but
> for you. . . . (254)

No principles are self-interpreting. Keeping on one's own to formulae
will end in conceit and meanness, in unreasonableness and injustice.
The only cure is criticism from and with another, the work of seeing
from a number of angles what it makes sense to say about one's judgments, responses, and actions. The *Bildungsqualitäten* of making and
accepting criticism have here come to maturity in Darcy's recognition
of the permanence of our need for them.

The maturation of these *Bildungsqualitäten* in both Elizabeth and
Darcy brings with it an immediate change in each one's sense and
appreciation of the other. Elizabeth, though she thinks it impossible as
a result of Lydia's attachment to Wickham, acknowledges that she and
Darcy might have made together a "marriage [that] could now teach
the admiring multitude what connubial felicity really was" (214)—a
marriage, that is, that lives through their mutual exercise of these
matured *Bildungsqualitäten*. Just after renewing his proposal of marriage, Darcy similarly connects his renewed affections with a change in
himself, brought about by Elizabeth, that enables them to go on with
one another as persons, in dignity and nonmanipulatively. ". . . dear-
est, loveliest Elizabeth! What do I not owe you! You taught me a lesson,
hard indeed at first, but most advantageous. By you I was properly
humbled. I came to you without a doubt of my reception. You shewed
me how insufficient were all my pretensions to please a woman
worthy of being pleased" (254–55). Where previously he had pre-
sumed on his wealth and appearance, treating Elizabeth as a thing that

might be caught by them, as a needle is drawn by a magnet, now he has learned to treat her, and accept treatment from her, as a person capable of an independent view of things. And he has learned both to value this mode of interaction and to live in it concretely, as it joins for him both seriousness and play, joins for him his ideal autonomy and the natural ways of the world and his sentiments. In the maturation of their *Bildungsqualitäten*, they have come to be for one another subjects, not objects.

The relationship that is here achieved is far from coldly intellectual or passionless. (Intellectualism, with its own underlying narcissistic passions, is rather associated with withdrawals and empty ideality, in the manner of Mr. Collins and Mr. Bennet.) Both Darcy and Elizabeth comment on the changed and deepened character of their feelings. Where he had previously been rightly thought by Elizabeth to be, as he puts it, "devoid of every proper feeling" (253), Darcy now finds in Elizabeth's acceptance of him a "happiness . . . such as he had probably never felt before" (252). Although Elizabeth has remained constantly the object of what he calls his "unchanged . . . affections and wishes" (252), he has, in his new understanding and appreciation of her capacities and his own, achieved a new quality of feeling, a new happiness. Elizabeth similarly comes to feel for Darcy not the delights she had once taken in Wickham's company, but rather an "interest . . . [that is] reasonable and just" (229). After she and Darcy have come to their understanding with one another, and as she contemplates the difficulties the announcement of her engagement will raise in her family, "Elizabeth, agitated and confused, rather *knew* that she was happy, than *felt* herself to be so" (257). This then is a happiness that is capable of being known, attended to, not something that simply sweeps over one, in the manner of a sudden pain. The happiness that is here in question is bound up with a lived understanding of oneself and the other and the relationship achieved. Just as one can be properly angry only if one has been wronged, so one can be happy in *this* way only in and through this relationship of being subjects for one another. Feeling and understanding have become intermingled through the progress of the relationship to produce a happiness that is different in kind from the satisfaction, and hence temporary extinction, of a given passion. This happiness in relationship more nearly resembles joy or enjoyment in activity than pleasant sensation. Its continuance both frees one from the consumption of experience and demands sanctification.

Austen herself explicitly stakes her claim as a novelist on our interest in the possibility and value of this sort of happiness, mingling feeling and understanding, for this pair. The work of *Pride and*

Prejudice has been to bring us to awareness and appreciation of its possibility and value.

> If gratitude and esteem are good foundations of affection, Elizabeth's change of sentiment will be neither improbable nor faulty. But if otherwise, if the regard springing from such sources is unreasonable or unnatural, in comparison of what is so often described as arising on a first interview with its object, and even before two words have been exchanged, nothing can be said in her defence, except that she had given somewhat of a trial to the latter method, in her partiality for Wickham, and that its ill-success might perhaps authorise her to seek the other less interesting mode of attachment. Be that as it may. . . . (190–91)

Gratitude, esteem, and affection, all intermingled, are the natural responses to the other with whom the maturation of our *Bildungsqualitäten* has been cooperatively achieved. So intermingled, they compose a way of happiness in relationship that fulfills the deepest demands of our nature.

The cooperative development of these *Bildungsqualitäten* that draws and moves us has no clear *archē*. One will find oneself aware of this development, and of these qualities, only, if at all, as one is already under way. As Elizabeth says of her love for Darcy, "It has been coming on so gradually that I hardly know when it began" (258). Darcy, having shared in this development, seconds this thought: "I cannot fix on the hour, on the spot, or the look, or the words, which laid the foundation. It is too long ago. I was in the middle before I knew that I *had* begun" (262). For a discrete need or desire that one in advance knows oneself to possess, it is typically possible to say when one first recognized that the means of satisfaction were at hand. For the deeper demand made on us by these *Bildungsqualitäten*, a demand that is discovered only as their development is already begun, the first awareness of the happiness achieved through their development will take the form of an awareness that one is already under way in relationship, that one has always already begun. Through the development of these *Bildungsqualitäten* we do not simply pleasantly fulfill a recognized lack, as a hamburger for a time fills a hunger. Rather we discover, exercise, and develop our capacities for deep attunement and shared purposiveness, in doing so flourishing and enjoying ourselves in actuality, as the members of an orchestra perhaps actualize their possibilities in playing with one another.

The development of these *Bildungsqualitäten* further has no perfectly achievable endpoint. It rather inhabits the continuous maintenance of a *way* of relationship, involving action and utterance proceeding from both spontaneity and discipline, individuality and principle, involving awareness of the impossibility, given our finitude, of the full perfection of self and relationship (the dark thought of the limits of education), hence involving awareness of the ongoing need for confession and forgiveness in order to stay in relationship. Confession and forgiveness each proceed from the internalization of a critical sense of the other—of the other's autonomy and intelligibility in judgment and expression, and of that autonomy as mirror and support of oneself. They are the sign of the inner acknowledgment of the other's perceptions and responses, of an achieved autonomy in relatedness. Within this way of relationship, the agent, who acts in a particular way against a background of norms, as Hegel puts it,

> does not merely find himself apprehended by the other as something alien and disparate from [him], but rather finds that other, according to its own nature and disposition, identical with himself. Perceiving this identity and giving utterance to it, he confesses this to the other, and equally expects that the other, having in fact put himself on the same level, will also respond in words in which he will give utterance to this identity with him, and expects that this mutual recognition will now exist in fact. His confession is not an abasement, a humiliation, a throwing-away of himself in relation to the other; for this utterance is not a one-sided affair, which would establish his disparity with the other: on the contrary, he gives himself utterance solely on account of his having seen his identity with the other; he, on his side, gives expression to their common identity in his confession . . . , [until there emerges from the other] the word of reconciliation [that] is the *objectively* existent Spirit, which beholds the pure knowledge of itself *qua universal* essence, in its opposite . . . —a reciprocal recognition which is *absolute* Spirit. . . . The reconciling *Yea*, in which the two "I"s let go their antithetical existence . . . is God manifested in the midst of those who know themselves. . . .[72]

Within this way of relationship, maintained by confession and forgiveness, that serves in furtherance of our *Bildungsqualitäten*, we can attain, within time and embodiment, to the self-understanding and fulfillment of which we are capable, remaining in the world and in relationship while exercising our autonomy against and with the other. And so Elizabeth and Darcy confess and forgive: "I have long been most heartily ashamed of ['what I then said' in rejecting you]" (254). But "my behaviour to you at the time . . . merited the severest reproof. It was unpardonable" (253). "I am convinced that [my letter] was written in a dreadful bitterness of spirit" (254). "The letter, perhaps, began in bitterness, but it did not end so. The adieu is charity itself. But think no more of [it]" (254).

That this way of relationship—furthering our *Bildungsqualitäten*, our very personhood, through criticism, confession, and forgiveness—is now in place does not guarantee that it will be maintained. There will be problems to be faced. Our finitude necessarily particularizes us along certain paths, which may grow apart. Education cannot perfect us or our relationships (again the dark thought). There remain the facts of gender and social role, and of class, where the possession of money must separate us from the concerns of many. These will remain problems for Elizabeth and Darcy, problems to which they may or may not be equal. Time and responsibility for one's activities and relations in the world are not stopped at the moment of even the happiest of marriages. Unanticipated tragedies can always happen: childlessness or death or the loss of fortune or bitterness in one's lot. It is possible to find oneself wanting to know how this pair will have lived together: how they have raised or refused children, abided with their neighbors, accumulated and disposed property, faced the problems of their gender and wealth, enjoyed and educated or antagonized and shunned one another. One may well wonder whether they will have continued in cooperative relationship with one another, in both seriousness and play, or whether, partially apart from the world and in reaction to its expectations of them, they will have lapsed into disengagement and exclusive self-concern. Yet, for all that one may wonder these things, one may also sometimes find oneself trusting that, in the achievement of this way of relationship, of criticism, confession, and forgiveness, Elizabeth and Darcy have entered, so far as we can judge, a way of happiness that is open to us as finitely embodied subjects in a shadowed world.

EPILOGUE: THE USES OF NARRATIVE—PARTIALITY AND DIFFERENCE, SELF-UNDERSTANDING AND VALUE

She passed a boy and girl who were standing in the center of the sidewalk, holding hands, the girl pivoting on her heels and giving the boy a shy smile. It was heartbreaking. She would have stopped to set them straight, but of course they wouldn't believe her; they imagined they were going to do everything differently. . . . Sometimes she thought the trouble was, she and Leon were too well acquainted. The most innocent remark could call up such a string of associations, so many past slights and insults never quite settled or forgotten, merely smoothed over. They could no longer have a single uncomplicated feeling about each other.

    Anne Tyler, *Morgan's Passing*

This crossing a letter is not without its association—for chequer work leads us naturally to a Milkmaid, a Milkmaid to Hogarth Hogarth to Shakespeare Shakespear to Hazlitt—Hazlitt to Shakespeare and thus by merely pulling an apron string we set a pretty peal of Chimes at work—Let them chime on while, with your patience,—I will return to Wordsworth—whether or no he has an extended vision or a circumscribed grandery—whether he is an eagle in his nest, or on the wing—And to be more explicit and to show you how tall I stand by the giant, I will put down a simile of human life as far as I now perceive it. . . .

    John Keats, Letter to John Hamilton Reynolds (3 May 1818)

There are these protagonists: Jim and Marlow, the poet-narrators of "Resolution and Independence" and "Frost at Midnight," and Elizabeth and Darcy. Each of them achieves an understanding and expression of our personhood, acknowledging both our peculiarly human autonomy and our essential embeddedness in nature and in society, in having and exercising our deliberative capacities. It is possible to take the careers of these protagonists abstractly described as manifesting a shared moral personhood and as exemplifying various dimensions of its best possibilities of expression in activity and relationship in the world.

But how consistent and coherent are these achievements? What do the careers of these protagonists have in common? Each achievement in understanding our moral personhood and expressing it in activity and social relations remains marked by particularity. In the various contexts of their careers, only certain expressions, different expressions, of our personhood are possible. Desires and fantasies that are in part particular to individuals—Jim's need to escape from life, Marlow's need to talk, Wordsworth's and Coleridge's fantasies of reception, Elizabeth's desire for security, and Darcy's need for possession—continue to be legible within each achievement. Signally, the ends to which the protagonists come are very different: Jim dies, Marlow talks, Wordsworth and Coleridge fantasize about their futures as teachers, and Elizabeth and Darcy marry. What sense can there be to the suggestion that these various achievements and ends manifest both a shared moral personhood and various yet coherent possibilities for its authentic and full expression in context?

In recent years, the thought has arisen that narrative accounts of careers, whether fictional or actual, if they are fully developed, *could not be* consistent and coherent in expressing a shared personhood, for any life must rest on and express quite particular choices among an unmanageable and incommensurable plurality of goods. It is particular desire, rather than understanding of a shared nature, that inevitably determines choices among these goods and hence gives each life its particular shape. As Bernard Williams puts it,

> The *I* that stands back in rational reflection from my desires is still the *I* that has those desires and will, empirically and concretely, act; and it is not, simply by standing back in reflection, converted into a being whose fundamental interest lies in the harmony of all interests. It cannot, just by taking this step, acquire the motivations of justice.[1]

We may, of course, try all at once to repress the particularity and the vagrancy of desire, to deny the incommensurability of the goods toward which desire points us, and to rationalize ourselves and our deliberations, hoping to make our deliberations approximate the working of an algorithm. But while these repressions, denials, and rationalizations are a possible mode of human life, are perhaps even, as Williams suggests,[2] a natural response to the dislocations and bureaucratizations involved in the processes of modernization, they are nonetheless possibilities of life that are rooted in denials of facts of our practical life, hence possibilities of life that are flawed, or self-mutilating, or regressive. In Martha Nussbaum's formulation,

. . . that much that I did not make goes toward making me whatever I shall be praised or blamed for being; that I must constantly choose among competing and apparently incommensurable goods and that circumstances may force me to a position in which I cannot help being false to something or doing some wrong; that an event that simply happens to me may, without my consent, alter my life; that it is equally problematic to entrust one's good to friends, lovers, or country and to try to have a good life without them—all these I take to be not just the material of tragedy, but everyday facts of lived practical reason.[3]

Against this background conception of the incommensurability of goods and of the primacy of desire in deliberation, morality—the effort to articulate universal principles for the fit expression of our personhood, principles understood as pieces of objective self-legislation on the part of persons in general—will appear as an imposition, as an effort to deflect the attentions of agents from their multiple natural concerns. As Williams sees it, morality, in seeking universal principles of value applicable to all actions, tries "to make as many [considerations that are relevant to action] as possible into obligations [that are commensurable]. . . . Morality encourages the idea, *only an obligation can beat an obligation*."[4] Morality asks us to see all our actions as properly structured and informed by the requirements of universal principles of duty or of obligation. But, given the ways in which people inevitably do come to act out of particular desires and multiple concerns, taking up the invitation of morality is a terrible mistake.

An obligation is a special kind of consideration, with a general relation to importance and immediacy. The case we are considering [furthering a political cause at the cost of failing to make a promised visit to a friend] is simply one in which there is a consideration important enough to outweigh this obligation on this occasion, and it is cleaner just to say so.[5]

The effort of the moralists to articulate general principles of duty or right conduct that will enable us to cast both considerations, furthering a cause and visiting a friend as promised, as commensurable obligations, one of which is evidently of greater weight in light of principle, is entirely misbegotten. Given who we are, beings who are essentially open to multiple considerations, "we must reject any model of personal practical thought according to which all my projects, purposes, and needs should be made, discursively and at once, considerations *for* me. I must deliberate *from* what I am."[6] To accept the claims of morality and to deliberate as it commands is to commit oneself to illusion, repression, and self-denial.

If this background phenomenology of deliberation is right, then no interpretation of the actions of persons as expressive of a genuine and genuinely valuable shared capacity for understanding our person-hood and what befits it can possibly be in order. Any such moralizing interpretation would necessarily rest on a denial of our particularity, our historicity, and our desire. Such a way of reading in defense of morality would necessarily involve, in Nietzsche's memorable image, a mummification of the person, the victory of death over life.

> You ask me which of the philosophers' traits are really idio-syncrasies? For example, their lack of historical sense, their hatred of the very idea of becoming, their Egypticism. They think that they show their *respect* for a subject when they de-historicize it, *sub specie aeterni*—when they turn it into a mummy. All that philosophers have handled for thou-sands of years have been concept-mummies; nothing real escaped their grasp alive. When these honorable idolators of concepts worship some-thing, they kill it and stuff it; they threaten the life of everything they worship.[7]

This thought—that to interpret actions in defense of morality is to worship death, killing what one interprets—finds encouragement in the forms of closure that appear in each of the texts under study. *Lord Jim* ends with Jim's death, or a narrative of it, the *Prelude* and "Resolu-tion and Independence" end with fantasies of a reception that con-tinues beyond death, "Frost at Midnight" offers as its closing image the poet as reflecting icicle melting toward death, Elizabeth and Darcy in agreeing to marry remove themselves from their active history of struggle and courtship, thus suggesting that temporality and on-wardness can be in this way defeated or suspended. To accept these events and fantasies and images as appropriate modes of closure to these narratives, as culminations of genuine achievements in the un-derstanding and fit expression of a shared moral personhood, is then seemingly to participate in and perpetuate the philosopher's forced and hysterical denials of the particularity of our condition.

And yet . . . . Is it so clear that these narratives do not reveal to us a common capability? Jim in his active presenting of himself to Doramin, expressing his sense of his dignity and connectedness to others, Marlow in his ongoing self-testing talk, Wordsworth in his active, present, self-recovering self-remembering through writing, Coleridge in his acceptance of his responsibility for and relatedness to his son as a mode of his active life, Elizabeth and Darcy in marrying so as to continue in sanctity what they have already begun—all these seemingly lend to the narratives that they conclude a closure that is at the same time a continuation for these protagonists in the active expression of a shared and acknowledged moral personhood. Do these protagonists, in coming to these ends, recognizably make progress on our behalf, reflecting to us our own capacities for understanding our personhood and fitly expressing it in activity in the world? It is at least an abstract possibility that this should be so. As Thomas Nagel observes in commenting on Williams's phenomenology of deliberation, "The I who desires and acts is also the I who reflects. Practical deliberation can be simultaneously first- and third- personal,"[8] can proceed simultaneously from our particular desires and yet also from a developing sense of what persons in general ought to do. Although we begin from the particular, from our given desires, classes, genders, family histories, and social contexts, in our development as agents and deliberators, it nonetheless seems possible that, as we go on, "a judgment about what I should do [should be] also, at least implicitly, a judgment about what the person who I am should do."[9]

To hold that there is this possibility—we may come to acknowledge our shared moral personhood and to act according to its requirements in contexts, in ways that mark out and exemplify the best possibilities of life of persons—is not to say either that the world will always receive and honor actions so motivated or that a life composed of such actions will be fulfilling, regardless of the reception of these actions in the world. Critics of Kantian morality often misconstrue it as committed to this latter point. Thus Nussbaum writes that

> the Kantian believes that there is one domain of value, the domain of moral value, that is altogether immune to the assaults of luck. No matter what happens in the world, the moral value of the good will remains unaffected. Furthermore, the Kantian believes that there is a sharp distinction to be drawn between this and every other type of value, *and* that moral value is of overwhelmingly greater importance than anything else.[10]

In one way, this is surely right. Morality will accept the thought that we are bound, above all else, and against the temptations of wealth, glory, and material happiness in particular, to the care of our souls, will feel the force of the questions put by Jesus: "For what does it profit a man, to gain the whole world and forfeit his life? For what can a man give in return for his life?"[11] But why is this so? Why are we, according to morality, bound to do what is right according to universal principle, or to the moral law? Not because any life so lived will be happy; the world is too dark a place for that. Accidents of nature, of disease, famine, injury, and so on, and accidents of social life, of accreted differences in habits of perception and judgment and in institutional life that make attentiveness and responsiveness among certain persons virtually sure to fail—these things will bring with them the tragedies of the failure of the reception of right action by the world. One is not made secure in one's happiness through the acknowledgment of morality's demands. Yet these demands are, according to morality's conception of itself, to have overriding force in motivating our actions and shaping our lives. Why?

It is not that the possession of a good will—a will motivated by respect for persons and for the moral law—of itself makes its possessors immune from fortune and guarantees the goodness of their lives. The good will should rather be understood as good unconditionally, but instrumentally.[12] Were everyone to come freely to possess a good will—that is, freely to develop habits of attending to and respecting persons because persons are worthy of such attention and respect—then, despite the remaining vicissitudes of fortune, we should have freely come as close as it is possible to come to establishing a kingdom of ends on earth. We should have come as far as possible toward living in a world in which freely chosen virtue is crowned with happiness and in which we would live with one another in harmonious expression of our shared nature as finitely autonomous beings in a material world. As Williams, who notes the force of this ideal even while arguing its impossibility, puts it, "The purity of morality itself represents a value. It expresses an ideal, presented by Kant, once again, in a form that is the most unqualified and also one of the most moving: the ideal that human existence can be ultimately just,"[13] where perfect justice comprises not only noninterference with others' rights, but further the cooperative fit expression of our shared nature as finitely autonomous beings.

It is a moving ideal. But how real can it be for us? Is the possibility of life that it represents only an idle and abstract one, one that fails to engage with the shaping forces of our deliberation and action, as Williams suggests? Or is it imaginably at least partially achievable, in ways that genuinely draw us toward them? What do these texts and these readings show us? What actualizations of the ideal, if any, are to be found in the careers of Jim and Marlow, Wordsworth, Coleridge, and Elizabeth and Darcy? To the extent that these figures acquire the motivation to be just, and further achieve apt expression of this motivation in activity and in human relationship, their acquisitions and achievements are surely *not* developed, as Williams has rightly seen, "simply by standing back in reflection."[14] Such acquisitions and achievements, if they are genuine, are the product of a concrete *Bildung* all at once in self-understanding, in motivation, toward certain activities, and in relationship. The motivation to be just, in the full

Kantian sense, and the further expression of that motivation appear not as the result of standing back from ourselves and our situations, but rather out of more fully appreciating our shared finitely autonomous nature and its possibilities of fit expression as they are already partially manifested to us in concrete activities and relations, which we then further value and deepen. What may happen, as Nagel puts it, is that "we begin with limited access to the truth, from a limited personal point of view, and in the course of our explorations we may go astray or get lost. But we can also make discoveries, and those discoveries will alter our motives and expand our perspectives as agents."[15]

Yet, again, how actualizable are these possibilities of development? What do these narratives show us? In Jim and Marlow, Wordsworth, Coleridge, and Elizabeth and Darcy, we have encountered what one may feel to be varying partial and anxious exemplars of the achievement of an understanding of our shared personhood and of its fit expression in actions, activities, and relationships. That these exemplars remain partial in being marked by desire, anxious in failing to achieve a self-certain discursive closure of understanding, and in tension in varying from one another means that the merger of philosophy and literature into a system of concrete moral knowledge can never be complete. Narratives of the particular, in acknowledging the continual presence and unruliness of desire in our lives, and philosophical theories, in elaborating systems of general terms that make narratives possible and intelligible to persons in general, continually call one another into question, even while requiring one another. The critics of morality are right to see how shadowed and haunted by the particularities of desire, class, gender, and background *Sittlichkeit* even the best achievements in understanding and expressing our personhood must remain. But that these protagonists are also receivable as exemplars, even though they are partial, anxious, and partially divergent, means that there may be more to the idea that we possess as persons a shared capacity for acknowledging the moral law and expressing that acknowledgment concretely than the critics of morality allow. The reshaping of desire need not always be entirely repressive. The ideal of justice, of acting according to the requirements of our shared finitely rational nature as persons, may have some power in part to move us of itself, naturally.

How shall we know? We have no access either to our capacities for self-understanding and motivation by justice or to our distinctive nature as persons that they, if they are real, define, apart from partial, anxious, and partially divergent exemplifications of our personhood such as these. There are no perfect exemplifications of our moral personhood. Even Jesus in his humanity must himself have shared in our embodiment and our particularity, whatever else he may have been. In that it emerges, in ways that remain subject to interrogation, only out of our confrontation with partial, anxious, and partially divergent exemplifications of our moral personhood such as these, morally significant self-understanding cannot form a closed system of theoretical propositions. Philosophy, or wisdom, or criticism, to the extent that it involves the pursuit of such self-understanding, must be an activity, not a body of knowledge. We must, as Wittgenstein reminds us, "plunge into the waters of doubt again and again"[16] in our attempts to come to terms with ourselves. Yet our ongoing efforts at self-understanding and the fit expression of our nature, our acknowledgments of our moral personhood as finitely autonomous, embodied beings, may, if we will let them, take some shape, or achieve some further development, from continuing recognitions of the complexities of the general achievements on the parts of particular protagonists that are evident in cases such as these.

NOTES

Chapter 1

1. The phrase in quotation marks derives from Stanley Cavell, who has remarked that "the motive to philosophy can be thought of as a desire to true this asymmetry [between teaching and learning]." *The Claim of Reason* (New York: Oxford University Press, 1979), 112.

2. This formulation derives from an as yet unpublished paper by Stanley Bates, "The Lined Horizon: The Sublime as Figure," delivered at Romantic Revolutions: An International Symposium, Bloomington, Indiana, March 3, 1988.

3. See Geoffrey H. Hartman, *Wordsworth's Poetry, 1787–1814* (New Haven, Conn.: Yale University Press, [1964] 1971), esp. "Retrospect 1971," xi–xx, and 225–42.

4. The importance of *acknowledgment* as lying at the center of the achievement of an understanding of oneself and one's humanity in relation to others and the world has been worked out and emphasized above all by Stanley Cavell, especially in *The Claim of Reason*, pt. 4, chap. 13, "Between Acknowledgment and Avoidance."

5. Charles Altieri has voiced a similar sense of the limits of knowing in noting "the dualities of timeliness on which the Enlightenment tradition would founder," therein engendering a turn toward "confessional narrative" of our experiences of self in relation to world. "Eloquent Nature: Contemporary Poetry and the Rediscovery of the Miltonic Sublime," delivered at Romantic Revolutions: An International Symposium, Bloomington, Indiana, March 2, 1988.

6. Immanuel Kant, *Foundations of the Metaphysics of Morals*, trans. Lewis White Beck (Indianapolis, Ind.: Bobbs-Merrill Company, Inc., 1959), 47.

7. John Rawls, *A Theory of Justice* (Cambridge, Mass.: Harvard University Press, 1971), 489.

8. Ibid.

9. Ibid., 490–91.

10. Stanley Bates, in "The Motivation To Be Just," *Ethics* 85, no. 1 (October 1974): 1–17, suggests the possibility of supplementing Rawls's account of the stability of a just society in this Hegelian way so as to yield an account of how "the conception of justice [Rawls] presents occupies some favored place historically." He then notes that "Rawls himself is far too modest and tentative to make such a claim directly" (16–17).

11. Rawls, *A Theory of Justice*, 504.

12. John Rawls, "Justice as Fairness: Political Not Metaphysical," *Philosophy and Public Affairs* 14, no. 3 (Summer 1985): 223.

13. Ibid., 251 n. 33.

14. Ibid., 230, 231, 223; emphases added.

15. William L. McBride criticizes *A Theory of Justice* in this way in his review essay "Social Theory *Sub Specie Aeternitatis:* A New Perspective," *Yale Law Journal* 81, no. 5 (April 1972): 980–1003.

16. Rawls, "Justice as Fairness," 224 n. 2.

17. Cf. ibid., 240–42, 245–46.

18. G. W. F. Hegel, *Introduction to the Lectures on the History of Philosophy*, trans. J. M. Knox and A. V. Miller (Oxford: Clarendon Press, 1985), 9.

19. Peter Brooks, *Reading for the Plot: Design and Intention in Narrative* (New York: Vintage Books, 1984), 3.

20. Aristotle, *Poetics*, trans. Ingram Bywater (Oxford: Oxford University Press, 1920); reprinted in *Aesthetics: A Critical Anthology*, ed. George Dickie and Richard J. Sclafani (New York: St. Martin's Press, Inc., 1977), book 1, chap. 9, 214.

21. Northrop Frye, *The Great Code: The Bible and Literature* (New York: Harcourt Brace Jovanovich, Publishers, 1983), xviii.

22. Martha Nussbaum, "Narrative Emotions: Beckett's Genealogy of Love," *Ethics* 98, no. 2 (January 1988): 250.

23. See Helen Vendler's essay "The False and True Sublime," *Southern Review* (Summer 1971); reprinted in her *Part of Nature, Part of Us* (Cambridge, Mass.: Harvard University Press, 1980), 1–15.

24. Harold Bloom, *Wallace Stevens: The Poems of Our Climate* (Ithaca, N.Y.: Cornell University Press, 1976), 23.

25. Wallace Stevens, cited in Vendler, "The False and True Sublime," 19.

26. Stevens, *The Letters of Wallace Stevens*, ed. Holly Stevens (New York: Alfred A. Knopf, Inc., 1966), 445; cited in Bloom, *Wallace Stevens*, 204.

27. Ludwig Wittgenstein, *Philosophical Investigations*, 3d ed., trans. G. E. M. Anscombe (New York: Macmillan Company, 1958), x.

28. In worrying about the vocation of poetry, Keats observed similarly that "I think Poetry should surprise by a fine excess and not by Singularity—it should strike the Reader as a wording of his own highest thoughts, and appear

almost a Remembrance. . . ." Letter to John Taylor, 27 February 1818, in *Selected Poems and Letters*, ed. Douglas Bush (Boston: Houghton Mifflin Company, 1959), 267. This formulation of the aims of poetry, taken alone, is, however, perhaps too aestheticist.

29. Charles Altieri, "From Expressivist Aesthetics to Expressivist Ethics," in *Literature and the Question of Philosophy*, ed. Anthony J. Cascardi (Baltimore: Johns Hopkins University Press, 1987), 147, 140. See also Altieri's "An Idea and Ideal of a Literary Canon," *Critical Inquiry* 10, no. 1 (September 1983): 41–64, esp. 44, 52, 58–59.

30. Anthony J. Cascardi, introduction to Charles Altieri's "From Expressivist Aesthetics to Expressivist Ethics," in *Literature and the Question of Philosophy*, 133.

31. Bernard Williams, *Ethics and the Limits of Philosophy* (Cambridge, Mass.: Harvard University Press, 1985), 6–7, 174–202.

32. Richard Wollheim, *The Thread of Life* (Cambridge, Mass.: Harvard University Press, 1984), 3.

33. Charles Taylor, "Design for Living" (review of Wollheim's *The Thread of Life*), *New York Review of Books* 31 (November 22, 1984): 51.

34. Wollheim, 21.

35. Ibid., 17.

36. Jon Elster, "Second-Decimal Arguments" (review of *The Thread of Life*), *London Review of Books* (23 May 1985): 6. Wollheim's other arguments are no better than this one that Elster criticizes. For example, Wollheim cites as argument the fact that "a constructionist theory" must allow the consequence, which "seems unacceptable," "that there could be events of the kind that normally make up a person's life but that turn out to belong to no one's life" (17). In reply to this, one might be tempted to say, "Of course there *could be* such events (as far as logic, say, shows), and it's perfectly acceptable that there could be; it just so happens (physically) that (so far as we know) there aren't." While Wollheim's view seems to me right, I do not know that I could show a contemporary reductionist that it is right, and that this remark is wrong, by demonstrative argument apart from a morally significant appeal to recognize oneself in one's activities and to transform them so as to express one's personhood better.

37. Taylor, Introduction and "What Is Human Agency?" *Philosophical Papers* (Cambridge: Cambridge University Press, 1985), 1: 3, 34–35.

38. Taylor, "Self-Interpreting Animals," *Philosophical Papers*, 1: 58.

39. See Taylor, Introduction, 12.

40. Cf. Richard Eldridge, "Criticism and Its Objects," *Glyph 6* (December 1979): 158–76.

41. Cf. Richard Eldridge, "Philosophy and the Achievement of Community: Rorty, Cavell, and Criticism," *Metaphilosophy* 14, no. 2 (April 1983): 107–25.

42. Cf. Richard Eldridge, "Problems and Prospects of Wittgensteinian Aesthetics," *Journal of Aesthetics and Art Criticism* 45, no. 3 (Spring 1987): 251–61.

43. Cf. Richard Eldridge, "'A Continuing Task': Cavell and the Truth of

Skepticism," in *The Senses of Stanley Cavell*, ed. Richard Fleming and Michael Payne, *Bucknell Review* 32, no. 1 (1989): 73–89.

44. See Richard Eldridge, "Hypotheses, Criterial Claims, and Perspicuous Representations: Wittgenstein's 'Remarks on Frazer's *The Golden Bough,'"* *Philosophical Investigations* 10, no. 3 (July 1987): 226–45.

45. See Richard Rorty, "Introduction: Pragmatism and Philosophy," in *Consequences of Pragmatism* (Minneapolis: University of Minnesota Press, 1982), xxxvii. See also the elaboration and criticism of Rorty's views in my "Philosophy and the Achievement of Community: Rorty, Cavell, and Criticism."

46. As Mark Timmons usefully observes (though he puts the point in the course of talking about *theories* and *systems*, not elaborations of readings), it is sufficient for the falsity of foundationalism—sufficient, that is, for the view that such things as intuitions, moral principles, and interpretations of their requirements are all always up for reconsideration and do not have a fixed deductive structure—that "relevant background theories that constrain choice among moral systems, especially those concerning persons, cannot be developed apart from moral considerations." "Foundationalism and the Structure of Ethical Justification," *Ethics* 97, no. 3 (April 1987): 607.

47. T. S. Eliot, "Poetry and Propaganda," *Bookman* 70, no. 6 (February 1930): 601. Eliot's later views on the relation of poetry and philosophy approximate more closely to the view here being urged. For a survey of Eliot's views throughout his career, see Richard Shusterman, "T. S. Eliot on Reading: Pleasure, Games, and Wisdom," *Philosophy and Literature* 11, no. 1 (April 1987): 1–20.

48. Wittgenstein, Preface to *Philosophical Investigations*, ix.

Chapter 2

1. Bernard Williams, "Persons, Character and Morality," in *Moral Luck* (Cambridge: Cambridge University Press, 1981), 18.

2. Ibid., 12.

3. Alasdair MacIntyre, "Relativism, Power and Philosophy," *Proceedings and Addresses of the American Philosophical Association* 59, no. 1 (September 1985): 9.

4. Ibid.

5. Julia Annas, "Personal Love and Kantian Ethics in *Effi Briest*," *Philosophy and Literature* 8, no. 1 (April 1984): 28.

6. Alan Gewirth, "Rights and Virtues," *Review of Metaphysics* 37, no. 4 (June 1985): 753.

7. Ibid., 744; emphasis added.

8. Ibid., 748.

9. Ibid., 743.

10. Ibid., 748.

11. MacIntyre, *After Virtue* (Notre Dame, Ind.: University of Notre Dame Press, 1981), 64–65.

12. Gewirth, 745.

13. Annas, 25.

14. This point is prominent in Martha Nussbaum's *The Fragility of Goodness: Luck and Ethics in Greek Tragedy and Philosophy* (Cambridge: Cambridge University Press, 1986).

15. The distinction between capacities and abilities has its original source in Aristotle: "Privation [which is contrary to potency] has several senses; for it means 1) that which has not a certain quality and 2) that which might naturally have it but has not it, either (*a*) in general or (*b*) when it might naturally have it, and either (*A*) in some particular way, when it has it not completely, or (*B*) when it has it not at all." *Metaphysics*, trans. W. D. Ross, in *The Basic Works of Aristotle*, ed. Richard McKeon (New York: Random House, 1941), 821. "One who possesses knowledge of a science but is not actually exercising it knows the science potentially in a sense, though not in the same sense as he knows it potentially before he learnt it." *Physics*, trans. R. P. Hardie and R. K. Gaye, in *The Basic Works of Aristotle*, 8.4. 365.

16. Jonathan Jacobs, "The Place of Virtue in Happiness," *Journal of Value Inquiry* 19, no. 3 (1985): 171.

17. Arthur C. Danto, "Philosophy as/ and/ of Literature," *Grand Street* 3, no. 3 (Spring 1984): 170–1.

18. Charles Altieri, "An Idea and Ideal of a Literary Canon," *Critical Inquiry* 10, no. 1 (September 1983): 52, 49.

19. MacIntyre, *A Short History of Ethics* (New York: Macmillan Publishing Company, 1966), 197–98; and *After Virtue*, 44–45.

20. Alan Donagan, *The Theory of Morality* (Chicago: University of Chicago Press, 1977), sect. 1.2, 9–17.

21. MacIntyre, *After Virtue*, 45.

22. Immanuel Kant, *Foundations of the Metaphysics of Morals*, 47.

23. MacIntyre, *Short History*, 197–98.

24. G. W. F. Hegel, *Phenomenology of Spirit*, trans. A. V. Miller (Oxford: Clarendon Press, 1977), par. 430, 257.

25. G. W. F. Hegel, *Philosophy of Right*, trans. T. M. Knox (Oxford: Clarendon Press, 1952), par. 135R, 90.

26. John Gardner's *Mickelsson's Ghosts* (New York: Random House, 1982) contains a nice descriptive phenomenology of self-uncertainty in acting, in particular in lifting weights.

27. Thus I think Donagan goes somewhat too far in defending the power of individual conscience to issue objective verdicts about permissibility. In particular, Jagerstätter's achievement in judging participation after 1943 in Hitler's war to be impermissible is not, I think (contrary to what Donagan holds [17]), the work of Jagerstätter's conscience and grasp of principle alone. It instead proceeds from conscience and principle coupled with a history of Christian communities and verdicts about just wars which provides this principle of respect for persons with a background of applications. This background was willfully ignored by the church hierarchy with which Jagerstätter came into contact, but it was nonetheless available to him.

28. Michael Oakeshott, *Rationalism in Politics and Other Essays* (London: Methuen, 1962), 64–5; cited in Donagan, 11.

29. Williams, 14.

30. Hegel, *Phenomenology of Spirit*, par. 588, 358–59.

31. Harry Frankfurt, Review of Bernard Williams's *Moral Luck, Journal of Philosophy* 81, no. 6 (June 1984): 335.

32. Hegel, *Phenomenology of Spirit*, par. 386, 231.

33. Ibid., par. 390, 234.

34. Ibid., par. 434, 260.

35. Ibid., par. 589, 359.

36. Such extreme situations are far from an empty, abstract possibility. Famine, for example, is a serious and regular natural occurrence. To illustrate the difficulty, consider the policy recently announced in the People's Republic of China of relaxing the restrictions on child-bearing: if, but only if, their first child is a girl, a couple is permitted to have a second child in the hope of having a boy. Here one wants to say that this new policy displays a radical failure of respect for persons in general *and* that the conception of the proper social and economic roles of men and women respectively is so woven through a culture far from being absolutely corrupt that mandating radically egalitarian treatment of the sexes might well destroy it and all its modes of expressing respect. In this case, the proper interpretation of the requirements of a principle of respect for persons might be *not* the immediate overturning of this policy, but rather the slow and progressive intermingling of some of the social and economic roles of men and women, as they find such intermingling appropriate.

37. Nussbaum, "'Finely Aware and Richly Responsible': Moral Attention and the Moral Task of Literature," *Journal of Philosophy* 82, no. 10 (October 1985): 524.

38. Cf. Immanuel Kant, *Lectures on Ethics*, trans. Louis Infield (Indianapolis, Ind.: Hackett Publishing Company, 1979), 175.

39. Ibid., 205–6.

40. Marcia Baron, "The Alleged Moral Repugnance of Acting from Duty," *Journal of Philosophy* 81, no. 4 (April 1984): 217.

41. Immanuel Kant, *Critique of Practical Reason*, trans. Lewis White Beck (Indianapolis, Ind.: Bobbs-Merrill Company, Inc., 1956), 87–88.

42. Iris Murdoch, "The Idea of Perfection," *Yale Review* (1964); reprinted in *The Sovereignty of Good* (New York: Schocken Books, 1971), 1–2. Her *The Philosopher's Pupil* (New York: Viking, 1983) attempts to illustrate the extent to which a person's commitment to principle weakens other motives, such as love, and the genuinely life- and value-nurturing attachments grounded in such motives. A critic might wonder, however, whether the philosophical protagonist whose life is wasteful, John Robert Rozanov, genuinely structures his life around respect for persons and the comprehensive and flexible attention it commands, instead of retreating into a prioristic defenses of principle and its requirements that lead to subjective legalisms. I would argue that his rather pathetic character and actions are informed by the latter sort of retreat and that the rather naive natural goodness supposedly exemplified in the unphilosophical Tom and Hattie does not in fact take us very far in living well.

43. Williams, 2.

44. Annas, 24. It will be clear that I would contest Annas's claim that in

Effi Briest Instetten, in finding his love stopped by his sense of duty, acts and feels as a Kantian moral agent must act and feel; he has instead, I would urge, pridefully misinterpreted the requirements of Kantian principle in his situation, and this misinterpretation of what he must do has warped his emotional life. (Outer action and inner response do not come apart as easily as Annas suggests.) Recently Marcia Baron has replied to Annas along these lines, in her "Was Effi Briest a Victim of Kantian Morality?" *Philosophy and Literature* 12, no. 1 (April 1988): 95–113.

45. Hegel, *Philosophy of Right*, sect. 161, 111.

46. Kant, *Foundations of the Metaphysics of Morals*, 9.

47. Ibid., 60.

48. Ibid., 17.

49. Kant, *Lectures on Ethics*, 140.

50. Ibid., 65.

51. Kant, *Critique of Practical Reason*, 122–23.

52. Ibid., 96.

53. Kant, *Lectures on Ethics*, 77.

54. Barbara Herman, "The Practice of Moral Judgment," *Journal of Philosophy* 82, no. 8 (August 1985): 414–36, esp. 418–19.

55. Donagan, 11.

56. Kant, *Foundations*, 40–41, 48.

57. Ibid., 48.

58. Kant, *Lectures on Ethics*, 121; cf. also 117–18: "Far from ranking lowest in the scale of precedence, our duties towards ourselves are of primary importance and should have pride of place. . . ."

59. Barbara Herman, in hinting (423–25) that the rules of moral salience, rather than merely marking out special moral problem situations, may define a kind of attention and sensitivity to persons that (rationally) must always figure in our coming to act is, I think, suggesting something like this.

60. Kant, *Foundations*, 52.

61. Kant, *Lectures on Ethics*, 146.

62. Kant, *Critique of Practical Reason*, 76.

63. Ibid., 83.

64. Ibid., 86.

65. Kant, *Lectures on Ethics*, 196.

66. Ibid., 139.

67. Kant, *Foundations*, 18.

68. Lewis White Beck, Translator's Introduction to Kant, *Foundations*, ix.

69. Kant, *Foundations*, 13–14.

70. Ibid., 16; emphasis added.

71. Robert K. Shope, "Kant's Use and Derivation of the Categorical Imperative," in *Kant: Foundations of the Metaphysics of Morals: Text and Critical Essays*, ed. Robert Paul Wolff (Indianapolis, Ind.: Bobbs-Merrill Company, Inc., 1969), 266; second comma added.

72. Kant, *Foundations*, 15.

73. Donagan, 59–66.

74. Kant, *Foundations*, 47.

75. MacIntyre, *Secularization and Moral Change* (London: Oxford University Press, 1967), 24; cited in Donagan, 11.

76. MacIntyre, *After Virtue*, 58, 32.

77. Kant, *Lectures on Ethics*, 138.

78. Ibid., 6.

79. Ibid., 152; cf. also *Critique of Practical Reason*, 162–63.

80. Kant, *Critique of Practical Reason*, 117.

81. Ibid., 118.

82. Ibid., 48; cf. also 94.

83. Ibid., 127.

84. Ibid., 129–30.

85. Ibid., 127.

86. Ibid., 4.

87. Ibid., 114.

88. Ibid.

89. Hegel, *Phenomenology of Spirit*, par. 631, 382–83.

90. John Wisdom, in "Gods," *Proceedings of the Aristotelian Society* (1944); reprinted in *Philosophy and Psychoanalysis* (Oxford: Basil Blackwell, 1953), 149–68, cites the following passage from Wordsworth with the suggestion that it records, perhaps obscurely, *some* authentic or appropriate attitude toward the world.

91. William Wordsworth, "Lines Composed a Few Miles Above Tintern Abbey . . . ," in *Selected Poems and Prefaces*, ed. Jack Stillinger (Boston: Houghton Mifflin Company, 1965), 110, ll. 93–102.

92. Kant, *Critique of Practical Reason*, 48.

93. Kant, *Foundations*, 70.

94. Ibid., 66.

95. Ibid., 90.

96. Ibid., 65.

97. Ibid., 64–65.

98. Ibid., 65.

99. Kant, *Critique of Practical Reason*, 4 n. 1.

100. Ibid., 89.

101. Ibid., 4 n. 1.

102. Ibid., 3.

103. Kant, *Foundations*, 13.

104. Ibid., 14.

105. Ibid., 14–15.

106. Kant, *Critique of Practical Reason*, 30, 159–60. Donagan's case, derived from J. L. Stocks, of the reluctant manufacturer (226–29) is similar to Kant's.

107. Kant, *Foundations*, 24–25.

108. Kant, *Critique of Practical Reason*, 12.

109. Kant, *Foundations*, 24.

110. Kant, *Critique of Practical Reason*, 148.

111. Ibid., 155.

112. Ibid., 158.

113. Ibid., 159–60.

114. Ibid., 167–68.

115. Donagan, 25. See also Manley Thompson, "On A Priori Truth," *Journal of Philosophy* 77, no. 8 (August 1981); Barry Stroud, "Wittgenstein and Logical Necessity," *Philosophical Review* 84, no. 4 (October 1965); Jonathan Lear, "Leaving the World Alone," *Journal of Philosophy* 79, no. 7 (July 1982); Richard Eldridge, "The Normal and the Normative: Wittgenstein's Legacy, Kripke, and Cavell," *Philosophy and Phenomenological Research* 46, no. 4 (June 1986); and, above all, Stanley Cavell, *The Claim of Reason.*

Chapter 3

1. Fredric Jameson, *The Political Unconscious* (Ithaca, N.Y.: Cornell University Press, 1981), 208–9.

2. Ibid., 209.

3. Ibid., 217.

4. Ibid., 250.

5. Ibid., 206–7.

6. Ian Watt, *Conrad in the Nineteenth Century* (Berkeley: University of California Press, 1979), 10–14.

7. Joseph Conrad, *A Personal Record*, in Collected Edition of the Works of Joseph Conrad (London: J. M. Dent Company, 1946–55), xvii; cited in Watt, 130.

8. Joseph Conrad, *The Mirror of the Sea*, in Collected Edition, 28; cited in Watt, 19–20.

9. See Watt, 28.

10. Tadeusz Bobrowski, in *Conrad's Polish Background: Letters to and from Polish Friends*, ed. Zdzislaw Najder, trans. Halina Carroll (London: Oxford University Press, 1964), 154; cited in Watt, 28–29.

11. Watt, 33.

12. Ibid., 32.

13. Ibid., 7.

14. Ibid., 3.

15. Ibid., 1–4.

16. Conrad, *A Personal Record*, 136; cited in Watt, 22.

17. Joseph Conrad, Letter to Edward Garnett, 1/20/00; reprinted in *Lord Jim: An Authoritative Text, Backgrounds, Sources, Essays in Criticism*, ed. Thomas Moser (New York: W. W. Norton & Co., 1968), 299.

18. Conrad, Letter to Edward Garnett, 11/12/00, ibid., 305.

19. *Lord Jim: An Authoritative Text* . . . , ix. Hereafter all references to the text of *Lord Jim* will be to this edition and will be given in the text by page number in parentheses. Quotation marks indicating Marlow's voice will be suppressed for convenience when the context makes the speaker clear.

20. Conrad, *Notes on Life and Letters*, in Collected Edition, 168; cited in Watt, 4.

21. Conrad, Letter to David S. Meldrum, 8/10/98; reprinted in *Lord Jim: An Authoritative Text* . . . , 293.

22. Watt, 337.

23. Philip M. Weinstein, *The Semantics of Desire: Changing Models of Identity from Dickens to Joyce* (Princeton, N.J.: Princeton University Press, 1984), 165.

24. Watt, 280.

25. Conrad, *Typhoon*, in *The Portable Conrad*, ed. Morton D. Zabel (New York: Viking, 1947), 208; cited in Weinstein, 157 n. 9.

26. Immanuel Kant, *Critique of Practical Reason*, 161.

27. Ibid., 158–59.

28. Kant, *Lectures on Ethics*, 137.

29. Hegel, *Philosophy of Right*, par. 140, 102.

30. Wordsworth, "Tintern Abbey," 109, ll. 75–76. Cf. also, e.g., *Prelude* 3.612–16; 231 in *Selected Poems and Prefaces*: "Of these and other kindred notices / I cannot say what portion is in truth / The naked recollection of that time / And what may rather have been called to life / By after-meditation."

31. Weinstein, 149.

32. Watt, 345.

33. Kant, *Lectures on Ethics*, 151.

34. Ibid., 150.

35. Ibid., 154.

36. See Eldridge, "The Normal and the Normative."

Chapter 4

1. Charles Taylor makes this point in *Hegel* (Cambridge: Cambridge University Press, 1975), 6–10.

2. Wordsworth, Preface to *Lyrical Ballads* (1800), in *Selected Poems and Prefaces*, 445; subsequent references to this work will be to this edition and will be given in the text after the abbreviation "Pref."

3. Wordsworth, *Prelude*, in *Selected Poems and Prefaces*, book 2, ll.233–34; 212; emphasis added. Subsequent references to the *Prelude* will be to this edition and will be given in the text by book and line numbers, e.g., (2.233–34).

4. Hegel, *Phenomenology of Spirit*, par. 344, 209.

5. W. G. Gallie, "Is *The Prelude* a Philosophical Poem?" *Philosophy* 22 (1947): 124–38; reprinted in William Wordsworth, *The Prelude 1799, 1805, 1850: Authoritative Texts, Context and Reception, Recent Critical Essays*, ed. Jonathan Wordsworth, M. H. Abrams, and Stephen Gill (New York: W. W. Norton and Company, 1979), 665.

6. James K. Chandler, *Wordsworth's Second Nature: A Study of the Poetry and Politics* (Chicago: University of Chicago Press, 1984), 194.

7. Gallie, 665.

8. Chandler, 188.

9. Gallie, 667.

10. Ibid.

11. Chandler, 215.

12. Cf. "Lines Composed a Few Miles Above Tintern Abbey . . . ," in *Selected Poems and Prefaces*, ll. 75–76, 109: "I cannot paint / What then I was."

13. Chandler, 199.

14. Ibid., 200.

15. Ibid., 193–94.

16. Stanley Cavell, *The Claim of Reason*, 125.

17. It is possible to hear something like this in the following remark of Wittgenstein's: "The criteria for the truth of the *confession* that I thought such-and-such are not the criteria for a true *description* of a process. And the importance of the true confession does not reside in its being a correct and certain report of a process. It resides rather in the special consequences which can be drawn from a confession whose truth is guaranteed by the special criteria of *truthfulness*." *Philosophical Investigations*, 3d ed., trans. G. E. M. Anscombe (New York: Macmillan Company, 1958), 222e.

18. William Wordsworth, "From *The Recluse*," in *Selected Poems and Prefaces*, l. 776, 45.

19. William Wordsworth, "Tintern Abbey," ll. 119–20, 110.

20. Ibid., l. 141, 111.

21. Ibid., ll. 146, 149, 111.

22. William Wordsworth, Advertisement; cited in Kenneth R. Johnston, *Wordsworth and* The Recluse (New Haven, Conn.: Yale University Press, 1984), 238; from Wordsworth, *Poems, in Two Volumes, and Other Poems, 1800–1807*, ed. Jared Curtis (Ithaca, N.Y.: Cornell University Press, 1983), 527.

23. Johnston, 238.

24. Harold Bloom, *The Visionary Company*, rev. ed. (Ithaca, N.Y.: Cornell University Press, 1971), 165.

25. Wordsworth, "Resolution and Independence," in *Selected Poems and Prefaces*, ll. 1–2, 165. All references to this poem will be to this edition and will be given by line numbers in parentheses in the text.

26. John Keats, "Ode on Melancholy," in *Selected Poems and Letters*, ed. Douglas Bush (Boston: Houghton Mifflin Company, 1959), ll. 21–24, 209–10.

27. Bloom, *The Visionary Company*, 165.

28. John Milton, "When I consider how my light is spent . . . ," in *The Complete Poetry and Selected Prose of John Milton*, ed. Cleanth Brooks (New York: Random House, 1950), ll. 10–11, 86.

29. Hegel, *The Phenomenology of Spirit*, par. 199, 121.

30. Ibid., par. 69, 43.

31. Keats, Letter to Richard Woodhouse, 27 October 1818, in *Selected Poems and Letters*, 279.

32. William Wordsworth, "Remark to Henry Crabb Robinson," cited in M. H. Abrams, Foreword to *William Wordsworth and the Age of English Romanticism*, ed. Jonathan Wordsworth, Michael C. Jaye, and Robert Woof (New Brunswick, N.J.: Rutgers University Press, 1987), x.

33. See the passages cited in the penultimate paragraph of sect. 2 above.

34. See par. 3 of sect. 3 above.

35. Geoffrey H. Hartman, "Was it for this . . . ?" Paper delivered at Romantic Revolutions: An International Symposium, Bloomington, Indiana, March 1, 1988. See also Hartman's discussion of Wordsworth's experiences of apocalypse and akedah in his *Wordsworth's Poetry*, xi–xx, 225–42.

36. John Keats, Letter to John Hamilton Reynolds, 3 May 1818, in *Selected Poems and Letters*, 274.

Chapter 5

1. Richard Rorty, *Philosophy and the Mirror of Nature* (Princeton, N.J.: Princeton University Press, 1979), 383.

2. Harold Bloom, *Wallace Stevens: The Poems of Our Climate*, 398; see 5 for Bloom's expansions of the meanings he assigns to *ethos* and *pathos*.

3. On Emerson's and Heidegger's views on "the epistemology of moods" and on which moods ought to be sustained and why, see Stanley Cavell's essay "Thinking of Emerson," in *Essays in Kant's Aesthetics*, ed. Ted Cohen and Paul Guyer (Chicago: University of Chicago Press, 1982), 261–70.

4. David Hume, *An Enquiry Concerning Human Understanding*, ed. E. Steinberg (Indianapolis, Ind.: Hackett Publishing Company, 1977), 31.

5. David Hume, *A Treatise of Human Nature*, ed. L. A. Selby-Bigge (Oxford: Clarendon Press, 1888), 268–69.

6. Ibid., 269.

7. Ibid., 269–70.

8. Wordsworth, *Prelude*, in *Selected Poems and Prefaces*, 11.306–14, 337.

9. Ibid., ll. 321–25.

10. M. H. Abrams, *Natural Supernaturalism* (New York: W. W. Norton, 1971), 96.

11. Ibid., 95.

12. S. T. Coleridge, Letter to Sir Humphry Davy, February 3, 1801, in *The Portable Coleridge*, ed. I. A. Richards (London: Penguin Books, 1950), 271.

13. Coleridge, Letter to Thomas Poole, March 16, 1801, in *The Portable Coleridge*, 271.

14. Coleridge, "Frost at Midnight," in *The Portable Coleridge*, 128–30. All subsequent references to this poem will be given in the text by line numbers in parentheses.

15. Geoffrey Hartman discusses whether-or formulations and Wordsworth's habits of surmising in *Wordsworth's Poetry*, 8–12.

16. Harold Bloom, *The Visionary Company*, 204–5.

Chapter 6

1. Sir Walter Scott, Review of *Emma*, *Quarterly Review* 14 (1815); cited in Richard Whately, "Modern Novels," *Quarterly Review* 47 (1821): 352–63; reprinted in part in Jane Austen, *Pride and Prejudice: An Authoritative Text, Backgrounds, Reviews and Essays in Criticism*, ed. Donald J. Gray (New York: W. W. Norton and Company, 1966), 316–17.

2. Whately, "Modern Novels," 320.

3. "Mrs. Gore's *Women as They Are* or *The Manners of the Day*," *Edinburgh Review* 51 (1830); reprinted in part in *Pride and Prejudice*, 322.

4. George Henry Lewes, "The Novels of Jane Austen," *Blackwood's Magazine* 86 (1859); reprinted in part in *Pride and Prejudice*, 327.

5. Richard Simpson, "Jane Austen," *North British Review*, 52 (1870); reprinted in part in *Pride and Prejudice*, 335.

6. Reginald Farrer, "Jane Austen," *Quarterly Review*, 228 (1917); reprinted in part in *Pride and Prejudice*, 342.

7. Marvin Mudrick, *Jane Austen: Irony as Defense and Discovery* (Princeton, N.J.: Princeton University Press, 1952), 94–126; reprinted in *Pride and Prejudice*, 409.

8. A. Walton Litz, *Jane Austen: A Study of Her Artistic Development* (New York: Oxford University Press, 1965), 97–111; reprinted in *Pride and Prejudice*, 443.

9. Whately, 317.

10. Lewes, 325.

11. Samuel Kliger, "Jane Austen's *Pride and Prejudice* in the Eighteenth-Century Mode," *University of Toronto Quarterly* 16 (1945–46); reprinted in part in *Pride and Prejudice*, 357.

12. Litz, 442–43.

13. Alistair M. Duckworth, *The Improvement of the Estate: A Study of Jane Austen's Novels* (Baltimore: Johns Hopkins University Press, 1971), 142.

14. Julia Prewitt Brown, *Jane Austen's Novels: Social Change and Literary Form* (Cambridge, Mass.: Harvard University Press, 1979), 76.

15. Mary Poovey, *The Proper Lady and the Woman Writer: Ideology as Style in the Works of Mary Wollstonecraft, Mary Shelley, and Jane Austen* (Chicago: University of Chicago Press, 1984), 178.

16. Ibid., 212.

17. Ibid., 182.

18. Duckworth, x.

19. Simpson, 336.

20. Ibid., 332–33.

21. Ibid., 334.

22. Ibid.

23. Ibid.

24. Mudrick, 403.

25. Ibid., 403–4.

26. Ibid.

27. Ibid., 404–5.

28. Ibid., 405.

29. Ibid., 408.

30. Poovey, 196–98.

31. Ibid., 197.

32. Ibid., 201.

33. Ibid., 236.

34. Ibid., 229.

35. Rachel Blau DuPlessis, *Writing beyond the Ending: Narrative Strategies of Twentieth-Century Women Writers* (Bloomington: Indiana University Press, 1985), 7.

36. Mudrick, 408.

37. 1 Corinthians 7:2–4.

38. Augustine, "The Good of Marriage," from *Treatises on Marriage and Other Subjects;* reprinted in *Philosophy of Women,* 2d ed., ed. Mary Briody Mahowald (Indianapolis, Ind.: Hackett Publishing Company, 1983), 261.

39. John Milton, "The Doctrine and Discipline of Divorce," in *The Complete Poetry and Selected Prose of John Milton,* 625, 629.

40. Hegel, *Phenomenology of Spirit,* par. 456, 273.

41. Stanley Cavell, *Pursuits of Happiness* (Cambridge, Mass.: Harvard University Press, 1981), 241.

42. Hegel, *Philosophy of Right,* par. 163, 112; par. 162, 111.

43. Ibid., par. 163R, 112.

44. Denis de Rougemont, *Love in the Western World,* rev. ed., trans. Montgomery Belgion (New York: Pantheon Books, Inc., 1956), 292–93.

45. Ibid., 280.

46. Ibid., 307–8.

47. Emile Durkheim, *Suicide,* trans. J. A. Spaulding and George Simpson (Glencoe, Ill.: Free Press, 1951), 271.

48. Jessie Bernard, "The Paradox of the Happy Marriage," in *Women in a Sexist Society,* ed. Vivian Gornick and Barbara K. Moran (New York: Basic Books, Inc., 1971), 90.

49. Robert N. Bellah et al., *Habits of the Heart* (Berkeley: University of California Press, 1985), 111. Bellah et al. are drawing on Joseph Veroff et al., *The Inner-American: A Self-Portrait from 1957 to 1976* (New York: Basic Books, 1981), 178.

50. Letter from a college freshman to her brother, cited in Mirra Komarovsky, "Cultural Contradictions and Sex Roles," *American Journal of Sociology* 52 (November 1946): 186.

51. Alexis de Tocqueville, *Democracy in America, Part the Second: The Social Influence of Democracy* (New York: J. & H. G. Langley, 1840), 227; cited in Bernard, 85.

52. Friedrich Nietzsche, *The Gay Science,* trans. Walter Kaufmann (New York: Random House, 1974), 319.

53. Shulamith Firestone, *The Dialectic of Sex: The Case for Feminist Revolution* (New York: William Morrow, 1970), 128.

54. Ibid., 132.

55. Ibid.

56. Ibid., 129.

57. Simone de Beauvoir, *The Second Sex,* trans. H. M. Parshley (New York: Alfred A. Knopf, Inc., 1949), 472.

58. Bertrand Russell, *Marriage and Morals* (Liveright Publishing Corporation, 1929); excerpted in *Philosophy of Women,* 146.

59. de Beauvoir, 425–26.

60. DuPlessis, xi.

61. Ibid.

62. According to the *Statistical Abstract of the United States: 1986* (106th ed., compiled by Glenn W. King et al., [Washington, D.C.: Bureau of the Census, 1985], 38), 31.7% of ever-married women 15–44 years old had their first marriages dissolved by the time of the survey; 60.5% of these women

had remarried by that time. According to the 1980 census, of divorced women aged 35–44 with a 1979 income of $50,000 or more, 59.9% have remarried (U.S. Dept. of Commerce, *1980 Census of Population*, Vol. 2: *Subject Reports: Marital Characteristics*, PL80-2-4C [March 1985], 140). This remarriage rate exceeds that of divorced women with incomes $25,000–$49,999 (52%), with incomes $15,000–$24,999 (51.9%), and with incomes $10,000–$14,999 (57.3%); it falls below that of divorced women with incomes $8,000–$9,999 (61.5%) and $0–$7,999 (75.8%) (ibid.). It seems reasonable to suppose that economic necessities do play a considerable role in remarriage by women with low incomes. Yet the remarriage rate is higher for women who are presumably materially independent than for women either less clearly independent or on the margins of independence. Perhaps wealthier women are more attractive matches than women of middle income. Still, they choose to marry. It remains a matter of conjecture whether their remarriage rate is a function of serious commitments to an ideal or of illusions that have yet to be undone. Expressions of support for the marriage ideal are, however, virtually unanimous: "A 1970 survey found that 96 percent of all Americans hold to the ideal of two people sharing a life and home together. When the same question was asked in 1980, the same percentage agreed" (Bellah et al., 90).

63. de Beauvoir, 472.

64. Ibid., 473.

65. All references to *Pride and Prejudice* will be to the edition by Gray, cited in n. 1 above, and will be given in the text by page number from this edition in parentheses.

66. Dorothy Van Ghent, *The English Novel* (New York: Holt, Rinehart and Winston, Inc., 1953); reprinted in part in *Pride and Prejudice*, 358.

67. Here I take issue with Mary Poovey's assessment of both Lydia's character and Austen's judgment upon it. Poovey remarks that "Austen never really dismisses [Lydia] or the unruly energy she embodies" (*The Proper Lady and the Woman Writer*, 205), citing the passage describing Lydia's return to her family in support of this. Poovey goes on to argue (206) that "even Austen's concluding comment on Lydia acknowledges that she finally finds a place within the same society that Elizabeth superintends. 'In spite of her youth and her manners,' the narrator informs us, Lydia 'retained all the claims to reputation which her marriage had given her'" (267). This passage seems to me, in contrast to Poovey, to stand as sharp criticism of Lydia's character. Her wildness is insipid, irresponsible, and destructive. Her claims to reputation, though perhaps publicly accepted, are empty, as the context makes clear: "[Wickham's] affection for her soon sunk into indifference; her's lasted a little longer; and in spite of her youth and . . ." (267). It is entirely accurate on Poovey's part to cast *Pride and Prejudice* as an "aesthetic solution" to the problem of closing "the gap between imaginative desire and social reality," or to the problem of reconciling our ideal aspirations for ourselves with the conditions of our embodiment (Poovey, 206). In contrast to Poovey, however, I am arguing that this solution is not an escapist one but rather, especially through its depiction of the possibilities of self-understanding and transfiguration through courtship, continuously alert to material develop-

ments, plausible, and largely successful. One of the ways to see this is to consider the criticism and education Elizabeth and Darcy give one another through the courtship process and to see that Darcy in particular learns from Elizabeth, rather than merely acquiring her.

68. Poovey (196–98) puts forward a compelling analysis of Elizabeth's "liveliness" and "impertinence" toward Darcy in their initial conversation during the Lucas party as a defensive reaction against Darcy's deflation of her image of herself and her eligibility for marriage to a handsome aristocrat.

69. Simpson, 336.

70. I owe this point, again, to Poovey (196–98); see n. 68.

71. I am led to this image (obviously) by Carlyle's *Sartor Resartus* and by J. Hillis Miller's "The Stone and the Shell: The Problem of Poetic Form in Wordsworth's Dream of the Arab," in *Mouvements Premiers: Études critiques offertes à Georges Poulet* (Paris, 1972), 125–46, esp. 130.

72. Hegel, *Phenomenology of Spirit*, par. 666, 405; par. 670, 408; par. 671, 409.

Chapter 7

1. Bernard Williams, *Ethics and the Limits of Philosophy*, 69.

2. "The drive toward a *rationalistic conception of rationality* comes [not from within our actual experience of deliberation, but] instead from social features of the modern world, which impose on personal deliberation and on the idea of practical reason itself a model drawn from a particular understanding of public rationality." Ibid., 18; see also 8.

3. Martha C. Nussbaum, *The Fragility of Goodness* (Cambridge: Cambridge University Press, 1986), 5.

4. Williams, 179, 180.

5. Ibid., 187.

6. Ibid., 200.

7. Friedrich Nietzsche, "'Reason' in Philosophy," *Twilight of the Idols*, trans. W. Kaufmann, in *The Portable Nietzsche*, ed. W. Kaufmann, sec. 1, 479.

8. Thomas Nagel, "Book Review—Bernard Williams: *Ethics and the Limits of Philosophy*," *Journal of Philosophy* 82, no. 6 (June 1986): 358. I have inverted the order of the two noun phrases flanking "is also" in the first sentence; this inversion does not affect Nagel's thought.

9. Ibid.

10. Nussbaum, *The Fragility of Goodness*, 4.

11. Mark 8:36–37.

12. Christine M. Korsgaard has established that this is Kant's understanding in her "Two Distinctions in Goodness," *Philosophical Review* 92, no. 2 (April 1983): 169–95.

13. Williams, 195.

14. Ibid., 69.

15. Nagel, 359.

16. Ludwig Wittgenstein, "Remarks on Frazer's *The Golden Bough*," trans. John Beversluis, in *Wittgenstein: Sources and Perspectives*, ed. C. G. Luckhardt (Ithaca, N.Y.: Cornell University Press, 1979), 61.

INDEX

Abilities, distinguished from
  capacities, 31, 193 n. 15
Abrams, M. H., 130–31
Absalom, Absalom!, 31
Acknowledgment: compared to
  theory, 4; lived by
  protagonists, 4, 9; of moral
  principle, 5, 66; narratives of,
  102–3, 185, 187–88; in relation
  to interpretation, 9; social
  conditions of, 23
Adorno, Theodor, 10
Agency: Aristotelian, 29; Hegelian,
  29–30; Humean, 29, 31; and
  modern physics, 104–5;
  Nietzschean, 29, 31
Altieri, Charles, 17, 33, 189 n. 5
Annas, Julia, 41
Anomie, moral, 28, 30
Aristotle, 12, 29, 143, 193 n. 15
Associationism, 127–28, 131
Augustine, Saint, 21, 152, 154
Austen, Jane (*Pride and Prejudice*):
  acknowledgment of materialist
  motivations by, 159–60; on
  confession and forgiveness,
  179–80; courtship of Elizabeth
  and Darcy, 168–80; failures of
  realism of, 145–50; on figures

of empty ideality, 166–67; on
  figures of excessive
  materiality, 161–6; and
  qualified praise of marriage,
  160–61; realism of, 142–45; on
  silliness and reasonableness,
  165–66
Autonomy: and community, 23,
  120; and confession, 179; and
  determinism, 104–5; and fit
  activities for persons, 22–23;
  and modern philosophy, 2–4;
  and modernist literature, 14;
  and moral worth, in Kant, 42,
  44, 51; and negative freedom,
  in Kant, 57–59; as object of
  acknowledgment, 15; and the
  sublime, in "Resolution and
  Independence," 127, 131 and
  theories of criticism, 13

Baron, Marcia, 194–95 n. 44
Bates, Stanley, 189 n. 1, 190 n. 10
Beauty, 3, 56
Beauvoir, Simone de, 157–59
Bloom, Harold: on "Frost at
  Midnight," 138–39; on
  "Resolution and
  Independence," 116–18;